ISLAM
Our
CHOICE

PORTRAITS OF MODERN
AMERICAN MUSLIM WOMEN

Edited by

Debra L. Dirks
&
Stephanie Parlove

amana publications

First Edition
(1424AH / 2003AC)
Second Printing
(1427AH / 2007AC)

© Copyright 1424AH / 2003AC
amana publications
10710 Tucker Street
Beltsville, Maryland 20705-2223 USA
Tel: (301) 595-5777 / Fax: (301) 595-5888
E-mail: amana@igprinting.com
www.amana-publications.com

Library of Congress Cataloging-in-Publication Data

Dirks, Debra L.
  Islam our choice : portraits of modern American Muslim women / Debra
L. Dirks & Stephanie Parlove.-- 1st ed.
     p. cm.
  ISBN 1-59008-018-1
1.   Muslim converts from Christianity--United States--Biography. 2.
Muslim women--United States--Biography. I. Parlove, Stephanie. II.
Title.

  BP170.5.A1D57 2003
  297'.082'0973--dc21

                                                      2003007772

Printed in the United States of America by
International Graphics
10710 Tucker Street
Beltsville, Maryland 20705-2223, USA
Tel: (301) 595-5999 Fax: (301) 595-5888
E-mail: ig@igprinting.com
www.igprinting.com

Table of Contents

Editors' Preface

Bismillah Al-Rahman Al-Rahim

In writing this book, all the authors were blessed with sharing an improved sisterhood relationship with each other. May Allah extend His kind blessings upon all our readers and bring us all together under His love and protection.

We dedicate this book to Allah and Allah alone. *Insha'Allah*, He will bless the reader with the understanding and openness to bridge any gaps between culture, religions, experience, and background.

Before providing a context in which to understand the sisters' stories, three basic bits of housekeeping need to be accomplished.

Firstly, the reader will find a number of Arabic terms sprinkled throughout this book. These Arabic words either have become a normal part of the language of most Muslims, or have no simple equivalent in English. For the ease of the reader, we have tried to transliterate these Arabic words in a consistent manner into English letters across this book's individual chapters. Further, following the first occurrence of each Arabic term, we have given an English definition within the text. Moreover, we have listed all of these Arabic terms and their English definitions in a glossary at the end of this book.

Secondly, it is customary for Muslims to use certain phrases after mentioning Allah, one of the prophets recognized by Islam, and the *Sahabah* (companions) of Prophet Muhammad. For example, after mentioning Allah, it is customary to use the phrase *Subhanna Wa Ta'ala* (glorified and exalted is He). After mentioning the name of a prophet, a Muslim typically says *Salla Allah 'Alayhi Wa Salam* (the peace and blessings of Allah be upon him, or simply, peace be upon him). After saying the name of a *Sahabi*, a Muslim usually says *Radhi Allaho Anho* (may Allah accept him). The use of such phrases by Muslims is an expression of honor and respect. However, as most non-Muslim readers find that the repetitious use of such phrases is disruptive to their ease of reading and comprehension, the editors have elected to use the English equivalent of each such phrase only upon the first occurrence of each individual name in each chapter. The sole exception to this procedure is that some of the authors have elected to use the simple declarative "peace" after mentioning one of the prophets of Allah, and the editors have allowed this use throughout each such author's chapter.

Thirdly, while most Americans readily understand concept of conversion, many Muslims prefer to use the word *reversion* when talking about someone becoming a Muslim. As Muslims, we reject the Christian concept of original sin, and believe that all babies are born Muslim. We further believe that all babies and children automatically remain Muslims until reaching the age of accountability, reason, and self-determination. When someone follows the road home to Islam from some other religious tradition, he or she is technically returning to his or her state as a baby. Thus, many Muslims prefer the terms *reversion* and *revert* to *conversion* and *convert.* However, the editors have elected to leave this choice in terms up to the individual authors.

As editors we could acknowledge all the different people in our lives. However, with this limited space, we would like to recognize the special and decisive guidance and tender care of four wonderful sisters.

The first of these is Sahar bint Zacariah Al-Soos who provided the brilliant backdrop upon which Allah introduced us to Islam.

Suha bint Ribhee Al-Khateeb who ushered the soft wind of Allah's will into our lives.

Hanadi bint Yasser Al-Hawari whose sparkle and gaiety blend seamlessly with the modesty demonstrated by the wives of the Prophet Muhammad, peace be upon him.

And last, but not least, Nura Al-Fallahah who beautifully demonstrates the intense generosity and care of the Islamic sisterhood.

Our thanks to each of them, and our thanks to Allah, *Subhanna Wa Ta'ala.*

Stephanie Parlove
Debra L. Dirks

Introduction

America and Islam in the 21st Century:
Welcome to the Sisterhood

DEBRA L. DIRKS

*A*t the present time, there is a rapidly growing number of modern American women who were born in America to non-Muslim parents, who later converted to Islam, who worship Allah (glorified and exalted is He) as the One God, and who have become united in a very special way as sisters-in-Islam. This book presents the personal accounts of six different American sisters-in-Islam, all of whom have been kind enough to share their first-person stories of the winding roads that they traveled en route to embracing Islam. In giving their personal portrayals of their individual journeys to Islam, some of these sisters-in-Islam have publicly proclaimed far more about their personal lives than they normally would be willing to share. In essence, they have sacrificed some of their personal privacy, as well as some of their normal reticence and modesty about their personal and private lives, for the sake of Allah, and for the sake of witnessing to the truth of the message of Allah as revealed to Prophet Muhammad (peace be upon him), the last of Allah's prophets.

In our individual journeys to Islam, American sisters-in-Islam have traveled different roads and pathways than those traveled by our sisters-in-Islam who were born into an Islamic society, and who were raised as Muslims in Muslim households. The life-roads traveled by American sisters-in-Islam also differ from those taken by our European sisters-in-Islam, reflecting the sometimes subtle, yet pertinent, differences between American culture and the various Western cultures of Europe. As American sisters-in-Islam, our backgrounds, upbringings, and culture, as well as certain aspects of our basic value structure, are firmly rooted in our American heritage. Our thought processes and conceptual skills were honed by American school systems. Our identities were influenced by stories of Clara Barton, Rosa Parks, Eleanor Roosevelt, Susan B. Anthony, Carrie Nation, and Annie Oakley, and our self-images were indelibly marked by our impressions of such Hollywood celebrities as Lucille Ball, Marilyn Monroe, Harriet Nelson, Rita Morino, Shirley Temple, Ruby Dee, and Grace Kelly. As American sisters-in-Islam, we are the heirs of a rich American legacy. Regardless of whether we traveled a scenic route, a highway, a byway, or a backwoods country road of dirt and gravel, those roads were all American roads that conformed to an American topography and wound through American vistas, and by traveling them we were led home to Islam.

What the authors of the following chapters share with other modern women in America is immense, and cannot be easily overstated. Within the pages of this book, each non-Muslim American reader will probably be able to relate to and identify with the pre-Muslim background of at least one of the authors. However, despite all the things that we share with our fellow Americans who are non-Muslims, what we have come to share with our worldwide sisters-in-Islam is especially sweet and appealing. While each of us remains an American, we are Americans who have joined a very special and caring sisterhood that transcends biological inheritance, personal genetics, ethnicity, race, and socioeconomic status. We have come to understand and to love the fact that what is important is individual righteousness, not superfluous considerations of language, skin color, ethnicity, etc. We are one family in our descent from Prophet Adam (peace be upon him), and we have come to know our sisters-in-Islam as fellow members of that one family. The ethnic, national, and racial differences among us are not causes of division, but are opportunities to learn from each other and to enrich ourselves in the process. Allah says in His glorious *Qur'an*:

> O mankind! We created you from a single (pair) of a male and a female, and made you into nations and tribes, that ye may know each other (not that ye may despise each other). Verily, the most honoured of you in the sight of Allah is (he who is) the most righteous of you. And Allah has full knowledge and is well-acquainted (with all things). (*Qur'an* 49: 13)

The authors of the following chapters are both Americans and sisters-in-Islam. This duality in our self-identities has resulted from our passing through the maze of American society and culture, and from finding our spiritual and religious home in Islam. We are since then personally enriched by sharing an American cultural legacy with an Islamic religious heritage. Nonetheless, it must be admitted that while our dual heritage as American sisters-in-Islam is very precious to us, it can also be challenging at times. As American sisters-in-Islam, we each have had to find our own way to blend the American culture of our homeland with our religion of Islam, while still preserving each of the two facets of our dual self-identities in pristine form. At times, we may experience this dual self-identity as being more like a juggling act, than like a seamless synthesis. At worst, we may sometimes feel like we have one foot in each of two worlds, while not completely belonging to either world. Yet, at its best, the synthesis of our American heritage and our submission to Allah in Islam brings a spiritual peace and comfort that exceeds anything we have ever known before. *Al-Hamdulillah* (praise and thanks be to Allah), the time and energy we expend in this effort not only strengthens us spiritually, but also contributes to the gradual enhancement of American society and culture as the melting pot of the world.

In this politically correct and patriotic era, it is essential to look at the paths that we have followed, in order to appreciate that choosing Islam is not a rejection of everything American, but is rather an embracing of the special spirituality and religious truth of Islam. As American sisters-in-Islam, we are still Americans, even though we are Muslims. After all, if it weren't for the freedom of religious choice guaranteed by the First Amendment to the American constitution, our individual journeys to Islam would probably have been far more difficult. Being American sisters-in-Islam does not mean that we are any less zealous than other Americans in cherishing our rights as Americans, and it does not mean that we are any less patriotic. Furthermore, it does not mean that we are any less distressed by the senseless, abhorrent, and decidedly non-Islamic violence of September 11, 2001.

Like all Americans, we Americans who are also sisters-in-Islam do not always agree with every aspect of American policy, and with every decision of the American government. Such disagreement is our guaranteed right as Americans. However, that does not mean that we are terrorists or that we advocate the violent overthrow of the American government. Like all Americans, we can express our agreement or disagreement with American policy at the ballot box in a peaceful and constructive manner.

As American sisters-in-Islam, we are modern women who have embraced an ancient religion — far more ancient than the average American realizes. As Muslims, we believe that Islam is the first and most ancient religion. While most Americans have been and, indeed, still are being taught in their schoolbooks and world history courses that the first monotheistic religion was Judaism, and that both Christianity and Islam were later derivations of Judaism, this is an interpretation of religious history that is rejected by Muslims. As Muslims, we see the beginning roots of Islam starting with Allah's creation of Prophet Adam. We trace the growth and evolution of Islam through the pre-Israelite patriarchs (e.g., Prophets Enoch, Noah, Abraham, Lot, Ishmael, and Isaac, peace be upon them), through the various Israelite prophets and notables named or alluded to in both the *Bible* and the *Qur'an* (e.g., Prophets Jacob, Moses, Joseph, Samuel, David, Solomon, Elijah, Elisha, Jonah, John the Baptist, and Jesus, peace be upon them), and through various non-Israelite prophets (e.g., Hud, Saleh, and Shu'ayb, peace be upon them), before culminating in the final revelations given to Prophet Muhammad. The revelations received by Allah's last prophet, Muhammad, were not the beginning of Islam, but rather the culmination of the progressive revelations received throughout time by many prophets of Allah.

In contrast to the Judaeo-Christian interpretation of religious history that results in both Islam and Christianity being seen as derivations of Judaism, the Islamic perspective is that, Judaism and Christianity began as ritualized and codified deviations from Allah's true religion of Islam. As Muslims, we believe that such deviation resulted from the alteration of the original revelations given by Allah to the various prophets that preceded Prophet Muhammad.

It should be noted at this time and place that the Arabic word Allah simply means the One and Only God. Further, Allah is linguistically linked with the Hebrew word "*Elohim*" that is typically translated as God in the *Old Testament*. Thus, Arabic-speaking Jews and Christians use the term Allah to refer to God. Nonetheless, many Americans react negatively to the word Allah, as though the word had the connotation of some distinctly foreign and specifically un-American deity. While most Americans do not react negatively to someone using the term "*Gott*", the German word for God, they frequently do react negatively to the term Allah. This conditioned reaction is really quite remarkable, as changing the foreign language that is being used should not cause such an emotionally negative reaction. *Insha'Allah* (God willing), the reader will now be able to overcome any potentially negative reaction he or she might normally have to the word Allah, and will be ready to appreciate the core beliefs and practices of Islam.

Fortunately, the fundamental essence of Islam is not complicated. In its basic form, there are six articles of *Iman* (faith) and five pillars of Islamic practice. While, the six articles of faith are far less known by most non-Muslim Americans than are the five pillars of practice, these articles of faith lie at the very heart of Islamic faith and belief. In their core essence, the six articles of *Iman* consist of believing in:

1. Allah — in His existence; His Oneness (*Tawheed*); and His attributes; and that He is the only one deserving to be worshipped.

2. Allah's angels — beings created by Allah from light for the purpose of obeying Allah's orders and praising Him.

3. Allah's books of revelation, which include the *Qur'an* plus the original versions of the *Torah* (the book of revelation received by Prophet Moses) the *Zabur* (the book of revelation given to Prophet David), and the *Injil* (the book of revelation given to Prophet Jesus).

4. All of Allah's messengers and prophets, some of whom are directly mentioned in the *Qur'an*, and some of whom are not.

5. The last day or the Day of Judgment when all mankind will be judged by Allah according to their deeds, and when Allah will accord them their appropriate punishment or reward, as tempered by His abundant mercy and forgiveness.

6. *Qadar* — the timeless knowledge of Allah, His power to plan, and His ability to execute His plans.

Islamic religious practice consists of five basic acts, which are known as the *Arkan* or pillars of Islamic practice. It is useful to note that the Arabic word for pillar (*Rukn* is the singular form, while *Arkan* is the plural form) also has the connotation of corner, cornerstone, or essential ingredient, thus emphasizing the indispensable nature of these five pillars of practice. Simply stated and without detailed elaboration, the five pillars of practice consist of the following.

1. *Shahadah* consists of saying, with full understanding, *Ushhadu an La Ilaha Illa Allah wa Ushhadu anna Muhammadan Rasulu Allah.* In English translation, the *Shahadah* states "I testify that there is no god but Allah, and I testify that Muhammad is the messenger of Allah.

2. *Salat* is performing to the best of one's ability the five mandatory and daily prayers in which one worships Allah.

3. *Ramadan* is the month of the lunar Islamic calendar in which a Muslim observes *Sawm* (fasting or avoiding all intake of food and liquid, as well as refraining from sex) from the first light of dawn until sunset.

4. *Zakat* is the mandatory giving in charity of a set portion of one's agricultural harvest and economic surplus to those who are in need.

5. *Hajj* is the pilgrimage to Makkah that every Muslim must make once in his or her lifetime, provided he or she is physically, mentally, and financially able to do so.

These six articles of faith and five pillars of practice have stood the test of time throughout almost 14 centuries, and currently bring spiritual peace and comfort to over 1.2 billion Muslims around the world. There has been no need to abrogate or modify these articles of faith and pillars of practice to fit any particular temporal or cultural situation. They are the unchanging and universal truths and fundamentals of Islam, which are in no conflict with nor inconsistent with modern advances in the sciences and technology. Islam is not a backwards religion, but is a religion that embraces new knowledge, while holding fast to its religious, spiritual, and ethical roots. While

Islam is not in conflict with technological progress, Islam refuses to sacrifice its basic values and core religious beliefs on the altars of fad, fashion, and politically correct expediency.

In marked contrast to Islam, most other religions in America are currently plagued with the crisis of simply trying to survive within the context of contemporary modernity. Within many of these religions, articles of faith and modes of worship are ever changing in a desperate attempt to "fit in" with the prevailing mood and fancy, and to adapt to the "Age of Aquarius". This phenomenon has been part and parcel of American religious life since the 1960s ushered in the then new theology of "God is Dead", and the decades since then have done little to reinvigorate a belief in the divine. The end result is that for many Americans religious life has become a mere manifestation of temporal and cultural relativism, and that the worship of an absolute deity has become decidedly secondary to the glorification of the individual human experience of "religiousness", both of which eventually leave the spiritual core of the individual feeling much like an empty void that is adrift from any higher guidance and inspiration.

When modernity is built on a firm ethical and religious foundation, it is a blessing to a humanity eager for knowledge and technological progress. In the absence of that essential foundation, modernity is not all that it is cracked up to be. It takes its toll, leaving a stressed out society trying to justify its lack of morality, while refusing to admit that anything is amiss in America. However, many Americans are beginning to yearn for something better and more meaningful. These Americans are left reminiscing about the trust and security they once experienced in the American society of yesteryear. They are left searching for God, for His religious structure and guidance, and for the inner peace of spirit that comes with proper worship of Him.

Against this backdrop of moral decline in American life, and given the unchanging spiritual focus and unconditional morality of Islam, it is no wonder that Islam is currently the fastest growing religion in both America and Europe, and numbers over 1.2 billion adherents throughout the world, the vast majority of which are not Arabs. With regard to that last point, there are over 160 million Muslims in Indonesia, over 100 million Muslims in Bangladesh, over 100 million Muslims in Nigeria, over 100 million Muslims in India, over 90 million Muslims in China, over 60 million Muslims in Turkey, several million Muslims in Germany, France, and Great Britain, and the list goes on and on.

In point of fact, Islam is the second largest religious faith in America today, and is the only rapidly growing and expanding religion in America, with at least one study suggesting that the number of Muslims in the United States has doubled during the 11 years between 1990 and 2001! While estimates of the number of Muslims in America vary according to the sampling procedures and statistical methods used, the most reliable estimates suggest that there are currently over seven million adherents to Islam in the United States.

Contrary to what many Americans might think, this escalating growth in the Muslim Ummah (community) in America is not simply the result of foreign-born Muslims emigrating from their country of origin to the United States. This growth is largely reflective of the vast numbers of Americans who have left their traditional religious affiliations in order to convert to Islam, with estimates ranging as high as 25,000 new converts each year in the United States. Furthermore, despite what might be expected by many Americans in the wake of the tragedy of September 11, 2001, the number of conversions to Islam appears to have quadrupled since then. In fact, there is every reason to believe that at least a third, and possibly as high as half, of the Muslim population in the United States consists of native-born Americans, whose parents belong or had once belonged to some other religious tradition.

The reasons behind all these conversions are simple. Islam offers the worship of the One God, an unconditional morality that is free of the trappings of cultural and temporal relativism, and a fellowship of believers who submit themselves to God and His directions. Islam thus speaks to the nostalgic yearnings of middle-aged Americans who vaguely remember a once better and more spiritual way of life. Islam also speaks to the younger generation of Americans, a generation which has always been more willing to expand its horizons in search of a higher calling.

One of the most important aspects of the Muslim Ummah in America is that it is home, regardless of where one lands, and regardless of one's origins. New Muslims instantly have a family of believers looking to help them, and wishing and praying for them, as all Muslims are taught to wish and pray for their brothers and sisters as they wish and pray for themselves. This is one of the very special features of Islam, and is a blessing that is part and parcel of what it means to be a Muslim. It is reflective of the example of religious life provided by Prophet Muhammad, and it is a matter of honor and duty to Allah to care for each other, and to provide for each other's needs.

What is more, we have Prophet Muhammad's guarantee that Allah will reward us for each and every little effort we make in doing these good deeds, even if our good deed is merely to smile at our neighbor. Throughout America, there are a growing number of Muslim brothers and sisters just waiting to welcome any interested American into the family of Islam. What is more, many of those brothers and sisters are homegrown Americans.

What keeps surprising so many women in our American society is that a large majority of these homegrown Americans who convert to Islam are women. Some estimates place the percentage of American converts to Islam that are women as high as 80%. One simply cannot ignore this fact, which elegantly and dramatically illustrates that Islam speaks to an obvious need among modern American women. It is not the objective of this book to define this need to which Islam is speaking so very clearly. Rather, the authors intend to present some vistas through which modern American women have journeyed to the absolute freedom, security, and peace of the Islamic sisterhood. However, it is crucial to emphasize that the erroneous stereotype of women being subjugated and oppressed by Islam is flatly and unmistakably refuted by the fact that a large majority of American converts to Islam are women.

Modern American women like to describe themselves as self-assured, liberated, secure, and independent individuals, and they set out to prove that they are just that. Only a couple of centuries ago, their European ancestors prohibited women from owning property in their own behalf, of inheriting from their deceased relatives, and of having any say in whom they married. They were little better than chattel throughout most of Europe until at least the 19th century. Further, it was only at the beginning of the 20th century that American women won the fight for the right to vote. Still further, during the 19th and early 20th centuries, American women automatically lost their United States citizenship if they married a man who was not a United States citizen. During the same time period, a woman who was not previously a United States citizen automatically became a United States citizen upon marrying a United States citizen.

Just as their female ancestors fought for women's suffrage and equality under the law, modern American women have also struggled and fought to have successful professional careers, and to be upwardly mobile on the corporate career ladder. In marked and dramatic contrast, Islam gave women independence and security so long ago, almost 15 centuries ago, that most of our Muslim sisters-in-Islam who were born into Islamic societies do not feel any need to prove their independence, they simply accept it as a their God-given right. Just as one does not need to fight to breathe unless and until air is being restricted to one's lungs, Islamic women do not need to fight to be liberated, as their breathing has not had the history of restriction that America and the West have inflicted on their women. While the American press and media seem to celebrate each instance of the oppression of women that they can find in some so-called Muslim country, such oppression, where it actually exists, is a violation of Islam, and a perverse and unwarranted expression of some local, cultural tradition.

In this book we present a brief, glimmering insight into our lives, both before and after our surrender to Allah in His religion of Islam. Each author was asked to write her own story of coming home to Islam using the following general outline:

1. Personal Background/Personal History
2. Introduction to Islam
3. Considerations and Decision to Come Home
   – What propelled you forward
   – What held you back
4. Reversion - Now What?
   – Family
   – Learning to live in Islam
   – Societal norms
5. *Insha'Allah*, an uplifting conclusion

As the reader can see, the outline provided to each author was quite general, with the idea being to let the diversity and splendor of each story be told in each author's own words, manner, and style. To that end, we have confined editorial revisions to standardizing format, the spelling of Arabic words, etc. Each author is a modern American woman, and each tells her story in her own individual way.

As modern American women who have surrendered to Allah in Islam, we had our own unique pasts, and have traveled our own individual paths to Islam. We were each ambling down the individual pathways of our personal lives when Allah granted us guidance. Some of us were traversing across busy city streets, some were speeding over four-lane interstates, and some were strolling down dusty, country lanes.

It is the very variety of the roads and pathways that we have traversed to come home to Islam, which illustrates the universality of Allah's message and the potential for other Americans to find spiritual peace, contentment, and support as practicing Muslims. In the chapters that follow, the reader will be introduced to six different American sisters-in-Islam. *Insha'Allah*, the authors' individual writing styles, their adaptation of the above-stated general outline to their personal stories, and their own word usage will enable the reader to see and appreciate the individual differences among the various authors. However, these differences can also be highlighted by a few demographic variables.

Our authors' current ages range from 28 to 54 years, with an average age of 46.2 years. Thus, the authors represent a cross-section of the adult population of modern American women. In age, they are no different than the American women the reader might randomly encounter in any given day.

Our authors vary greatly in terms of how old they were when they accepted Islam. Among the six authors, the youngest convert to Islam was 21 years old, the oldest was 50, and the average age at conversion was 34.7. As can be seen, conversion to Islam is not a phenomenon that belongs exclusively to any age group. Modern American women are converting to Islam across the whole expanse of chronological maturity. As can be seen by this data, conversions to Islam are neither the searching for one's youthful self-identity, nor the doddering of old age. The authors are strong women who undertook their own personal quest for God, and Allah answered their search with His guidance to Islam.

Our authors also vary according to how long they have been Muslims. In terms of length of time being a Muslim, our senior sister-in-Islam has been a Muslim for 27 years, while our most recent sister-in-Allah has been a Muslim for three years. On average, our authors have been Muslims for 11.7 years. In reading the following chapters, the alert reader will notice that this difference in longevity within Islam is occasionally reflected in the different viewpoints expressed by the individual authors.

In traveling down their own unique roads to find God, our authors encountered many stops and rest areas along the way to worshiping Allah, the One and Only God. As reported to the editors, the former religious affiliations across our six authors included stays in such rest areas as atheism, the Baptist Church, the Born-Again-Christian movement, the Catholic Church, the General Conference Mennonite Church, the United Methodist Church, the Nation of Islam, New Age movements, and the Southern Baptist Church. The above indicates that modern American women are converting to Islam from a wide variety of prior religious affiliations.

Our authors come from all across the United States. Various individual authors were born or grew up in the North, the South, the East, the West, and the Midwest. Conversion to Islam is not something that is confined to any one geographical region of the United States, but has spread across the depth and breadth of our country.

Since America has historically been the great melting pot of the world, many Americans cannot easily distinguish or select just one ethnicity that contributed to their individual heritage. When asked about how they would classify their own ethnicity, our authors variously responded with the following descriptors: African-American; American-American; German-American; Euro-American; and "blonde-haired, blue-eyed hillbilly". As can be seen, American converts to Islam cannot be easily pigeon-holed as coming from any one ethnic background, but cover the gamut of ethnicities that contribute to America.

Our authors also vary according to the amount of formal education they have received, with years of formal education ranging from 12 to 17 years, with everyone having had at least some college courses, and with the average length of formal education being 14.8 years. Two of the authors have completed their bachelor's degree. Clearly, the modern American women who are converting to Islam are not predominantly coming from the undereducated classes of our society. Islam is speaking not only to the spiritual needs of American converts, but also to their intellect.

Our authors have or have had a variety of careers, including that of being an artist, a creative writer, a designer and illustrator; a real estate agent, a customer service representative, and a horse farm owner and manager; public school teacher and anger and conflict management trainer. All of the authors have been mothers, and one is actively home-schooling her children at this time.

One thing that all of the sisters who wrote for us have in common is that they are all currently married, though their current marriages stretch in length from three years to 33 years, with an average of 17.5 years.

As you read our stories, I am sure you will discover that another thing the authors have in common is the strength of their own individuality.

There are many roads leading travelers through the land of religion to the shining mansion that is Islam. While each of the authors was traveling her own individual road, all of the authors have found their lives permanently uplifted and forever changed by being heralded with "there is no god but Allah, and Muhammad is His messenger." Likewise, there are many doors to that mansion that is Islam, and each of the authors has entered Islam through her own individual door. Further, the mansion of Islam is large, and the different authors may occasionally find themselves standing in different spaces within that mansion. Indeed, our journey has not ended by entering that mansion, but has only just begun, as each of us further struggles to strengthen her *Iman* (faith) and to worship and serve Allah to the best of her ability.

As one looks at the diversity of our authors, it should come as no surprise that each contributor stands in a slightly different place within that mansion that comprises Islam. *Insha'Allah*, this is a blessing not only to ourselves, but also to the reader who can thereby experience some of the breadth of the Muslim *Ummah* in America and what it has to offer. Not all of us would necessarily agree with everything that another sister-in-Allah has written. However, Islam is a religion of tolerance and inclusiveness, and whatever differences may exist in the spaces each of us momentarily chooses to occupy within the mansion of Islam, we are all still unequivocally bound together as sisters-in-Islam. As such, the editors have refrained from insisting that each author' chapter conform to the editors' own interpretation of Islam, and have granted each author the freedom to describe Islam as she sees it. Thus, each author, including the editors, assumes liability and responsibility only for what she herself has written.

"There is no god but Allah, and Muhammad is His messenger." All of our non-Muslim sisters around the world who now hear that heraldic message must sooner or later decide how they, as individuals, will respond.

The Peaceful Essence

CAREMA COOK

In the name of Allah, the Merciful and Compassionate. This is my story of how I came to follow the teachings of the Qur'an. This is a narration from my perspective. It is my understanding that others may not hold my views, and I honor their truth. I seek forgiveness from any of you whom I may offend, or who may disagree with my truth. May Allah, Glorious and Most High, accept the efforts made in this work with the intentions of others' gaining an understanding of how individuals come to and maintain Islam. May peace and blessings be upon Muhammad, the Final Messenger of Allah, and upon all the Prophets of Allah.

The Search of Islam – Finding Peace through God

I love hearing the stories of what brought people to learn about the beliefs and the lives of Muslims. I am intrigued with how those who have embraced the faith decide to make the life-altering decision to revert to Islam, finding peace through God. Many have very fascinating stories where they traveled a deeply intellectual journey of various faiths, and through reason they deduced Islam to be the faith they sought to embrace. Yet other academics or theologians sought to discredit the teachings of Islam and the *Qur'an*, but instead found the teachings sound and could do nothing but submit to them. Others were charmed with a culture of people who are Muslim and, through inquiries about the lives of Muslims, discovered Islam. Yet others began their quest by studying the history of Muslims where the teachings of Islam are deeply imbedded, and again came to find the teachings a way of life they desired to adopt. My story is not as fascinating as the academics, theologians, and travelers of the world. My conversion story begins with my simply looking for a quotation to use in my wedding ceremony. But before I get too ahead of myself, allow me to interject a little of the early history on my path to Islam.

I am from the last of the so-called Baby Boomer era of hard-working, optimistic youth that followed the rules and enjoyed the easy life our parents worked hard to provide. My childhood was during the Civil Rights movement and the Apollo space missions of the sixties. My teen years were during the Watergate and Disco era of the seventies. This explains a lot about the nonconformist style of my aspirations to strive towards world justice and obtain high goals, all the while feeling the urge to shatter the established rules and spontaneously seek out fun. I grew up in Arvada, a suburb of Denver, Colorado. My traditional Kennedy-era family had five children, a hardworking father whose goal was to provide a better life for his family than his father had, and an accepting, generous mother who strived for a peaceful, loving home.

After serving in the Philippines during World War II, Dad sought an education as an architect. Because money remained scarce, he eventually landed a job with an oil company and did not complete his degree. At Amoco, he excelled to the position of lead draftsman and worked with them for over thirty years until his retirement.

Dad freely shared accounts of his painful childhood that focused on the bewildering behavior of my grandfather. Grandpa Cook was a quiet, loving man to his grandchildren, but was an abusive father, husband and neighbor who terrorized his family and community. Dad's family struggled through the depression, living, literally, on the other side of the tracks in Casper, Wyoming. He was the oldest of four children, and from early childhood he was given the responsibility of contributing to the meager family income. My passionate grandmother was a fundamentalist Christian and unintentionally turned my father away from most aspects of formal religion. In my childhood, visits to Grandma Cook's house usually included arguments around the dinner table with Grandma saying phrases like "evolution is an atheist's belief" and "the *Bible* says...", followed by my father saying "the *Bible* is just meant to be a book of lessons." These exchanges usually escalated to some form of name-calling and concluded with Dad ordering my mother to pack up the car, and we would soon be on an inconsolably silent ride home from Casper back down to Arvada.

My ever-patient mother had an easier childhood in her Iowan town of Cresco. Her lovely parents were calm, gentle people who never spanked, but who gave clear guidance as to what was expected of their four daughters. Mother was the youngest in her family, and did not need to seek employment until her graduation. Because Grandpa Webb died before my birth, I only knew Grandma May, and saw her attributes in my mother's kind face, gentle words, and easy laugh. Dad was raised in the Pentecostal faith, and Mother was raised as a Methodist. As mother and father raised their children, they decided to become active in the liberal Methodist Church close to home. My parents did not teach the doctrine of religion. Instead, they taught the values of generosity, truthfulness, and honest work.

My childhood summers were full of roller skating, bike riding, and games of "Mother May I." At night, in pitch dark, my neighbor-hood pals, siblings, and I played block-wide games of hide-n-go seek. The rest of the seasons were full of school and holidays. It was a wonderful childhood. And, oh, the

holidays! Halloween, Thanksgiving, Christmas, Easter and Independence Day. My father seemed to live to have memorable holidays. The house was decorated for each one, and holiday meals prepared by Dad were truly a culinary celebration. The presence of family friends was always welcome, and I remember few holiday meals where the table wasn't spread for extra company.

THE YOUNG COOK FAMILY DRESSED FOR EASTER SUNDAY IN 1967: Kim, Dona, Bob, Deborah, Scott. In front are LeAnne and Barbara

My belief in a Supreme Being was always significant to me. It is difficult to remember a time when I was not drawn to worship, a better under-standing of my inner-spirit, and the One who created me. Church was a vivid memory of my youth. I cherished attending Sunday school or working in the nursery, and then sitting in the long wooden pews for the Sunday service in our large United Methodist Church. I treasured standing to sing hymns with the congregation, and I loved the echo of silence when we bowed our heads in silent meditation. Then we would settle in to listen to the comforting, methodical tone of my pastor first sharing a joke, then an anecdote, and bringing it all home with the primary message to love one another, do good works, and seek worship by attending church instead of football games.

As we grew older, the family did not attend church as much. When all of their children were in school, mother became employed as an aid in a nursing home and worked every other Sunday. The pattern of going to services was interrupted. But, on most Sundays, Dad would drop me off at church for Sunday school, and, as I got older, to fulfill my job in the nursery, and later attend church service with or without my family. However, my family did consistently attend holiday services. Attending church on holidays was a joyous ritual. Families dressed in newly purchased clothes and smelling of fresh baths, packed the normally unfilled pews. As we filed in, the lit candles, potted flowers, and beautiful organ music, all granted an atmosphere of warmth that my siblings and I relished. Our lips would all follow in sync as our pastor read the homily of the Christmas Eve Candle Light Service. It was the same discourse every year. "Everywhere, everywhere Christmas tonight." When we lit the candles and the lights were turned down, my heart would leap with excitement. The tradition of it all was grand.

In seventh grade, I registered for the required classes to become a member of the United Methodist Church. I eagerly attended, because I wanted to learn more about my religion. I knew I believed in God as my Creator and Sustainer. I knew the Christmas and Easter stories of Jesus, and my Sunday school classes affected the memorization of the names of the books in the *Old* and *New Testament*. I owned a personal *Bible* earned in Sunday school class, but I had not read the text of it yet. Grandma Cook could quote passages from it. Dad spoke of it as a storybook. Mom would share that she couldn't quote the passages like her mother-in-law. So the event of membership classes was going to be my way to learn more about my Holy Book, and our beliefs in God. I knew to be charitable, honest, and hardworking, but I felt spiritually undernourished. I wanted more substance than the warm rituals my upbringing had offered. I needed to understand more about the teachings of God.

As students of the membership class, we were required to read a short book written by our pastor. If there were vocabulary we did not understand, we were to write it down on a page in the back of the book, and scribe its dictionary meaning. If we had a question about the book or our religion, we could ask it at the end of class. The class consisted of the reverend reviewing the chapter we were to read in his book, followed by the questions we were allowed to ask at the end. I once dared to ask the question about the Immaculate Conception. I asked how Jesus could be born from a virgin. I really did not understand what a virgin was, but I assumed it meant not having a husband. My pastor gave me a calm look, and proceeded to explain that we don't take everything in the *Bible* literally. From that I understood that he, like my father, believed that the story of the birth of Jesus was a tale with the purpose to giving a message to the believers. I was confused as to what that message would be. I was confused why the supposed Book of God would be thought of as a book of stories. But I felt shy to further my query.

In a following session, I asked how we are to believe in only one God as required by the Ten Commandments, but still call Jesus *Lord*. I recalled one of my earlier Sunday school assignments was to draw a picture of God. I left my paper blank because I felt pressure to produce, and I didn't have a clue what God looked like. The teacher loved my idea, thinking that my undeveloped work symbolized my feelings that God was like light and can't really be seen. Her acceptance of my non-work baffled me. As I thought about that concept, I was even more confused as to how God could have a son that looked like and lived like a man. My pastor's answer given to my bold question was not clear, except for the vision of his calm face and unwavering voice. I did not understand his explanation and felt overwhelmed by his numerous words. When I asked my Mom what she felt, she said that she thought Jesus was not the same as God, but perhaps a means to teach us about God. Although I learned the love of God from my pastor, he failed to answer the questions to my satisfaction. I completed my classes and was announced as a member of the Arvada United Methodist Church.

Soon after, I asked my mother to take me to other churches to fulfill a search. I wanted a faith that would give me all the answers. I was confused with the empty feelings I experienced within the everyday rigors of family, friends, and school. I felt like I did not have a connection with my soul, and I wanted to have more spiritual teachings in my faith. I wanted clearer instruction as how to live my day-to-day life. And finally, I was mystified by the belief that Jesus died for my sins. Wasn't I responsible to fulfill those wonderful values my parents taught me, in order to earn the reward of Heaven? I searched for the faith that would help me feel at peace, the one that would satisfy my questions and relieve my discomfort.

My search continued into high school. I searched for answers in meditation, in community service work, and in the newly popular self-help books. I also visited a Jewish synagogue. During my search, I continued to be active in the Methodist Church, teaching Sunday school and vacation school, and attending youth group meetings. As I taught Sunday school, I found that I always spoke to my young students of one God and the beauty of His love and creations. I spoke of Jesus as our teacher and example. This is how I came to reconcile my belief in Jesus along with my belief in one God. I was content with this proposal, but still felt confused on how to act on this faith. I finally read the *Bible* in a high school literature class. I found it to be filled with wonderful stories and pious counsel. I especially loved the poetry and guidance lent in *Psalms* and *Proverbs*. I enjoyed the stories in *Genesis* and *Exodus*, but was frustrated with the apparent contradictions my teacher pointed out.

As I graduated from high school and struggled with how to live in my future, I set aside my search for the one faith to which I could commit. I stopped going to church, concentrated on becoming a teacher by working at a school for developmentally delayed children, and attended college. At that same time, I met a student from North Africa. I was drawn to his energy, and the gracious kindness he granted everyone. Mohamed was in America to get his degree in engineering. At a gathering at one of his friends' apartment, Mohamed's friend, Fauzi, asked me if I wanted to learn about a faith that accepted all people no matter what their race or nationality. He asked me if I wanted to learn about a faith that taught people to be just. He asked me if I wanted to earn an eternal life in Heaven, not because of the belief in Jesus as the Savior, but because of the good works I do in this life. I was captivated. Growing up in the civil rights era, I had always been drawn to human rights. A religion that actually spoke to fair treatment of all caught my attention. Also, to be rewarded for my good deeds was a concept for which I was searching. He called this faith *Islam*. I had never heard of it before and was wary of its unfamiliarity. My search for a place to put my faith was dormant, and what he had to say did not arouse my attention enough to pursue the idea further.

In the meantime, I quit my job at the school. Up to that point, I had used my feet as my sole form of travel. I wanted a car, and the teaching job could not pay for my apartment, food, school, and car. I began working for a bank in downtown Denver, and a co-worker introduced me to the faith of Jehovah's Witnesses. It ensnared my interest because of the sincerity with which she lived her life. She lived what she believed through everything she did. I had a good friend in junior high school whose father was a pastor of the Church of Christ. Her family also lived their faith, but I did not feel the spirit I was searching for when I attended her church. The conversations I held with my co-worker revitalized my need for a formal way to worship. With a new faith to explore and a sincere believer with whom to explore it, I decided to re-open my search for faith and visited a

Jehovah Witness Kingdom Hall in Denver. I wanted to make it work but found the teachings harsh. It too was without the spirit for which I longed. I still was looking for a peaceful essence.

By this time, Mohamed and I had fallen in love and decided to marry. We began to plan our wedding ceremony for August of that year, 1980. We desired a simple backyard wedding, with Dad's wonderful cooking for our reception, and with just our close family and friends in attendance. My adoring uncle, Dad's brother in-law, was a judge and Pentecostal preacher. I wanted him to officiate at our wedding and received his permission to help write the service. It was my desire to include Mohamed's culture in our ceremony. I thought it would be appropriate to incorporate a quote from the *Bible* and perhaps one from Mohamed's traditions. I had learned a lot about his culture over the two years we had known each other, but not much about his faith. When I asked him what I could add to our wedding address from his family's beliefs, he referred me to the *Qur'an*. The peculiar word Islam was re-introduced to me. My future husband soon delivered an English translation of the *Qur'an*, borrowed from his friend Fauzi, the one who first told me about Islam. During my lunch breaks at the bank, I began reading this Holy Book in hopes of finding a quotation to insert in our impending wedding ceremony.

The book seemed unyielding to me. The translation was full of fancy language, and I soon felt overwhelmed. All I wanted was a quotation about love or relationships. On my next break, I decided to randomly open the book and leave it to God. The book fell open near the middle in a chapter called *Maryam*. As I read, I soon discovered that this book from an unfamiliar faith was speaking about Jesus, the Jesus of whom I had so many questions. According to this story, Mary did indeed miraculously conceive a child while being a virgin. This story said that God is capable of creating by any means, and a virgin birth was how He chose to create Jesus. It told me that the virgin birth was just a sign to humankind. Then I received confirmation of what I had previously decided to be my conviction. According to this book, Jesus was not considered the son of God, but rather the teacher from God. As the story ended it read:

> He (the infant Jesus) spake: Lo! I am the slave of Allah. He hath given me the scripture and hath appointed me a prophet, and hath made me blessed wheresoever I may be, and hath enjoined upon me prayer and alms-giving so long as I remain alive, and hath (made me) dutiful toward her who bore me, and hath not made me arrogant, unblessed. Peace on me the day I was born, and the day I die, and the day I shall be raised alive! Such was Jesus, the son of Mary: (this is) a statement of the truth concerning which they doubt. It befitteth not (the Majesty of) Allah that He should take unto Himself a son. Glory be to Him! When He decreeth a thing, He saith unto it only: Be! and it is. And lo! Allah is my Lord and your Lord. So serve Him. That is the right path. (19: 30-36 from the first translation of the Qur'an that I read – the translation by Marmaduke Pickthall.)

These verses not only confirmed my belief that God, not Jesus, is my Lord, but that my job is to serve God. It also answered my questions about the Immaculate Conception. It isn't just a story, rather it is a sign and a method of creation by God who can create anyway He wills. I decided to give up my search for my wedding quotation and just read the book. As I read the English translation of the Qur'an, I found more stories about prophets or teachers of God. I read about Noah, Joseph, and Moses. The Qur'an also repeatedly mentioned a prophet of whom I did not know. His name was Muhammad. Unlike my experience with the Bible, there were no contradictions among these stories. In fact, pieces of them were repeated throughout the book, using the same words and meaning. I also found verses about the acceptance and justice that Fauzi told me about.

> O mankind! We created you from a single (pair) of a male and a female, and made you into nations and tribes, that ye may know each other (not that ye may despise each other). Verily the most honoured of you in the sight of Allah is (he who is) the most righteous of you. And Allah has full knowledge and is well-acquainted (with all things) (*Qur'an* 49: 13).

> O ye who believe! Stand out firmly for Allah, as witnesses to fair dealing, and let not the hatred of others to you make you swerve to wrong and depart from justice. Be just: that is next to piety: and fear Allah. For Allah is well-acquainted with all that ye do. (*Qur'an* 5: 8).

I also found a description of the good deeds I was meant to do on this earth to earn the company of the virtuous believers in heaven. My mother and father had taught me the values that God wanted me to have.

> For Muslim men and women – for believing men and women, for devout men and women, for true men and women, for men and women who are patient and constant, for men and women who humble themselves, for men and women who give in charity, for men and women who fast (and deny themselves), for men and women who guard their chastity, and for men and women who engage much in Allah's praise – for them has Allah prepared forgiveness and great reward (*Qur'an* 33:35).

More importantly than the information I found in the *Qur'an*, I found the feeling of peace for which I was searching. I felt spirituality as I read the passages. I felt a connection with the Divine. My interest was also awakened upon learning that God is the One who knows all I do, including my intentions. I concurred with the idea that God is the only true judge of who is eternally rewarded with Heaven. This meant to me that everyone has a chance to be rewarded with Heaven through good actions. If everyone were living through peaceful and superior actions, promoted by faith in a superior being, then we would live in a just, peaceful world. This was all very compatible with my established beliefs, and I decided to learn more about the alien religion of Islam. It was about this same time, I found the Qur'anic quotation I wanted read at our wedding along with the passage from the Biblical book of *Ruth*. My wedding quotation from the *Qur'an* read:

> O humankind! Be dutiful to your Lord, who created you from a single soul and from it created its mate, and from them both scattered many men and women, and fear Allah through Whom you demand your mutual rights and not to cut the relations of the wombs. Surely Allah is ever a watcher over you. (*Qur'an* 4:1 from a modified version of the third translation of the *Qur'an* that I read – the translation of Muhammad Taqul-ud-Din Al-Hilali and Dr. Muhmmad Musin Khan)

Becoming Muslim – Submitting to Peace through God

Within the six months of my first reading of the *Qur'an*, I concerted an effort to learn more about this faith called Islam. I asked my new husband where I might go to learn more about Islam, and he arranged an appointment for me to meet a gentleman at a place called Masjid Al-Nur, the Mosque of the Light. The mosque was a small house around the University of Denver neighborhood. Mohamed and I were living in Capitol Hill, close to Downtown Denver, where I continued to work at the bank, and near to where Mohamed was busy with his studies at the University of Colorado's Denver Campus. It was February of 1981.

As I walked into this small, unmarked house, called a mosque, I walked into another world. There was no furniture. The men present were dressed in long shirts to their ankles and were sporting turbans and long beards. I truly had never seen such a vision, not even in the movies. I sat on the carpeting of a small room, and two men walked into the room and sat on the floor across from me. I noticed that, although I tried to make eye contact with them, they would not acquiesce and kept their gaze on the carpet in front of them. I had a sudden urge to announce the obvious mistake I had made and escape to familiar safety. But my ever-present courtesy would not allow me to leave. As one of the men began to converse with me, I noticed he spoke in the familiar accent of my Libyan husband, and I felt a little more at ease. The man everyone called Sheykh Mabrook, spoke in disciplined, silent tones, while the other man sat silently looking at the ground in front of him.

Sheykh Mabrook proceeded to tell me that the tenets of Islam included belief in one God, belief that God created angels that did not have free will and whose sole purpose was to worship and obey God, belief that God sent humankind teachers or prophets to teach how to worship and follow His path, belief that some of those prophets were given revelation to use in their teachings, belief in pre-destiny along with human free will, and belief in the Day of Judgment with reward in Heaven and/or punishment in Hell following for eternity. I need-ed to believe in this last aspect. My parents' belief that our Heaven and Hell were merely in this life did not satisfy my desire to have more reason, more promise than what I understood this short life to be. I knew I believed in the hereafter. It was comforting to have this gentleman speak of it. I was also interested to learn of the concept of free will along with God's providence. It all made sense to me – all is planned, God knows all, and how we accept, use, or react with what is given to us is our free will.

All this information was grand. But I was not satisfied. What I really wanted to know was how living this faith will affect my life. Would it fill this gaping hole in my soul? How would this faith clarify all my confusions of life? How would it complete me? The bare surroundings and reserved responses that I was receiving up to that point were causing me to rethink my path of investigation. I became so anxious that I did not know how to ask the multitude of questions resounding in my head. I decided to ask more concrete questions. What does a Muslim do in devotion to God? How does she behave in daily life? At these questions, the composed, mysteriously dressed man explained to me the pillars of worship. They included praying five times a day, giving alms once a year, fasting from sunrise to sunset during the month of *Ramadan*, and making pilgrimage to the city of Makkah in Saudi Arabia once in a lifetime if you have enough means and if all of your financial obligations are met. During that awkward meeting, everything felt surreal to me. I was frustrated as to how I could live this faith. He had answered what to believe and how to worship, but it seemed that the spirit I found in the *Qur'an* was missing from his explanation. My questions were not receiving the complete answers I wanted to hear.

Everything that I was experiencing up to this point was so alien to my understandings of the world. The dissonance caused great discomfort, and I wanted to leave. I wanted to return to reading the *Qur'an*, searching for peace within myself, and continuing on as usual. But I knew that continuing on as usual left me feeling unsatisfied. That was why I was in this small room with these peculiar men. Sheykh Mabook broke the silence and asked if I would like to profess my faith in Islam. I heard a sarcastic laugh roll out of my mouth and told the man that I would need to learn more. He then explained to me that learning about the way of God is like climbing a ladder. You cannot start from the top. He went on to say that, to climb a ladder, you must start at the bottom rung, and that is confessing your faith to God through Islam. He explained that I should not wait, because none of us know if we will die in the next minute. He asked what would happen if I were to die without faith. I sensed his genuine concern for me, but was confused as to what he thought he knew about me. I explained that I did have faith. I believed in God and was simply searching for a way to live out that belief. If I died that day, I would not die without faith. God knew what is in my heart, and I hoped that I would not be punished for working towards my enlightenment. I hold this belief still today. What belief each of us sincerely lives by is a personal choice. One's relationship with a Supreme Being is between the individual and God. He is the only judge.

The conversation with Sheykh Mabrook evolved into his applying pressure on me. My discomfort was now unbearable, and I quickly thanked the gentlemen and offered my hand in salutation. They left my outreached hand hanging in the air without the usual reciprocating handshake. Once I saw that they had their hands graciously at their sides, I realized enough to drop my hand and simply slid out of the room with a weak goodbye.

As the years passed, and I learned more about Islam, I came to understand that my handshake was not returned, because of their need to seek modesty and utmost respect for my gender. I disagree with the practice of not shaking the hand of someone of the opposite gender, but truly respect the belief of those who follow it. The humble scholar I met that day came to be my husband's mentor, and his wife and daughters came to be my faithful friends. I learned that his dress and mannerism were a display of how he chose to practice his Islam. Although he did not fully answer my questions during our first meeting, he nourished my faith on many other occasions. In 1986, Sheykh Mabrook was murdered while making *Hajj*, the pilgrimage to Makkah. The investigation concluded that Libyan nationals, who deemed him to be a threat to the dictatorship, stabbed him and left his remains in the desert. This peaceful man sought nothing but to live his life as a Muslim and to serve his community by sharing the teachings of God. May God accept his efforts and bless and protect his family.

On the way home from my visit to the mosque, I could not let go of the idea of becoming a Muslim. Maybe that decision would be too radical. I was raised to keep my religion private. Maybe professing to one faith is not a necessity. Then I reminded myself of the unfulfilled, empty sensation that I had continually had within my soul. My spirit was longing to be fed, and everything I had tried so far to nurture it did not fill that hole. I was twenty-one years old. I was married to an intelligent, thoughtful man. I had a supportive family and a good job. I lived an ideal life with the young professionals on Capitol Hill. Yet, I still felt unfulfilled. I went home to read more *Qur'an*. Reading the book continually calmed me and produced my inner solace. It caused me to feel spirit and purpose. Once again, I just let the book drop open and I read:

> By the Qur'an, full of wisdom – thou (Muhammad) art indeed one of the messengers, on a straight way. It is a revelation sent down by (Him), the Exalted in Might, Most Merciful, in order that thou mayest admonish a people, whose fathers had received no admonition, and who therefore remained heedless (of the signs of Allah). (*Qur'an* 36: 2-6)

I once again experienced that connection with the Divine. I was now even more determined to learn how I could live the faith of this book. This time, I wanted to speak to an American Muslim. I wanted to speak with a woman. I opened the phone book, looked under "mosque" in the yellow pages and came up empty. Then, I looked in the white pages. I found a number and began dialing. Within the next minute, I was speaking with a member of the Shriners at their meeting place in downtown Denver, which was called a mosque. I then tried the word "Islam," and found the Islamic Center in the white pages. For the next two weeks, before going to work, on my lunch break, and when I arrived home, I called this number in hopes of finding someone. All I received was endless ringing. Finally, one Friday, a strong voice with a stronger accent answered the phone. I asked the man if he knew of an American woman that I could talk to about Islam. After I repeated my question three times, each time using clearer, simpler words, the man on the other end of the line said that he did indeed know of an American Muslim and gave me the phone number to a Moroccan restaurant.

The frenzy of a busy kitchen full of hurried orders and clanging dishes greeted me with this phone call. At my request to talk to a lady named Ameenah, the young man who answered my call passed the phone over to a friendly voice with a mid-western accent like mine who easily understood me. She was surprised to get a call at that number. It was her husband's restaurant, and she herself was rarely there. Within a week, I was sitting in the comfortable living room of Ameenah, the first American Muslim I met. I don't know if we really spoke much about Islam at that meeting. She seemed to know that I simply needed to visit with a cordial face that belonged to a Muslim. Through our interchange, I saw how her belief in God through Islam gave her contentment even though her life seemed difficult. She seemed to have found resolution and peace through her faith. This serenity was a presence I wanted to possess. At my request, Ameenah started classes to teach Islam to English-speaking women. Our first class had only four women, three Americans and one Pakistani. Our community of Muslims was moderately populated, and the two known Denver mosques were small homes found in the old neighborhoods. It was satisfying to spend time with these ladies. I believe the first meeting spoke of prayer. My meeting with Ameenah instigated me to ease onto the first rung in climbing the ladder to Islam. I went home from the first women's meeting feeling elated at my newly found community. Mohamed was still at school, leaving me alone in our apartment. I sat at the edge of our bed and spoke to God. I had not asked for God's help or advice since high school. I asked God if I should convert to Islam. I told Him to give me a message if Islam was the right way for me to proceed. It was an immediate response. A calm feeling embraced my being while sitting on that bed. I knew that I should take that step and proclaim myself to be a Muslim.

I called my mother to share my revelation with her. At first she was apprehensive and asked why I felt I had to choose a certain religion. But soon she said a statement that reminded me of the devotion my mother possesses for her fortunate children. My mother said, "You have been looking for a religion since seventh grade. I am glad you found one, and hope it is everything you've searched for."

I borrowed a scarf from Ameenah to attend the Friday service at the Islamic Center. She had told me that I would need to wear a scarf on my visit to the mosque. I wore my flowered, wrap-around maxi skirt and long sleeved peasant blouse, topped off with the patterned scarf. My outfit did not match, but it was the best I could do. Although I felt awkward wearing the scarf – it was not my usual approach to style -- there was a feeling of accuracy to the act. I was a modest person, and the scarf represented modesty to me. I sought a way to worship God, and the scarf represented a way of worship to me. Wearing this scarf, I was now someone with a purpose, someone with clear intentions.

At that time, the now large Colorado Muslim Society's Islamic Center, currently a beautiful structure built as a modern, domed mosque, was then a small house on Ash Street. I was elated this day, because my husband Mohamed was escorting me to this momentous activity. Since he had come to the United States, Mohamed, as happens with many young international students, remained firm in his beliefs of God, but left his religious practices at home with his parents. I was happy that he would again offer prayer. This all seemed to fit perfectly. My reading the *Qur'an* to find a quote for our wedding brought us to a mutual means of worshipping God, rejuvenated the devotional spirit in both of us, and brought us to this spot where I would confess my faith in Allah, the One God. I would enter into Islam.

At the Islamic Center, in a curtained room that probably was a bedroom off a main living room in days gone-by, I sat on a red Persian rug listening to a man give a sermon in the Arabic language I had often heard my husband speak to his friends. There was then a short English translation. Then, the three women that shared our secluded room stood for what I assumed was the prayer. I watched the two teenaged girls in jeans and headscarves hesitantly bend and prostrate in prayer. Their mother was dressed in a long robe and long scarf. Her movements were more confident, smoother. I felt at peace watching her motions as she submitted herself to Allah and listening to the rhythmic sounds of the *Qur'an* being read in its original Arabic text. My husband announced to the *Imam*, the leader of the prayer, that there was someone who wanted to take her *Shahadah*, declaration of faith in Allah and belief in His prophets. I was then invited from behind the curtain to the main room.

Here, less than twenty men, dressed in pants and shirts, were sitting on the floor. I made eye contact only with the man at the front of the room. Like the men at the other mosque, this man was wearing a long white shirt with baggy cotton pants. Instead of a turban, he wore a small skullcap, and he was clean-shaven. Another difference was that he received my eye contact by returning a friendly glance. I sat in front of him listening to unfamiliar words that I was to then repeat. I stumbled over the Arabic words "*La Ilaha Illa Allah Wa Muhammad Al-Rasul Allah.*" The *Imam* then translated what I had just said, and I knew I had achieved a great feat in my life. There is no god but Allah, and Muhammad is the messenger of God. With that declaration, I acknowledged my faith in one God. I accepted the teachings of the Messenger Muhammad and all of the prophets of Allah before him. With that declaration, I was now confident that I would have a lifestyle that would be in daily remembrance of Allah through prayer and praise to Him. I felt I now had direction. I felt that this would give me all my answers and make my life perfect. I was confident that that hole in my soul would soon be filled.

My Education in Islam

With my recent reversion, I quickly purchased easily read books to better understand my faith. I devoured those books on the bus while going to work, on my breaks, and in any chance I could appropriate. From my book on Islamic prayer, I copied the English translitterated Arabic recitations on index cards, and taught myself how to make the ritual prayer of Muslims, called *Salat.* I felt comfort in wearing the scarf and the wholesome feeling I gained from it. I loved the distinction it gave me as a faithful person. I already owned a number of long maxi skirts. It was the fashion during high school. So I purchased some material for scarves and began wearing my new outfits to work. Soon after my conversion in fashion, I was called to the bank's personnel office with concerns about my breaking the established dress code at this conservative establishment. Women were to wear skirts or dresses and nylons, and head coverings were not allowed. As soon as I explained that I was wearing the scarf because of my religion, the human resource representative smiled, and all discussion was ended with her giving me permission to continue dressing in my Islamic attire. I never was asked about my scarf again.

I was even promoted to assistant supervisor within the next year.

This conversation gave me the confidence to ask if I could use the boardroom to make afternoon *Salat*. I was also granted that request and would slip into the unoccupied room after my lunch hour to practice my *Salat*. I felt very awkward during my untrained *Salat* and did not yet feel the spirit of it. My movements were stiff, like the young girls I had seen at the mosque, and my tongue tripped over the Arabic words. At that time, *Salat* was merely a ritual to me, and I was constantly concerned that someone might walk in and find me in an odd position. I did not know enough about this practice to explain it to my co-workers.

At the refreshing time of my conversion, I was so happy to have found a place to put my devotion that I even wanted to change my name. I knew a name change was not a necessity to become a Muslim, but I felt it would be a positive induction into my re-born faith. A new method of worship, a new mode of dress, and a new name – it all made sense to me. I sat on the couch in our apartment with Mohamed and asked him to start saying Islamic names. He said 'Aisha and Khadijah. I tried to say the names properly without success. Then, Mohamed came to the name Carema. I could say it easily and even spell it with a "C" to match my family name. Without deliberation, I adopted my name, not knowing its meaning or history. About six months later, a friend of Mohamed told me the meaning of my name, and that it was an attribute of Allah. I was humbled, and confirmed that generosity, the meaning of my new name, was the quality I would like to be remembered by most. I knew that more than just Mohamed and I were involved in the choosing of this name. Like Islam, Carema felt like a perfect fit. During just this one year, my nameplate at work had changed from LeAnne Cook, to LeAnne Cook-Masaud after my marriage, to Carema Cook-Masaud at the advent of my name-change. My co-workers quickly adapted, but my siblings and parents were slower to concede. I am still called LeAnne by some of my extended family, and it really makes no difference to me. I am the same person, the same soul that I was before my knowledge of Islam, no matter what my name.

With my change of name, change of dress, and occasional dismissals from the family group to perform my ritual prayer in the back bedroom, my extended family seemingly accepted my transformation without protest. I must admit that my family does not always greet conflict with open honesty. Although we are all gregarious, friendly people, it is not usually our custom to say what is on our minds if it might be met with controversy. One brother did ask questions, comparing the Islamic teachings of the prophets to the Christian teachings. I was relieved to be able to answer his questions and receive no discernment. My mother continued to ask questions regarding everything about my faith as they came to her mind. My father, however, constantly remained silent about the matter. My adoption of faith was an issue that was not approached by him. From his exchanges with his mother, he had learned it was better not to talk about religion. Grandmother Cook was actually the only one to state her protest of my conversion. She wrote a letter informing me that she fears I will find my abode in hell, and that all I need to do is turn on the television to hear the evangelists and accept the true way of God. I wrote her back, sharing my love for her and thanking her for telling me her concerns. When I told Mother about the letter, she comforted me, saying that Grandma believed her faith was the only way. Mother reflected on the occasion of the death of my eldest sister. She died from injuries of a fire when she was very young. My grandmother was clearly upset at the loss of her granddaughter and told my mother that this would not have happened if my parents had attended church more regularly. At that time, my mother was crushed, as I now felt. I continued to write Grandma letters about my life, but did not discuss my faith. She passed on not really knowing my four children or my husband, but I felt at peace with the love I showed her. Grandpa Cook soon followed her in death.

Through the silent acceptance, polite questions, and continued inclusion of Mohamed and me at family gatherings, I derived that my new faith was not a major concern to my family. By this time, both of my elder brothers had married delightful Catholic women and had quickly adopted their faith, joining them for Sunday mass. My older sister had long been married to a mellow, tolerant man who called himself an agnostic. My sister later became very active in the Methodist Church along with her children and continues to be happy with that faith. Mother attends Sunday service and is active in her women's church circle. And my younger sister maintains her custom of attending church on holidays with our mother. Having Muslims in the family does not seem to upset the family structure.

Although Mohamed and I did not feel the celebration of Halloween, Christmas, and Easter was compatible with our Islamic beliefs, we continued to join my family in those celebrations for the first three years after my conversion. We did not want to upset anyone. But when our first two children were toddlers, we felt that they might begin to anticipate the Christian holidays, and I became concerned. I wanted our children to anticipate our Islamic holidays of 'Eid Al-Fitr and 'Eid Al-Adha, holiday of the feast and holiday of the sacrifice. I knew that it would be tough competition in a country where Christmas and Easter are widely celebrated and marketed. I decided to begin teaching about the Islamic holidays and to exclude us from the Christian holidays. I approached my father and mother with my plan, and, although they looked slightly wounded, as one would completely understand, they accepted our wishes and saved the Christmas gifts for 'Eid. I am sure that our presence was missed on the holidays, and, sadly, the relationships of my siblings' growing families grew sounder amongst each other than with us. Our large family of uncles, aunts, nieces, nephews, and now a great-niece still gathers often, and we truly enjoy each other's company. Although my family has never protested, our absence at important family holidays and dissimilar religious practices are an obvious strain on our continued bonding. My relationships with my siblings are now a little more formal than I would like, and I work to ease that tension.

Mohamed had re-found his faith. Through Masjid Al-Nur, he became involved with the peaceful missionary work of the *Tablighi Jammah*, translated as the group that conveys, i.e.., conveys the message of Allah. Mohamed began to visit other cities, gathering Muslims at the mosques and holding circles of learning, reading from the *Qur'an* and the teachings from the peace-seeking traditions of the Messenger Muhammad. At home, I would host groups of women traveling to our city for the same reason. It was a very spiritual time, with frequent meetings of people wanting to increase their knowledge of Islam. I began to dress even more conservatively, wearing the *Jilbab*, a cloak from shoulder to foot. I also found myself wanting to live a sparser existence, and made my home less cluttered by pictures, furnishings, and music.

Mohamed graduated with a B.S. in engineering in December of 1983. I had recently quit my banking job to care for our two young children. With no current ties holding us home, we decided to travel to Pakistan to work with the *Tablighi Jammah* close to its center of conception. It was our intention to stay at various mosques and homes throughout the country and strengthen our Islam by conducting the spiritual gatherings.

We sold or gave away most of our belongings and stored the rest. On a gray day in January of 1984, Mother, Father, and my younger sister escorted us to the airport. Mohamed and I traveled the long trip to Karachi with our young sons, ShemsAdeen (then only two years old) and Yusef who was eight months old. Our two young sons were undemanding traveling companions. They enjoyed the long plane ride, finding play easy at our bulkhead seats. We landed in Karachi, and I stepped into a world that I could not have imagined. The colors were vibrant, the activity of the crowded populace was over-stimulating, and a language that neither Mohamed nor I spoke filled the air.

Mohamed immediately fell into role and began bargaining for the price of a taxi ride to our first host home. I was absorbed in the exchange as I observed the driver and my husband perform intense haggling. Mohamed stated a price and received a smile and soft laugh from the driver. In disbelief, I witnessed Mohamed walk away. I quickly gathered the children and bags and ran to join him, only to have the driver follow us. The price was negotiated a little while longer, and finally our things were placed in the trunk of the cab. These two seasoned hagglers acted out this transaction like a grand performance.

Once we were finally on the road, I witnessed a chaotic dance of vehicles that was marshaled at random. Cars, oxen, and carts shared the roads with cycle-powered rickshaws and people riding by twos on single-seated bicycles. Added to this milieu were wildly painted buses, packed with passengers sitting and standing inside the bus. Outside the bus were additional riders hanging on to the back ladder leading to the roof where even more passengers sat. The dance of vehicles sped along without incident. There were few traffic signs or lights. Civility was purposely left at home. This was the time and place to be aggressive, or one would be in the same spot watching the hours and vehicles go past. Maneuvering the intersections was a miracle to behold, and horn honking was all part of the movement. We finally arrived at a dusty street that was lined with adobe-like apartment buildings wherein lived our first hosts. The driver delivered our bags, and forgot to unload my large bag of disposable diapers. Knowing that disposable diapers sold for one dollar each, I figured the taxi driver got more than Mohamed bargained for in payment of our short transport.

I had a large supply of cloth diapers which was my normal mode of diapering, but, with no wash machines and dryers in the homes and mosques in which I resided, I was hoping to use disposables. I promptly learned to wash by hand just after sunrise, so the clothes could dry quickly in the daytime sun.. I was definitely not a world traveler. This was the first time I had ever gone out of my familiar boundaries of the United States. The largest city I had ever visited was my hometown of Denver. I felt I was prepared to travel, and I was, except for knowledge of the dangers of unfamiliar water. Mohamed and ShemsAdeen seemed to acclimate to the water easily. Yusef and I remained sick with diarrhea for our entire four-month stay. I managed to keep Yusef hydrated, but knew he would have many diaper changes. Except for the frequent diarrhea and occasional abdominal cramps, we had no other symptoms. My baby was never lethargic or pale until we traveled on an all-day bus ride to the north.

So far on our trip, we had stayed in the simple apartment homes of Muslim families in the city of Karachi, then in a larger, more wealthy home in the city of Lahore. Mohamed left us to rest in this slightly opulent home of a Lahore business owner while he visited Islamabad. Then we stayed at a mosque in the small village of Riwand. The sounds in each of the towns were spectacular. The *Adhan*, call to *Salat*, sounded five times a day. I never grew tired of the echoing cadence reminding us to stop everything to make the *Salat*. The street vendors also filled the city with their rhythmic cries for people to leave their homes and buy the vendors' wares. In Riwand, the resonance of hammering and Islamic chants was added to the potpourri of sound. Carpenters were building an addition to the school, and they would say praises to Allah while doing their work.

Now, two months into our trip, our travels took us north to Peshawar. I knew we would be on the bus all day, so I slightly held back on giving my children fluids. I reasoned that this commode-less bus would not be the best forum to change diapers and rush a child in toilet training to the facilities. Because of my withholding fluids on a hot bus, my infant son, Yusef, had a sudden rise in temperature. He then collapsed into a febrile seizure. I told my husband, who had learned more Urdu than me, to tell the bus driver to find a clinic and ask for cold water. I found a cloth and cooled my son down with the cold water acquired from a pump at the side of the road. I shouted for everyone to read *Surat YaSin*. This is a chapter of the *Qur'an* that when recited gains protection from Allah. We were in an extremely rural area of Pakistan, and it took us thirty minutes to find a city with a clinic. Yusef's seizure had ended, but we visited the doctor anyway. The doctor, like many professionals in Pakistan, spoke English and told me to be sure to keep Yusef hydrated. I knew that. It was my mistake. But one that unintentionally brought me even closer to Allah. I had never been one to panic. I am very cool in emergencies. But during my sheltered life in middle class, suburban North America, I had not experienced the degree of desperation I felt on that bus as I held my jerking son and realized that help was not close by. But I did not panic. I calmly turned to Allah in prayer, and I asked others to turn to Him in prayer. I methodically cooled my son's fever with a cold cloth. It was my choice not to give my son as much water, but it was Allah's will to give him the seizure. It was my choice to seek Allah's help and to cool my son with water. It was Allah's will to stop his seizure and ward off sickness. This is *Qadar*, the combination of providence and free will. I just experienced Allah's *Qadar* in a momentous way. To some, this may seem like an averted tragedy. To me it was the most spiritual event I had experienced up to that time.

I had never met such warm, genuine people as those that I

had the blessing to experience in Pakistan. I was amazed at how each family welcomed my children and me into their homes. We were in the homes of city people and village dwellers of all different means. Some people I met in the neighborhoods were so poor that a week's dust covered their skin and clothes, their feet were thickly calloused from walking without shoes, and they showed unrelenting appreciation for the couple of dollars I presented to them in charity. I felt truly embarrassed and humbled by their displays of gratitude. I knew that the little amount of money I gave so freely would feed their family for a month. Back home, that same amount was just enough for the occasional ice cream cone in which we would indulge. We stayed in many homes throughout different areas of Pakistan. We stayed with large families in small village homes or apartments and with small families, like ours, just starting out and living in city apartments. We stayed with other traveling families in mosques, sleeping on straw mats and eating simple food. We stayed with families in large, well-furnished homes with an abundance of extravagant food. The homes were all different. But no matter what the families' financial standings, we were truly welcomed at each place we stayed. We were treated as if we were doing the hostess a favor by staying with her, rather than the opposite. No matter how much they had or didn't have, we were given royal treatment. The food, like the sounds and colors of the city, was a true stimulation to the taste buds. But with all the sights and sounds I experienced, it was the serenity I felt that remains most in my memory. Absorbing myself in reading *Qur'an* and learning *Ahadith*, the traditions of the Prophet, were a haven from the stress of balancing work, family care, and time for spirituality. I enjoyed every moment of our stay.

Our travel home had a transfer in Athens, Greece. In our rush to leave the States, we did not sense the need for separate passports for our small children. In Athens, they required the passports to board the plane to the United States. I had their birth certificates, proving their American birth, but the TWA counter agent and her supervisor insisted on the passports. We immediately called the embassy which was closed, and we were advised by the off-hours attendant to stay in a motel until Monday when we could visit the embassy and receive emergency passports for our children. My husband was a permanent resident of the United States, but had not yet received his citizenship, and he was traveling on his Libyan passport. Being a citizen of the United States, I was allowed to leave the airport without a visa, but my children and husband were not permitted to leave without permission from the airport police. The ticket counter supervisor, a calm and helpful soul, escorted me to the airport police. I was wearing my *Jilbab*, scarf, and now a veil to cover my face. I stood in front of a dark, burly man in a tight-fitting, blue uniform. He did not speak English, so the ticket counter supervisor was my translator. The airport police asked where I was from, where my children were born, and where my husband was from. He then asked how much money we had. I was hesitant to answer that last question, because I was unclear of his intentions. He became annoyed at my indecision, and loudly yelled at me in Greek. The response, in Greek, by the supervisor seemed to be an attempt to calm the fuming, imposing figure of the policeman, while begging for reconsideration. The police refused, and I was gently escorted away.

The ticket counter supervisor hesitantly and apologetically explained that the airport police yelled, "You have made your own grave. You have grown up in the land of opportunity, and you stand in front of me dressed like a Muslim peasant. I will not help you." This was the first time in my life that I was aware of being a casualty of prejudice. Amazingly, praise Allah, I did not panic or become incensed, I felt at peace with the fact that this was a grand trial to again test my acceptance of the *Qadar* of Allah.

We found a cafeteria, ordered meatless spaghetti, and then settled into the hard, black seats of the Athens airport. The next day, a Sunday, I once again called the embassy and explained that my family was not allowed out of the airport. The clerk on the phone agreed to open the embassy so that I could obtain a letter of permission allowing my United States-born children to re-enter our own country. I left my children and husband behind to take a taxi ride through the city of Athens. Although my mind was not on touring the town, I did enjoy viewing the breathtaking hills, and the taxi driver pointed out the historic ruins of the city. Fully covered in a veil and *Jilbab*, I walked up to the guards at the gates of the embassy and explained my appointment. I was accompanied through the empty building to a friendly face and familiar language. The embassy official apologized for not meeting with me yesterday and explained that she was sure the airport police would grant leave for my family.

With my letter in my hand, I returned to the airport. We were on the next plane to New York City. The immigration clerks looked at our letter from the embassy and asked what was the reason for it. I shared the abridged version of our adventure caused by our ignorance of passport policy and world travel. She replied that the letter was not necessary, and the official birth certificates were enough documentation for the re-entry of our children. According to her, the airlines should have let us board the plane with the birth certificates, and our stay in the Athens airport was unnecessary. *Qadar*. We can prepare and be unprepared, but what occurs is within the great plan of Allah. I experienced prejudice, and we learned patience through that ordeal.

Living Islam – Struggling For Harmony – Still Looking For Peace

We were in Pakistan for four months. The culture shock of seeing our affluent country after leaving a land of dismal poverty was profound. We returned to Denver to face the reality of living in this life in this country. In Islam, we are taught to work and play in our earthly life, while keeping worship and devotion to Allah. Living the constant life of a monk or a person traveling with the *Tablighi Jummah* is not permissible. We need to have families and to provide for them. We need to contribute to our communities. We need to be active in our faith and be part of the society. Isolation is not advised in Islam. A balance is to be maintained. So, back in Denver, I sought to find harmony between living the life of this world and doing good works to earn Heaven in the hereafter. While in Pakistan I had prayed to Allah to provide us with enough sustenance to be comfortable, but not so much as to gain greed and pull us away from our dedication to Allah. We have been granted this blessing.

Mohamed was able to land a nice job performing computer drafting. He trimmed his beard to a groomed length and saved his long shirts and baggie cotton pants for the weekends. I was soon pregnant again. So we decided that Mohamed would be the financial support, and I would stay home and be the home-making support. We had sold most of our belongings, so our roomy and nicely carpeted apartment with a patio had no furniture. And honestly, that was just fine with us. We slept on quilts on the floor, ate our meals on mats on the floor, and lounged on pillows. When Mom and Dad came to visit, they surprised us with a card table and chairs. Eating on and sitting on the floor were not experiences they wished to encounter.

Upon my arrival back in the States, I immediately established a weekly *Taleem*, a circle of learning, in my home. There was not a consistent gathering for English-speaking women. There were wonderful meetings for men, in Arabic, but women who spoke English were not served. During the meetings, we would memorize verses of *Qur'an* in Arabic, read from *Ahadith*, and learn about the life of Muhammad and the *Sahabah*, his companions. I was met with disagreement as to how the meeting was run. Some felt the meetings were too restrictive and wanted to do more than read from Islamic texts. I altered the *Taleem* to please those who protested. I was then encountered with different protests from those that liked the previous format. I struggled to please my fellow Muslim sisters only to find myself in the middle of controversy. I was now being accused of not following my Islam properly.

On the Thursday night before the next meeting, I had a dream of the Messenger Muhammad. We are taught in Islam that having a dream of the Prophet is an extraordinary occasion. It was an exceptional occurrence for me. My dream was filled with white light. A man with a moderate hue of skin in a dark beard and white robe walked towards me. His face held a gentle smile that comforted me. I wanted to embrace him, but, in awe, was unable to move. In a gentle voice full of grace and kindness, this man who I understood to be the Messenger of Allah, told me to continue as I was doing and to always follow my heart. The light then engulfed him, and my dream ended. I woke with a feeling of serenity. I had gained some wisdom. I cannot please everyone. Some will disagree with me. People interpret their path of Islam in diverse ways. All that I can do is what I feel is best for me at the time and pray for guidance. I also reminded myself of the *Hadith* that prompts us to understand that we are judged by our intentions and that only Allah and I know my intentions. I need to serve my community by doing good works, but I cannot expect a general consensus from my brothers and sisters in Islam as to how those good works should come into fruition. I asked forgiveness for my weaknesses and continued with the *Taleem* in the original format. The meetings continued in one form or another for the next decade.

My attire had changed to an even more conservative mode while I was in Pakistan. Now I was wearing a veil to cover my face. In my previous Islamic dress of a scarf and dress, I might have been the object of a double take. The onlooker was just making sure they saw what they thought they saw. At that time, the presence of various Muslim women's attire was not as widely apparent as it is now. But I usually was able to share a congenial smile to comfort the onlooker, and would sometimes then receive curious questions that I gladly answered. In Pakistan, the veil was not a source of alarm. Back in he United States, in 1984, I felt my veil and black *Jilbab* actually frightened people. I know I frightened young children, because they ran from me at the park. If I found a way to talk to the children, they would relax and ask if I was a Ninja. I would then usually manufacture a fake karate move to generate laughter and put the children at ease.

In my veil, I also found that conversations with my son's preschool teacher were strained. Since we only had one car, I also found myself at home a lot, and depended on Mohamed to take me on errands. It was vital for me to be involved in the community and my children's school, and I felt stifled with my loss of freedom. I did not like the self-imposed isolation I had seemingly selected. I was becoming more and more resentful of my Islamic dress and lack of freedom. We soon acquired another car, so I could transport ShemsAdeen to preschool and ease Mohamed of being my chauffer. As far as my veil, I prayed to Allah for a week, asking what I should do. With each completion of prayer, the message received in my heart was to once again adjust my mode of Islamic dress. I returned to loose dresses, or pants and a long shirt, and a headscarf. I once again felt part of my wider community.

I become frustrated with the amount of attention received about Muslim women's attire. While wearing a scarf, I am either seen as backwards and oppressed or as too liberal by my more conservative Muslim cohorts. I believe that how a Muslim decides to act out her

Hijab is a personal choice. The word *Hijab* literally means partition or curtain, and is meant to be a means of modesty between men and women. My choice not to wear the face veil was a private decision, and it does not denote my disagreement for those women who choose to wear the veil. In fact, I have a great deal of admiration for them. My choice to wear a scarf is also personal, and does not indicate my disagreement with those Muslim women who choose not to wear a scarf. I also have a great deal of respect for those sisters in Islam. My initial decision to wear a scarf was as a form of worship and to establish my distinct character as a Muslim. It gave me peace. As my Islam develops, the scarf continues to signify a form of identity for me. Along with being an act of worship, I wear my scarf to be recognized as a Muslim.

I have heard that if a Muslim woman wears a scarf in the United States that she is discriminated against and probably cannot find an occupation outside of the home. I am not aware of this experience in my life. While wearing my scarf and concealing attire, I have been interviewed and hired for wonderful jobs. These jobs have been from a customer service representative at a bank, to a receptionist at a tennis association and a financial industry, to public school teacher, to a workshop trainer at a non-profit organization. In my scarf, I have made wonderful relationships with neighbors, shopkeepers, and school personnel. It is my belief that I receive this good treatment because I grant, and expect in return, kind and just dealings. I am proud to sport my scarf and feel free to do so in my country of the United States. In the states, I do not feel the least bit of oppression because of the scarf.

My fourth child and my only girl was born at home like her brothers, Yusef and AbdAllah. My decision to have my children at home was out of a need to better control my children's birthing. My first son was delivered by emergency Caesarian section when the doctor's decision to speed the process caused a compressed cord and caused my son's heartbeat to stop. With my second pregnancy, I found a talented midwife that kept careful watch over us before, during, and after the births. When I was pregnant for the fourth time, I had conceded to being a mother of sons, and was pleasantly surprised with my blessing of a daughter. Fatimah came so quickly that no one was close enough to catch her. I reached down to receive my child and knew that I finally had a girl. With each homebirth, Mohamed would be the first to hold our child and quietly call the *Adhan* and *Iqama*, calls to *Salat*, in their ears, welcoming our children to the world with the promise of Islam. I would then cradle our newborn, signifying the comfort and safety we would provide for them in this life.

When Fatimah was born, I had planned on naming her Sakinah, meaning tranquility from Allah. At the last minute, and with protest from Mohamed, I decided to name her after my mother-in-law and the daughter of the Messenger. Mohamed and I chose the name ShemsAdeen, because Shemsi, meaning sunshine, was his favorite name, and Sunshine was mine. As a teen, I dreamed of naming my child Sunshine. It was a John Denver thing. *Deen* means faith and was added to our son's name to inspire spirituality. Yusef, Joseph in English, is the name of one of the prophets I read about in the *Qur'an* when I worked at the bank. AbdulAzziz, the same friend who informed me of the meaning of my adopted name, suggested we name our second son Yusef. Like the prophet Yusuf, our large, nine and a half pound son had a pleasant appearance. We both decided on the name of AbdAllah for our third son. The meaning of this name is servant of Allah. With Mohamed's last name, Ben-Masaud, our son would be named after one of the companions of the Messenger who memorized the *Qur'an* and transmitted some of the authentic *Ahadith*. We were now a family with four children between the ages of five and newborn and were living in a two-bedroom apartment. It was time to purchase a house. We found a nice home at an unbelievably low price. It was a real "fixer upper," as they say, in a pleasant neighborhood within walking distance to schools.

I became very active in my children's elementary school. I served on the community accountability board and volunteered in the classrooms. I ran an after-school reading group and helped with all the field trips I could. Because we did not celebrate Halloween, Christmas, or Valentine's Day, I would explain to the teachers our desire to pull our children out of school during the parties. They easily acquiesced, and the children and I would usually find a wonderful activity to do instead. On the days of the two 'Eids, we would keep our children out of school to celebrate our holidays. Because of these absences, my children would miss out on the perfect attendance award. This especially perturbed my young activist, Yusef. In fourth grade, he wrote letters to his senator, his congressman, the president of the Board of Education, and his school principal asking for a floating holiday in the school schedule. Nobody conceded to that request, but the school did change its definition of perfect attendance, and my children received their certificates that and the following years. When my older sons started high school, they also precipitated change in the attendance policy. Perfect attendance at the high school and a B average meant dismissal from semester and year-end finals. Through their protest, the schools added to their policy two floating holidays that would act as excused absences and allowed my sons to forgo their finals.

Throughout the years, the teachers all got to know our family well and frequently asked us to give presentations about Islamic holidays and the Libyan culture to their classes. It became a ritual that every 'Eid Al-Fitr we would share holiday goodies and stories about Islam to a least one of my children's classes. Even with these procedures put in place, it was a challenge to initiate traditions for our holidays at home in a state where only a minority celebrates 'Eid. We also had the challenge of joining the traditions of two cultures, the Libyan and North American. My holiday tradition was decorating the house, staying at home with a family gathering, gifts and a large dinner. Mohamed's holiday tradition was friends, visiting various homes, and parties with Islamic music. Visiting friends is wonderful, but Mohamed's friends liked to visit without their wives, segregating parties between women and men. I like spending time together visiting as a family. It truly was an effort to find mutual ground on this issue.

THE BEN-MASAUDS AT EID BREAKFAST. (L to R) Mohamed, Fatimah, Yusef, AbdAllah, ShemsAdeen and Carema

We came to a favorable settlement. During the holidays, we decorate the house with embroidered Arabic calligraphy and ribbons with crescents and stars. We then join our community at either the Islamic Center or Masjid Al-Nur for the holiday morning service. This ritual provides me with the same excitement I entertained during the holiday services at church. The Muslim congregation also dresses in their best clothes, and the mosque bursts at the seams with more attendants than during our usual Friday Sabbath. After taking holiday pictures and greeting all our friends at the mosques, we then have a family breakfast. This is then followed by a treasure hunt or the opening of gifts. In the evening of our holiday, Mohamed leaves to spend time with his friends. As our sons grow, they also join the all-male parties. Fatimah and I either arrange or find a women's gathering to attend.

On the weekend after our holiday, we have my parents over for a holiday dinner and gift giving.

In the second chapter of the *Qur'an*, called the Cow (*Al-Baqarah*), Allah states that a husband and wife are garments to each other. I love this verse. We are garments to each other. We protect each other. Adorn each other. Wrap ourselves around each other. Marriage is a truly blessed gift from Allah that is also a great challenge. Mohamed and I have said to each other, and to anyone else who will listen, that marriage is difficult in the best circumstances. Marriage to someone from a culture different than yours is grueling. We know that our adoring friendship with each other, our commitment to family, and the will of Allah has kept us married these twenty-some years. It was surely not the ease we felt in our relationship, at least in the beginning. We have learned a lot over the years, and ease comes more frequently. No matter how enlightened one may be, he or she comes into a marriage with unspoken expectations. Someone of a similar prospective easily understands those expectations. When the couple is deeply embedded in their differing cultures, as is the case with Mohamed and I, understanding the paradigm of the other is at best difficult. Communication is the key, but if the two have different means of communication, more creative methods are needed. Our method is to try to talk, drop the subject, seek out each other in comfort, and then depend on prayer.

In the summer of 1992, we packed up our family of six and took a trip to visit Mohamed's clan on the family farm in his hometown of Tripoli. There, I learned volumes about my husband's family culture. I definitely gained an improved understanding of him. It all made sense to me now. My family avoids conflict, but may simmer with unresolved resentment. His family loudly meets conflict head on, but quickly forgets it again without resolution, but with acceptance. It was a revelation to see how our family conflict styles were so different. With this revelation, I learned that I should forgive quicker and let some things slide. The visit was wonderful, not only because of my new knowledge, but because the children and I got to meet Mohamed's family, feel their warmth, and appreciate his place of birth. We all fell in love with this sociable crew who did so much to make us comfortable in the new environment. My sons found playing different forms of soccer all day on the dirt roads a true adventure, and quickly picked up the language of their cousins and neighborhood playmates. Fatimah and I tolerated the frequent tea parties, but missed our freedom of visiting libraries, playing in parks, and going shopping on a whim. Fatimah was more shy than the boys, and depended on my company in Libya. She did enjoy playing with her cousins, but tired of staying inside. Our visit was for six weeks, and although Mohamed and ShemsAdeen were not ready to leave, I am sad to admit that I was anxious to return to my own home. The other children also seemed ready to get back home.

When we returned home, Fatimah started kindergarten. With our children now all in school, Mohamed and I decided that I should return to work outside of the home in order to help out with the expenses. Working in the business world soon proved to be unrewarding, and I returned to college to re-start my schooling in psychology and education. Being on the Auraria campus with people striving to learn was an exhilarating experience. Sitting in classes and soaking in all the knowledge that was presented was wonderfully fulfilling. Trying to find that balance between work for this life and maintaining faith yet eluded me. I was still a student in all aspects, and the perfect life I thought I would have by becoming Muslim was still yet to happen. I was busy with home, family, and school, but did have time to realize that the hole in my spirit was once again growing inside me.

During the summer of my third year of college, I had planned on traveling with my parents to visit my mother's sister and family on their Iowan farm. All of my grandparents had died years before, and this aunt's family was all that remained on Mother's side. I was excited about the pilgrimage and the time I would spend with Mom's family. A couple days before our planned departure, Mom called to break the news that Dad was sick and felt he couldn't make the trip. Dad had experienced years of diabetes and arrhythmia which required the installation of a defibulator and pacemaker. He had looked weak and pale during the past months, but he was still very lucid and mostly involved, and we didn't notice how sick he really was. Before the end of the week, Dad was in the hospital with pancreatitus. The risky surgery weakened him further, and he died on June 5, 1998. Losing a parent deeply affects a person's resolve of faith. It can either strengthen faith, or find any holes and start draining the spirit.

That week, I had planned our monthly Muslim women's gathering to be held at a friend's house, because of my planned trip to Iowa. With the events of the week, the meeting was now held as I was attending my father's funeral. There were some Muslim ladies at that meeting who decided that my father was a *Kafir*, an unbeliever, and that the usual visits of condolence should not be granted to me because of that. I am always amazed at the self-perceived power with which some people delude themselves. How can we possibly judge the position of faith a person possesses when he is living or dying? Is not Allah the only one who can see in our hearts? How could any human judge another as a non-believer? My father's place with Allah is between him and Allah. What I felt at the time was sadness for the loss of my father, and I needed condolence. Only three Muslim sisters from our now large community visited me during the weeks after my father's funeral. The kindness of these devoted friends kept me afloat during this trying time. The lack of support from the others crushed me and further weakened my resolve.

Within a year, I completed my student teaching and graduated with a degree in psychology and with a certification in elementary and special education. My husband and children, all of my siblings and their families, and my mother were at my graduation loudly cheering me on. My enchanting husband planned a surprise party in our beautifully finished backyard. He gathered teachers and principals from our children's elementary school. He invited my favorite professors and the teachers who sponsored me during student teaching. Of course, all of my family was there along with close family friends. It was a wonderful day. I wished my father could have been there.

I accepted the second grade teaching position at the school where I student-taught. I was buried in planning and grading and assessing and more planning. My children were now in middle and high school, and I attempted to remain active on their campuses. My husband's sisters were also in town on their first visit to the United States. And we were moving into a new home, after living in our other home for eleven years. Mohamed had a great technical support position with Hewlett Packard, and we could afford a larger home. It is amazing how worldly possessions pile up. As I filled this large home with furniture and decorations, I thought back to the simplicity of our unfurnished apartments back in the eighties. The amount of stress I felt seemed unbearable, and my *Salat* began to suffer. I had abandoned organizing the women's meetings the summer before, and found going to the mosque more suffocating than inspiring. In Islam, we are taught to turn to Allah with gratitude in prosperity and hardship. We understand that all we receive from Allah is a blessing. We are taught to understand that a thing we may perceive to be a blight to our lives may actually bring about good for us. We are taught that we at least learn patience through our trials and gain rewards thereby. Even with this knowledge, I was finding it more and more difficult to show gratitude through my stress. My earthly support system was falling short of my needs, and I felt too overwhelmed to turn to Allah.

During my second year of teaching in a public school, I began to experience anxiety attacks. They came in the form of an intense pressure in my chest. I felt as if my heart was being crushed. My principal suggested that I visit the doctor where I got the report I expected. My heart was fine. I was suffering from panic attacks. With great trepidation, I asked for a leave of absence starting at the end of the school year. I spent the summer gardening and trying to improve my *Salat.* Even though the pain in my chest was alleviated, I still often found myself in tears.

Summer was over, and it was time to find another job. I did not want to go back to the business world. I felt most fulfilled helping others by teaching or counseling, but I was afraid to work in schools again. I polished my computer skills and arranged for interviews at various businesses. I was unhappy with all the companies I visited. I was a lost seed floating aimlessly in the wind. This was the uncomfortable feeling I remembered from my high school days. I was once again struggling with what to do with myself. One morning, I awoke asking Allah what direction to take. The Conflict Center then came to mind. Through the years, I had worked in some capacity with a place called the Conflict Center. I had taken parenting classes from the center while my children were in primary school, my children had taken conflict management classes there in school, and, as a teacher, I was privileged to have the center's teaching staff work with my students. I had called the center the spring before and inquired what type of degree was required to work there. I learned that my teaching certification would be accepted, but there were no current openings, and the pay would be less than my teaching salary. After praying for guidance that morning, I called the Conflict Center to see if a job was available. There was, and an interview was arranged on the spot. I had one other interview that Tuesday morning. It was for a computer job in which I had no interest. I slid through that interview and got in my car to grab some breakfast before my interview at the Conflict Center.

I turned on my radio and heard reports that two planes had crashed into the side of the twin towers of the World Trade Center, and that another plane had collided with the Pentagon. It was September 11, 2001. My heart sank. Mohamed and I were in Washington, DC, and Manhattan just the previous spring. I drove Mohamed crazy pointing out the Twin Towers at every turn of the corner. How could those magnificent buildings be damaged? With that, I thought of the people. I prayed that they would all get out safely. My thoughts then went to suspicions. This was obviously an attack. Who would do such a thing? I began to fear what the nationality was of these misled, violent beings. It was such a drastic act. While being with my Muslim husband, I had experienced the tense reports of the Iranian hostage-taking, the explosion of the plane over Scotland and the subsequent US bombings on Libya, the Persian Gulf War, and the bombing in Oklahoma City. Each time, the attention received within our Islamic community resulted in anxiety. Our mosque would swarm with reporters, and uncomfortable attention would be placed on the undeserving Muslim population. Any attacks my family might have received during those stressful times are really inconsequential. Our small maltreatments have been just harmless soaping of our car during the hostage taking, a few verbal attacks during the Gulf War, and the fear of the safety of any Muslim, including Mohamed's family, during any US-led attack. These were all selfish thoughts. I prayed again that the people would be safe. I prayed for solace.

As tears of frustration ran down my face, I decided to go home to freshen up. This next interview was for a job I wanted. By the will of Allah, I needed to prove to them that I was the teacher they wanted. As I arrived for the appointment, I opened the glass door that revealed a sign saying "Violence Not Welcome Here." I felt at immediate ease. I was hired at the Conflict Center and started that same month. I had found an occupation that would help decrease violence in our neighborhoods, by teaching conflict and anger management. I was now working with a group of hopeful, spiritual people who welcomed me without hesitation.

It was about this time that I visited the Islamic Center to hear a male Muslim scholar in Washington, D.C. area, speak to Muslim women. As usual, his first subject to approach was proper Islamic dress, and I immediately felt deflated. Do these men feel that the Muslim women's intellect can expand no further than how to dress and how to behave? I sat through the rest of the talk trying to glean some information, some kind of peace from his lecture. The Muslim scholar then proceeded to say that there is no reason for a Muslim woman to work outside the home. He added the query as to what could she possibly contribute to the community outside of the home. I felt so dishonored by his statements. By the will of Allah, I contribute a lot to my community outside of my home through my community work, my occupations, and my time spent in my children's schools. My chest closed in on my heart again, my breathing became rapid, and I had to go outside for air. I felt completely suffocated. Islam liberates me, but there are some Muslims who cause me to feel stifled. The lectures of some stifling scholars that I have heard over the years were not for the purpose to enlighten us and to find the beauty in Allah, but rather to restrict us. It seemed that their purpose was to tell us what not to do, without telling us what to do to feed our spirit.

At the Conflict Center, I loved my work, but the hours were long, and I still had not mastered juggling work and home. My depression had now gone so deep that I was wishing for a way to gain permission to be absent from my world for a while. I fantasized about checking into a hospital just to rest. One Sunday, my tears became so incontrollable that I was distressing my family. I got in my car and began driving. I headed west thinking to visit my mother, but felt my desperation would upset her. I came to an exit and pulled the car into a vacant lot. With tears streaming down my face, I screamed, "Just tell me what to do, Allah. I am so lost. So overwhelmed. Just tell me what to do." Again the answer came through my heart. Go home. Go home and rest. Go home and hug your children. Go home and hug your husband.

As I turned the car around, a homeless person was at the side of the road. I have the habit of stopping to talk to homeless people and share whatever small change or food I had in the car. I pulled up to him and gave what change I had. He looked at my tearstained eyes and asked if I were okay. His warmth touched me, and I shared that I was having a horrendous day. He then laughed and said, "It couldn't be as bad as mine. You at least have a car."

He was right. I am so blessed. I have beautiful, pious, intelligent children. My faithful husband is a caring teacher and passionate companion. I have a mother and siblings who have been by my side for everything. I have friends that care about me and are wonderful allies. I am happy with my work. I have health. I have shelter. I have nourishment. And I know my faith. But where is my faith? I thought that just finding a way to worship God that complemented my beliefs would be the answer. Remember? I would then have a perfect life. It was easy to be full of faith and worship in the safe environment of my secluded life in Pakistan. But the real test of faith is living the drudgeries of the day-to-day existence of this world while persevering in my devotion and beliefs. My depression was from my dissatisfaction that I still did not have all the answers. I was unforgiving of myself and expected perfection. I had let ingratitude and hopelessness creep into my world. I had lost my fortitude, and was not as acceptant of *Qadar* of Allah. I was letting the hole in my soul grow instead of filling it with internal peace and thanksgiving. I was also making the pursuits of this life more important than my work towards the eternal life. I did not have balance in my life. I was still in search of harmony. Twenty years after finding Islam, I again was lost and felt discontented.

With all these thoughts riveting in my brain, I came to the epiphany that all the answers are still within the *Qur'an*, the teachings of Allah. As I drove home, I reminded myself of the verse of the *Qur'an* that states:

> Ye shall certainly be tried and tested in your possessions and in your personal selves; and ye shall certainly hear much that will grieve you, from those who received the book before you, and from those who worship many gods. But if ye persevere patiently and guard against evil — then that will be a determining factor in all affairs (*Qur'an* 3: 186).

I needed to turn to Allah for my assistance. I needed to rejuvenate the graciousness and gratitude I knew in life. I needed to remind myself of the beauty in my life. I needed to accept *Qadar* and gain balance in my life. I needed to forgive myself and to turn to Allah.

Giving Life to a Muslim Spirit – Nearing Peace

Soon after my day of desperation, my children invited me to attend a lecture they had organized through their youth group at Masjid Al-Nur. Like the Islamic Center, that mosque had moved to a larger building. A few years back, my children and their friends started a youth group to hold weekly meetings, plan social activities, and arrange for speakers. The speaker they had engaged this time was named Dawud Warnsby. I had listened to one of his tapes and enjoyed his songs for Muslims, but I did not have much desire to attend a Muslim lecture. My oldest son, who was now twenty, was insistent. I felt compelled to go to please my son.

The speaker had a welcoming responsiveness to his voice, and a warm and affable appearance. I settled in to listen to what he had to offer. In his talk, this brother proceeded to remind me that Islam was entering into peace through Allah. I needed peace, Allah. He then reminded me that our spirits identified with truth. I was resuscitating my spiritual identity. He reminded me that our lives on this earth were just a short trip between the birth and death. He reminded me that the diversions in this life steer us away from finding peace through Allah. He reminded me that we choose to enter into peace, or we choose to be sidetracked by the chaos of life. I needed to alleviate stressful chaos in my life and to choose to enter into harmony and peace. The brother had my attention.

Next, brother Dawud tested his audience by asking what the various faiths offer. Through his quizzing, we agreed that most faiths offer the belief in God, the belief in the hereafter, the need to perform acts of worship, and the expectation of doing good to others. We pretended to put each of those entities into a box. He then asked which box has God. Where is God? The audience sat stumped for a long minute. Then a dear young friend sitting next to me said, "God is everywhere." God is everywhere. We cannot box Allah. The boxes are the institutions of religion. Allah is not an institution. The sounds of the room became mute to me, and I sat still in the midst of that revelation.

Allah is not contained within our acts of worship. That is a way to get closer to and to remember Him in our lives. He is not contained in our mode of dress and manners. That is a way to remain on a straight path. Allah is not contained in my family. That is a means to provide happiness, support, and a true test in this life. He is not contained in what occupation I hold. That is a means for me to live and contribute within my earthly community. Allah is Mercy. He is Compassion. He is Kindness. He is Generosity. He is our Protector and Provider. He is Forgiving. He is Truth. He is the Guide. He is the source of Peace. The *Qur'an* is His gift to us for guidance in this world to the hereafter. Allah gave His *Qur'an* to me years ago, because I was searching for answers. I praise Allah that I was given a guide. After the brother finished his lecture, I felt obligated to thank him. He was Allah's means to drag me out of the pit of desolation and back on the path toward peace.

Since that lecture, I decided to continue my community work at the Conflict Center, but on a part-time basis. I now have more time to read the *Qur'an*, maintain my worship, and be with my family and friends. Allah has also introduced me to an Islamic organization called Muslims Intent on Learning and Activism. The purpose of this group is to help others learn more about Islam and to provide community service. Through this group, I relish in the opportunity of listening to diverse, uplifting Muslim speakers. I am honored to help organize and speak at inter-faith events and various workshops on Islam. And I am privileged to be part of a group of Muslims working within the community on several different service projects. Through this group, I have also been blessed with many new and renewed friendships.

I know I will continue to receive many trials. Allah has promised me that, and that my faith will wax and wane as does the cycles of the moon. But through all my trials, my faith in Allah has remained firm. I strive to live with more patience and graciousness. I have learned to accept my limitations and make every effort in balancing the time I give to services in this life and time for spiritual nourishment. I am now finding that ever-illusive balance of family and friends and occupation and worship. And I have learned once again to turn my adversities over to Allah, seeking His guidance and help. I accept my free determination and His plan for me, His *Qadar*. I pray that He keeps me under His guidance as a truthful believer in constant gratitude of His beauty and bounties and continually doing good works in His Name.

There's a Whale in My Bed!

LINDA "ILHAM" BARTO

iLham is an artist and writer in the foothills of North Carolina. The following account and opinions are her own, so don't blame anybody else.

A straw-covered dirt floor, walls of cardboard-covered two-by-fours, benches made of planks, and a red-faced preacher who fell to his knees and beat the floor with his fist while he preached a sermon of hell and damnation – that's my earliest recollection of church. The youngest of five children, I bobbed through the yellow waves of a hay field to the temporary structure that made do while the preacher built a little, brick church by his own hands. I was well into my twenties before I figured out that all preachers don't scream until the veins pop out on their necks and their faces flush scalding red.

Despite his transformation during preaching, Preacher Martin was a kind, generous man who truly ministered to his congregation and his neighbors. I absolutely adored him, and I always had a big hug for him as I waited in line to shake the preacher's hand as the congregation departed from Sunday morning worship service.. Nearly a half-century later, I still remember his big smile and glasses as thick as an old Coke bottle. He died years ago without my ever telling him how positively he affected my life. That's okay; I'll tell him when I get to Heaven.

Gran'ma was a moonshiner in the hills of North Carolina. To make the babies sleep, she gave them homemade whiskey. Perhaps that's how Daddy became an alcoholic; perhaps it was because of the memories of World War Two in which he was a flame-thrower in the Marine Corps. At age twenty-one, he was called "Pop" by the other troops who were just kids sent out to face the probability of the supreme sacrifice. At Iwo Jima, many died, and Daddy was so riddled with shrapnel that he was unable to walk for four years. As a child, I used to watch him use his pocketknife to cut out pieces of shrapnel that had worked their way to just under the skin. We had to walk softly around Daddy; if he was startled, he would jump up fighting, and I think he fought World War Two almost every night in his sleep.

Mama was a martyr. She put up with constant emotional pain and abuse, but never slacked in raising crops, caring for the farm animals, canning vegetables, baking bread, making all our clothes, and performing a long list of other day-to-day chores in addition to the occasional jobs of things like carpentry, upholstery, and plumbing. (Actually, I was fourteen years old when we got indoor plumbing; Preacher Martin put it in for us and closed the episodes of my dashing out to the "blackhouse" and stepping barefooted into fresh chicken poop or losing my slippers in the snow.)

Mama never considered leaving Daddy, as his drinking got worse. She always believed that, if she stayed with him, someday he would eventually "give his life to the Lord." We missed church when Daddy was on one of his drinking binges. At Christmas, Preacher Martin would bring us the little goody bags of fruits and candy that we had missed out on because Daddy was too drunk to take us to the church play.

When Daddy took a spell of drinking, he wouldn't stop until he couldn't stagger around any longer and usually passed out across the kitchen floor. We would have to step over him for a week or so while Mama kept him rolled over on his side so he wouldn't choke on his vomit. When he finally came to and sobered up, Mama had to scrub the floor with disinfectant to clean up the vomit and urine.

The worst part, of course, was the beatings. I usually made myself as little as possible as I curled up in a dark corner and listened to my mother's crying and screaming, and her begging, "Bill, please don't hit me again." When he was finally through with her, she was a bloody, bruised lump collapsed on the floor while he went out to the shed for his bottle of poison.

When I was fourteen (not long after we got indoor plumbing), I stayed home with Daddy after he had just begun a bout of drinking. Mama had her driver's license then, so she took the rest of the family to church. Daddy made some comment (I don't remember what) that indicated that he was unhappy with the life he was living. I didn't know much about witnessing and certainly not about counseling my own father, but I got my Sunday School booklet, and Daddy and I had church together.

A few weeks later, when Daddy was sober and we were in the brick church, Preacher Martin gave the call to come to salvation. I had just come to the realization that, by Southern Baptist definition, I was "lost." It was required that a believer make "a public confession of faith in the Lord Jesus Christ," and I wanted to do the right thing, so I walked up the aisle. Right behind me came my daddy; he rededicated his life to God that day; he never drank again. Our lives improved greatly as Daddy studied the *Bible* and devoted his life to being a better Christian. Within a few years, he was a deacon in the fast-growing church and one of the church's and community's most-respected leaders. Today he is posthumously honored in the church's historical museum as a significant contributor to the ministry. Daddy's life was a testament to the fact that God changes sinners who come to Him.

As a Christian, I had many close encounters of the divine kind. One of the most memorable was a rescue when I was seventeen. One of my favorite places was in the woods behind the old homestead. I liked being alone, communing with nature. A creek ran through the woods, and my black, shaggy dog Choo-choo and I could often be found wading with the tadpoles and crawdads. One fine, sunny day I climbed over the neighbor's fence, outran the bull, tore the seat of my pants on barbed wire as I scrambled over the far end of the fence, and laughed in the face of the bull I had barely escaped. Soon Choo-choo and I were exploring patches of wildflowers and holes where critters lived. We were about ready to head back when we came to an embankment with a steep incline to the creek. In a pool within the water's rock-studded swirls, two smooth, black, water snakes were playfully chasing each other in circles. I wanted to take a closer look, but there was no trustworthy place down which to climb. Then I spotted a bar of sand in the middle of the creek. I jumped from the bank, but when my feet hit the sandbar, it's deceptive mask gave way, and I fell straight down into a miry bog. It was a mushy type of quicksand, and, against my body, I felt the jabbing and rubbing of what I imagined to be the bones of other reckless teenagers. Choo-choo was barking helplessly as I sank underneath the slush and debris, and I too was helpless as there was nothing to grab onto. I was doomed to be swallowed forever into a camouflaged black hole and leave my parents to always wonder what became of me. With my head underneath the muck, I pitifully thrust my hand above me with a last, vain attempt to grasp the air I would no longer breathe. Suddenly, a force grabbed my hand and encircled my arm. I was simultaneously pulled and thrust (perhaps by gases in the bottom of the bog) and thrown against the side of the embankment. I waded upstream where I washed off some of the mess and found an easy exit from the creek bed. When I walked into the kitchen, Mama was adding wood to the cook stove on which supper was cooking. She looked at me, dripping wet with dead stuff stuck in my hair, and said, "You oughta be ashamed of yourself!"

One of my favorite verses has since been: "He drew me up from the desolate pit out of the miry bog and set my feet upon a rock making my steps secure" (*Psalms* 40: 2).

Another miracle occurred much later in my life. I was in training for my black belt in karate and kickboxing when I suffered a neck injury. A disc ruptured and bone fragments damaged a nerve; my left arm became numb and barely useable; surgery was necessary. The doctor warned that there was a forty percent chance that the operation would fail, and I could lose the use of my arm completely. Days after the operation, I returned to the hospital to have an x-ray of the doctor's handiwork. The bone graft he had taken from my pelvic bone had slipped from its position in my neck and was wedged in muscle tissue beside my spinal cord. The doctor said there was no choice but to redo the procedure. After making a new appointment to schedule the operation, I returned home depressed. The operation had been extremely painful and difficult to overcome; I couldn't stand the thought of having to go through it all again. In a moment of desperation and inspiration, I opened the phone book, haphazardly plopped a finger, and called a number. A woman answered the phone; I explained my situation and asked her to pray for me. As it turned out, she and her husband were actively involved in the ministry, and they offered a special prayer for me. When I returned to the doctor a couple weeks later, I asked him to take a new x-ray. I waited as he viewed the negative, then he excitedly shouted for me to come into the viewing room to see the x-ray for myself. The piece of bone had worked its way back into position and had properly fused into place. The doctor was amazed, and I went on to get that black belt!

I have experienced many other miracles and signs, so I never doubted the reality of God or His involvement in my life. One night when I was a senior in high school, I was sitting on the back porch and wondering about my future, so I took a few minutes to pray for God to jump ahead of me and smooth out the road. While I was praying in the darkness, a soft, white light in the shape of dove's wings fluttered in front of me, and then disappeared as my prayer ended. The next morning, after the mail had arrived, I spotted the new Southern Baptist magazine on my sister's bed. The picture on the front cover was exactly the vision I had seen. "What's this!?" I asked, and my sister answered, "It's just an artist's conception of the Holy Spirit." (In Christianity, "Holy Spirit" means the Spirit of God.) I then realized that the vision and the interpretation from the magazine cover were a sign from God that I could always depend on Him.

Without intending to be a pioneer, I managed to be among the first of women paving the way into certain areas of a man's world. At age eighteen, I was the first female to build furniture in the shop where I got my first full-time job. I experienced the cliché of having "to work twice as hard to be considered half as good," and I did it for minimum wage while the men got raises. At only five-foot three and one hundred and sixteen pounds, I had to wrestle non-stop with the need to prove myself adequate. One of my tasks was unloading trucks of glued-up blocks of wood which were my equal in size and weight. With skillful maneuvering and a precarious balance of leverage and stubbornness, I managed to lift those blocks and stack them up over my head.

At age twenty-one, I joined the WAF (Women's Air Force) before the women's services were incorporated into the men's. My recruiter made me stand on the scale and eat bananas until I weighed enough to get in. I was in the first group of women to be assigned to the weather school. The older men despised us; the young men loved us. When the plane carrying us women landed at the base, the young men had con-gregated by the hundreds around the flight line. They were cheering, and many were holding up signs saying things like, "I love You," "WAF are beautiful," and "Will you marry me?"

USAF, 1970-1973

In weather school, women were discriminated against by the all-male staff that constantly debased and harassed the women. Students were tested by timed exercises; i.e., three minutes to calculate and plot the expected course of a hurricane. Twice during such tests, I was called into the administration office to make coffee for the male officers, so I received zeros on those required exams. When men failed a class, they were allowed to be set back to an under class and start fresh; women were dismissed without second chances. One man was set back for the seventh time while I was there. In addition to the school's male chauvinism, I created my own problems. I didn't take time to study because there were too many handsome men to date, and I was too busy growing up. I didn't do anything wrong—no drugs, tobacco, alcohol, or sex; I just wanted to have fun all the time and enjoy the experience of being away from home for the first time in my life. I quickly washed out of weather school.

I was sent to a desk job where I assisted in the training of bombardiers and navigators being shipped out to Viet Nam. It was then that I met my first Muslims; they were Iraqi airmen trained by the United States Air Force. I was among the first women ever stationed at the navigational training base, and I was likely the first blond, blue-eyed, female soldier the Iraqi navigators had ever seen; they were so intrigued by me that they heard nothing being said by their instructors as long as I was in the room. I just giggled a lot and was polite to them, but I didn't try to learn anything about their strange religion.

I caught a man in the Air Force! Ironically, Tom had joined the Air Force with the recruiter's promise that Tom would go to weather school, but we didn't meet there. After basic training, Tom discovered that recruiters lie! He begrudgingly accepted orders to the military police academy after being given the explanation that "the needs of the Air Force come first." After police training, Tom received orders for Viet Nam. His orders were put on hold, however, because he was a witness to an accident still being investigated. He was to stay behind temporarily while the rest of his group shipped out. Weeks after the deployment, every military policeman with whom Tom had trained was killed during the invasion at Cam Ranh. He would have been among the dead if it had not been for the accident investigation. After the massacre, Tom's orders were changed, and he was sent to the Aleutian Islands where he helped monitor Russian activity in the North Pacific and Bering Sea.

After the Alaskan assignment, Tom was sent to the navigational training base where we met. It was a whirlwind courtship; we had known each other less than ten weeks when we eloped. As *they* say, "When it's right, you know it." Tom also was a devout Christian and had never been involved with anything immoral. We made "the perfect couple" according to our friends who often accused us of being "lost in a world all (our) own."

Several years later, I gave birth to a son who came at a financially difficult time in our lives. Tom and I had left the service and gone to school full-time on the GI Bill. After the pregnancy, I got a serious case of phlebitis that left me unable to work for quite a while. We soon found ourselves with medical bills and a baby for whom to provide. I stayed home to care for the baby while Tom worked, but his job didn't pay very well, and most of the money paid debts. Often we had no food except what I could scavenge. I picked wild blackberries, persimmons, and apples. Sometimes I collected wild violet leaves and tossed them with a little mayonnaise to make a salad. I even swiped potato peelings out of a neighbor's compost heap; washed and cooked in oil, they weren't too bad.

Often in the dead of winter, we had no heat. We reserved money to buy oil, but after we invested in a month's supply, the man who rented us "the ol' stinky house" (as we called it) sneaked over during the night and siphoned out a few gallons for himself.

When we finally started climbing out of our financial pit, we returned to college where I studied art and Tom studied printing. Today, I work as a freelance artist who writes, and Tom is involved in the printing industry. We live in a house built by our own hands. It is in the country where we gather eggs from our chickens, and cook food we raise in a garden that begins in our small, backyard greenhouse.

Our son, Duston, was an inquisitive, thoughtful child who has grown to be a responsible, honorable young man. He loves art and, while holding down a job in retail sales, is studying to be a photographer. Soon after the terrorists' attacks of September 11, 2001, he was a guest on a local radio talk show where he answered the interviewer's and callers' questions about Islam. He explained, "The true validity of a religion is not found within the madmen who claim to practice it." It was the first time that many people in our rural area were exposed to an American-born Muslim's perspective.

DUSTON WITH TANA: shortly after her adoption

We adopted a child when she was five years old. Tana is a lovely girl with a delightful personality. She was born with Fetal Alcohol Syndrome (FAS). Most people don't know that FAS causes life-long problems. When a woman drinks during pregnancy—especially during the first few weeks when the baby's nervous system is forming—permanent brain damage can occur. We have been advised to "accept the reality" of Tana's condition, but we refuse. Our *Jihad* (struggle) is not, as stated in the famous "Serenity Prayer" of Alcoholics Anonymous, "to accept the things that cannot be changed," but to enlist God's power in helping Tana overcome the evil of FAS. Our *Qur'an* says "...Allah is the only reality..." (31: 30a), and "...Allah hath power over all things" (5: 40b). When the public school accepted "the reality" that Tana could not learn, Tom and I took her out of school and began teaching her ourselves at home. She's learning! As Tana faces greater challenges, our God remains the God of Impossibilities!

Years after the Viet Nam War, Tom and I both re-entered the military when we joined the North Carolina Air National Guard. I worked in flight line management to insure that the flight plans were approved for the aircraft to occupy air space, and I kept in radio contact with outgoing and incoming aircrews. Tom's job involved packing medicines and food supplies for airdrops in disaster areas. He remains in the guard, but my career, along with many other soldiers' careers, was abruptly ended when President Clinton did all those crazy cutbacks in the military. I was a decorated soldier having received, in addition to many ribbons, the George Washington Medal of Honor, the Air Force Commendation Medal (twice), and the first-awarded North Carolina Achievement Medal.

Tom and I and the children were always involved in church and Christian ministries. We donated time and money to spreading the Gospel of Jesus Christ. As volunteers, we spent many hours with

Bibles for the World as we prepared address labels and wrapped *Bibles* for residents of various foreign countries; we taught Sunday School and supported the local Christian radio station. We were unlikely prospects for Islam. If anyone had prophesied that I would become a Muslim, I would have joined the mob to burn him at the stake. It would have seemed a ridiculous idea to speculate that a devoted Christian and independent woman like myself would even consider joining the Muslims on their way to hell. Every civilized, sane person in the *Bible* Belt knows that only Christians are going to Heaven!

I never read any of the *Qur'an* until I was doing some research for a manuscript on how to legally accommodate religious diversity in the public schools. In preparing to write, I acquainted myself with various religions, including Islam. I got a translation of the *Qur'an* from the library, and the part about Jesus' not being the Son of God was a real turn-off for me. I thought, "There's some goodstuff in this book, but whoever wrote it didn't know anything about Jesus."

Although I certainly wasn't looking for a new religion, I became unhappy with church in general. I was constantly being criticized for my views, which often conflicted with the traditional church stance. Some public schools followed the examples presented in my book about accommodating religious diversity, but the suggestions inflamed Christian religious leaders. Entitled *The E Pluribus Unum Connection*, the document was a well-researched, legally sound plan for including religion in education. My argument was that a child's education is incomplete if he or she knows nothing about any religion except his or her own, and he or she is inaptly equipped to enter our diverse society. I received threatening phone calls, and portions of my book were even read and criticized nationally on Christian radio stations. I realized that a great number of Christians wanted religious freedom only for themselves and not for people of any other religions. I was hurt and alienated by the abuse I received.

My son picked up an old copy of the *Qur'an* at a flea market. It was a reprint of 'Abdullah Yusuf 'Ali's original 1934 version of his English translation. In his original manuscript, the Arabic was hand calligraphied, so the book was quite a masterpiece. I don't know why my son bought that book; it sat on a shelf unread for many years. In Judaic literature, the Spirit of Wisdom is the attribute of God that links Him to humanity and guides each person in the way of knowledge and understanding. I was not yet at a point in my spiritual journey where I could read the *Qur'an*, and accept guidance from the Spirit of Wisdom.

Since my teen years, God has revealed things to me in dreams and visions. There are many stories I could tell, but probably the most incredible (though morbid) event involved a murder. A Jane Doe was found in a wooded area; she had been dead for several days during which her body had been exposed to rain. The detectives assigned to the case asked me to come up with a portrait of what I thought the woman looked like before her face was blown off with a shotgun at close range. I'm not a forensic artist, but I agreed to do the best I could. The only features I had to go by was part of a misplaced nose, swollen eyes, and half an upper lip. Most of what was left of her face was fragmented, exposed muscle, and her hair was covered with a matted mess of mud, blood, and rain. It was quite a gruesome sight, and I was at a loss as to how to begin my sketch. I prayed for help, and suddenly a ghostly image of the woman stood before me. I quickly sketched her, then she faded away. Was it actually her spirit or just an image presented to me? I don't know, but after the body was identified, the detectives borrowed a photograph from the family so we could see how closely I came to capturing her likeness. The detectives were amazed at the accuracy of my drawing, but the most surprising detail was the hairstyle I had given her. The woman's daughter testified that the hairstyle I had drawn was the new look the victim had just received at the beauty shop the very day of her murder.

In late summer of 1998, after I had withdrawn from any church activity, I began having dreams about a country to which I had never been and about people I had never met. Over the course of several months, I learned from my dreams that the country was an Islamic state on the Mediterranean Sea, that it had gained its independence within the latter part of the twentieth century and that its government had built homes and schools for the citizens. One night I even dreamed that I was a child watching TV with my parents, and the news was about that country's progress. Eventually God revealed to me that the country was Tunisia.

Tunisia? I had to look it up in the encyclopedia. When I did, I found that my dreams were accurate. God proceeded to take me on a fantastic spiritual adventure, and He taught me many things in my sleep and through the research He inspired.

I believed that God was leading me toward being an apostle for the Islamic world. I borrowed my son's old, worn copy of the *Qur'an*, and I began reading with the attitude that I was preparing myself for witnessing to those lost in the false religion of Islam. I began writing the message I thought God wanted Muslims to understand. I explained why Jesus is called "the Son of God," and I explained the doctrine of the Trinity. Christianity teaches that God is One but He appears in three forms: God the Father (the Creator), God the Son (Jesus), and God the Holy Ghost (the Divine Presence of God's Spirit). When I was a Sunday School teacher, I explained "God in Three Persons" by baking one bread stick made of three strips of braided dough. In my written message, I said that God's being is like the three components of an individual human being: the Father is like an individual's mental self; the Son, like the physical self; and the

Holy Ghost, like the spiritual self. It made perfect sense to me, but God didn't like it! In my dreams, angels tore it up! I rewrote it several times, and He still didn't like it! I explained that one person could be a father, a son, and a servant; and so it is with God; but God disagreed with that analogy also. I felt as if angels took my brain out and played basketball with it all night. I woke up a basket case every morning! What does God expect from me? I wondered.

Unlike the *Qur'an* I borrowed from the library, 'Ali's translation had footnotes to help the reader understand. Despite my stubborn Southern Baptist stronghold, 'Ali's explanation of why Jesus is not the Son of God made sense to me. Much to my dismay, the verses about the Trinity also made sense. In order to strengthen the armor that the *Qur'an* was beginning to penetrate, I had to confirm for myself that Jesus is God and the Son of God. I couldn't remember, however, just where the Trinity verses were in the *Bible*. I had a *Bible* concordance, but "Trinity" was not listed. I had many Christian books, so I referred to some of them. I looked up the *Bible* verses used as examples to support the Trinitarian doctrine, but those verses were interpretive, not conclusive. Jesus' saying, for example, "The Father and I are one" (*John* 10: 30), could simply mean that Jesus and God are united in purpose—in the pursuit of bringing people into the Light of God's love and mercy. Also, a Messianic verse from the *New Testament* claimed that "of course all things" under Christ's authority does not include God Himself and that Christ will submit to God (*I Corinthians* 15: 27-28). Should God submit to Himself? Of course, when preachers are questioned about the Trinity, they dismiss concerns with responses like this: "The Trinity is one of the great mysteries of God that humanity is not capable of understanding."

I was confused. Where did that Trinity stuff come from? I made a trip to the library and brought home a stack of books. I studied the history of Christianity and learned how the Trinity doctrine had evolved in an environment of politics and controversy. I was suddenly thrust into a position of having to evaluate everything I had been taught my whole life!

Despite my sudden spiritual trauma, God assured me (through inspiration) that He wanted me to take a message to Tunisia, but first I had to unlearn. I had to come to grips with the idea that Jesus is not the begotten Son of God. The King James Version of *John* 3: 16 says:

> For God so loved the world, that he gave his only begotten Son, that whosoever believeth in him should not perish, but have everlasting life.

The Greek word translated to "only begotten" is monogenes, and it means *unique*. Jesus taught that all those who do what God requires have the right to be called His Children—not by any physical means, but by the power of God. Jesus' unique relationship to God is apparent by the miracles he performed and the lives he has changed, but to call him "the begotten Son of God" is blasphemous because of its literal implication. According to the *Gospel of Thomas* discovered among the Nag Hammadi Codices found by a Muslim in 1945, Jesus said, "When you see the One not begotten of a woman, prostrate yourselves and worship Him, for that One is your Heavenly Father."

I hit a snag when I read:

> That they said (in boast), "We killed Christ Jesus the son of Mary, the messenger of Allah"—but they killed him not, nor crucified him, but so it was made to appear to them, and those who differ therein are full of doubts, with no (certain) knowledge, but only conjecture to follow, for of a surety they killed him not—nay, Allah raised him up unto Himself: and Allah is exalted in power, wise— (*Qur'an* 4: 157-158).

Belief in the crucifixion, resurrection, and ascension of Jesus was too intrinsic to my faith to simply discard, so I didn't want to think about it anymore. All that pondering was giving me a screaming headache. When the angels starting shooting baskets with my brain, I just wanted to be left alone. "Huh-uh," I protested. "Let me dream about being abducted by Martians, fighting monster alligators, getting stomped by King Kong – anything but this *Qur'an* business. I'm perfectly satisfied with my ignorance." But I got no rest from God's persistence.

Referring to several translations of the *Qur'an*, I found that *Qur'an* 4: 157-158 has been interpreted many different ways: that Jesus looked dead, but was taken from the cross barely alive; that a phantom image of Jesus was crucified; that a man resembling Jesus was crucified by mistake; that the face of Jesus was superimposed over the face of another man; and that Jesus faked his own death. One view, however, was adapted from some early Gnostic Christian sects and it is in perfect harmony with the *New Testament.* They believed that Jesus is a spirit and that his human appearance was only an obscure reflection of his true self; therefore, he could not experience normal death.

I began to examine the words of the Qur'anic verses, and compare them to *New Testament* (NT) verses.

Qur'an: "...they killed him not, nor crucified him..." (4: 157) NT: "this man, handed over to you according to the definite plan and fore-knowledge of God, you crucified and killed by the hands of those outside the law (*Acts* 2: 23). The unbelievers did not execute Jesus themselves, but devised a plot wherein they executed him by having wicked men crucify him. The crucifixion, however, did not take Jesus' life.

Qur'an: "...but so it was made to appear to them..." (4: 157). NT: "Jesus told his disciples, For this reason the Father loves me, because I lay down my life in order to take it up again. No one takes it from me, but I lay it down of my own accord. I have power to lay it down and power to take it up again. I have received this command from my Father" (*John* 10: 17-18). The *New Testament* implies, then, that, although it appeared that the crucifixion killed him, Jesus himself actually determined the moment his spirit left the body. From the cross Jesus prayed, "...Father, into your hands I commend my spirit..." (*Luke* 23: 46). He said this and expired. Jesus suffered physical death, but remained alive spiritually (*I Peter* 3: 18).

Qur'an: "...and those who differ therein are full of doubts, with no (certain) knowledge, but only conjecture to follow..." (4: 157). NT: Those responsible for the plot against Jesus thought they had succeeded, but God used their evil scheme for victory! In accordance with His own plan, God had already decided that Jesus would be betrayed (*Acts* 2: 23). Jesus, however, was not abandoned to death; his body did not rot in the grave. God raised this very Jesus from death (*Acts* 2: 1-32). God preserved Jesus' body and revived it on the third day in order to symbolically fulfill a prophecy from the Jewish *Bible*. In two days, God will make Israel whole again; on the third day, Israel will be raised up and redeemed and whole (*Hosea* 6: 2). This was a sign that Israel's old sins had been forgiven, and a new covenant begun (*Hebrews* 9: 15).

Qur'an: "...for a surety they killed him not..." (4: 157). NT: "...He was put to death in the flesh, but made alive in the spirit, in which also he went and made a proclamation to the spirits in prison..." (*I Peter* 3: 18-19). The Good News was preached to those who had died as unbelievers, so that in their spiritual condition they may choose to live as God commands (*I Peter* 4: 6). It appears obvious that Jesus did not experience true death, but rather his spirit was set free from its physical confines in order to serve God unencumbered.

Qur'an: "nay, Allah raised him up unto Himself..." (4: 158). NT: After Jesus' resurrection, he was raised up to Heaven to sit at a place of honor (*Mark* 16: 19). In all His wisdom and insight, God did what He had proposed (*Ephesians* 1: 8-9). The *Qur'an* confirms that the unbelievers planned and schemed, but God too planned, and the best designer of plans is God (*Qur'an* 3: 54).

Ha! God pulled it off! He showed me that those troublesome verses from the *Qur'an* were actually a brilliant summary of the somewhat complicated message of the *New Testament*. I can accept this after all!

I believed, and still believe, in the overall message of the *New Testament*, despite the obvious contradictions, additions, and distortions. The writers promise:

> For we did not follow cleverly devised myths when we made known
> to you the power and coming of our Lord Jesus Christ, but we have
> been eyewitnesses of his majesty (*II Peter* 1: 16).

Although the manuscripts were written in Greek (instead of Jesus' Aramaic) many years after Jesus' ascension, the four Gospel accounts were reportedly based on eyewitness accounts. (*Luke* 1: 1-3; and *John* 21: 24; 19: 35). I was comforted by the fact that the *Qur'an* did not eliminate existing scriptures, but confirmed them (*Qur'an* 3: 3 and 29: 46). The *Qur'an* compelled me to look deeper into the *Bible* for a better understanding of its true message.

To atone for sins, Mosaic Law requires priests to annually offer animal sacrifices (*Leviticus* 16: 15-19). The loss of an animal's life is a reminder of the shame of sin. Jesus' life, however, is much more valuable than a sheep's, so his sacrifice is a greater reminder of the need for sincere repentance. God has prepared a sacrifice and consecrated those He has called (*Zephaniah* 1: 7). O Jewish people, you have suffered long enough for your sins. Jerusalem is forgiven! Your account is paid in full! (*Isaiah* 40: 1-2).

The *New Testament* was written for Hebrew-speaking Jews and Greek-speaking Jews across the Diaspora, so the message of Jesus' sacrifice was of great importance in relationship to Jewish heritage. The *Qur'an*, however, emphasizes Jesus' life. Although Jesus was sent first for the Jews (*Matthew* 10: 5-6), God had revealed in prophecy:

> ...It is too light a thing that you should be my servant to raise up the tribes of Jacob and to restore the survivors of Israel; I will give you as a light to the nations that my salvation may reach to the end of the earth (*Isaiah* 49: 6).

This verse has been interpreted to refer to the Jews as "a light to the nations," but the *New Testament* offers a secondary meaning as it refers to the Light of Jesus and the Gospel message (*John* 8: 12; *Acts* 13: 47-48). One interpretation of "the Light" mentioned in the *Qur'an* 57: 28 is that in his spiritual existence Jesus is a Light to guide people to the Straight Way, so they may be forgiven for their sins. According to the *New Testament*, Jesus instructed "that repentance and forgiveness of sins is to be proclaimed in his name to all nations, beginning from Jerusalem" (*Luke* 24: 47). The Lord God of Islam says, "...'(We wish) to appoint him (Jesus) as a sign unto men and a mercy from Us': it is a matter (so) decreed" (*Qur'an* 19: 21).

The virgin birth was a sign for all people, so they might believe the message of one covenant community for all humanity (*Qur'an* 21: 91-92). The Arabic word for the covenant community is the same as Jesus' Aramaic word, *Ummah*. Translators use the word church in the *New Testament*, but *Ummah* is also used in Aramaic portions of the Jewish *Bible* to indicate the Jewish community.

My brain was bubbling like Gran'ma's moonshine as God kept cramming more information into my head. Every time I got stuck on a verse in the *Qur'an*, God guided me to new understanding. I said to my husband Tom, "Ya know, the more I read this stuff, the more sense it makes." Finally, he started reading it too, and we discussed verses and shared information.

I knew God wanted me to take some kind of non-controversial Gospel message to Tunisia, but I did not think that He meant me personally, so I proceeded to try to find someone who would take the message after I developed it. I wrote letters to Christian ministries all over the country, but they did not believe in my dreams, and they responded with very critical, hurtful replies. They told me that there was great danger in taking a message about Jesus into an Islamic country where I might be imprisoned, and that there would be no merit in a message that did not refute Islam. I was even told that I should stay home with the laundry, and leave the witnessing to missionaries who knew what they were doing.

I did receive two positive responses. The president of a ministry in Alabama called to encourage me and to tell me of reports he had heard of Muslims seeing visions of Jesus on their pilgrimage to Makkah; and, the president of the International *Bible* Society (IBS) called and offered to personally take the message to Tunisia. He

had lived in Tunisia and explained that, although Tunisia is an Islamic country, its society is secular.

I was discouraged when the IBS president later resigned without ever following through on his offer, but evidently it was part of God's plan. When God began whispering to my soul that He wanted me to take the message to Tunisia myself, I tried my best to ignore Him. He kept smacking me up side the head, and I kept doing the laundry. When I went to sleep, I was chased around the bedpost by a crazed whale with graffito on his tonsils: "Jonah was here."

It was now winter of 1998, and I felt that God wanted me to leave for Tunisia before my next birthday, which was May thirteenth. I had never traveled overseas, I spoke no foreign languages, and I argued that I could not go to Tunisia, because I just didn't have the money.

Two days later I received a phone call from a customer: "Linda, have you ever thought about going to Paris to see the art museums?" I answered that I would like to do that, but I doubted I would ever be able to afford it. He said, "You and Tom plan on a trip for sometime in the spring, and I will pay for it." (Tunisia is just south of France.) Shortly after that, I received two big art projects and made enough money to cover the rest of the expenses for going to Tunisia with Tom and Tana. Okay, God; you win. Now can you call off Moby Dick?

Before God inspired the message that I would deliver, He continued to condition my mind and change my perception of Islam. I had to separate true Islam from the political and cultural problems reported by the news media.

In some countries where Islam is not only a religion but also a government, Muslims who convert to Christianity are considered traitors and are punished, but I became convinced that the teachings of the New Testament can be shared without such trauma. All truth is God's truth, and true Islam encourages each believer to seek God's guidance in search of truth. God made me realize that His true message did not have to be smuggled in by secret missionaries who are illegally trying to convert Muslims to the organized religion of Christianity. True Christianity is not so much a religion as an attempt to follow the life example of Prophet Jesus. A Muslim woman commented, "To be good Muslims, we must be good Christians." I began to realize that Jesus' spirit already walks within the sacred mosques.

I developed a vision of unity among the three Abrahamic faiths. Since then, groups of Christians have organized walks through Islamic countries for the purpose of apologizing to Muslims for the Crusades; Dr. Robert Schuller (Crystal Cathedral) was invited to give a message of peace to 15,000 Muslims at the Abu Nour Mosque in Damascus, Syria; and the Pope, after apologizing to Muslims and Jews for the crimes of the early Catholic Church, accepted a three-page document from Islamic leaders outlining a request for interfaith communication. I believe many more good things will happen when we learn to share spiritual insights as we respectfully receive the insights of others whom God loves and guides. No one has all the truth there is. God is glorified best when we continue to seek His truths and when, in ways that are peaceful, kind, and loving, we help others on their spiritual journeys.

As Tom and I continued to study the *Qur'an* and Islamic philosophy, we gained, not only respect, but also genuine love for the religion. We gradually became drawn into Islam, and began to identify ourselves as Muslims. Our son absorbed our enthusiasm, and he too began to seek the truths within Islam. After months of using my brain for play-dough, God revealed the message I should take. It was the simple message of Jesus' Gospel: you must be born again—not physically, but by the Spirit of God (*John* 3: 3-6).

Wait a minute! That is way too simple! Everybody knows you have to submit your whole life to God, be forgiven of your sins, and become renewed by His saving grace. Right? Well, apparently many people needed a reminder. In France, I met a Tunisian man who told me: "Tunisians like God; they just don't pay much attention to Him. They are Muslims because they are born Muslims, but many are not Muslims at heart."

In my dreams, I saw the face of an *Imam* (Muslim prayer leader) to whom I was to take the message. But why, I wondered, would he believe me, a blond Christian woman from America. The whole idea seemed wacky! But God gave me a vision of a painting I was to create and present with the message; this would be a sign that the message was truly from God.

After visiting the famous museums of Paris and touring the French countryside, Tom, Tana, and I got on a plane to Tunisia. We made no arrangements; we had no contacts, no reservations, no travel guide, no plan, no itinerary, nothing—not even any sense. We were like Paul in the *New Testament,* who wrote that when he started his mission to spread the Gospel to the non-Jews, he didn't consult with anybody about anything; he just went straight to Arabia (*Galatians* 1: 15-17).

So there we were in a foreign country with no idea of what to do. Noticing that we had no sense, people volunteered to help us, and eventually we had all our baggage crammed into a tiny car and were driving around the countryside looking for a man I had seen in a dream. Good grief!

We must have been an odd sight. Wherever we went, people stared, and many ventured to ask us why we were there. When we told them that we had a message from God, they didn't laugh or throw tomatoes at us. Instead, they were excited and wanted to hear the message. I had managed to get it translated into Arabic and printed, so I was able to share the message easily. People were happy and wanted us to come to their homes and the homes of their friends, so that everyone could meet us and receive the message.

By the time we arrived in Kairouan, we were famous! We were escorted to a hotel; and, as we ate supper at the hotel's restaurant, people waited for us outside. We were quite tired, but we didn't want to disappoint them, so we went wherever they took us and met many different people who rejoiced over hearing the message.

We were taken from house to house, and finally, the next day, I found myself sitting across from the man in my dream. He was the Grand Imam at the Great Okba Mosque. Across from me, he sat erect and stared suspiciously. I thought he seemed like a king who only needed to direct his thumb down, and I would lose my head.

He was older and his features less remarkable than in my dreams, but the depth, wisdom, and mystery of his penetrating eyes were unmistakably the same as that of the man I had spoken with for months in my dreams. He understood no English, but his son knew just enough to be able to translate for me. "We are Christians from the United States, and I came with a message from God," I explained.

He was not impressed. "Christians cause us nothing but trouble!" he scoffed. "I don't want to hear anymore."

I had a copy of the Arabic *Qur'an*, and I pointed to a portion that he read aloud:

> ...and nearest among them in love to the believers wilt thou find those who say, "We are Christians": because amongst these are men devoted to learning and men who have renounced the world, and they are not arrogant (*Qur'an* 5: 82b).

"We are not the arrogant ones," I told him.

Finally the *Imam* nodded, and I continued. I explained that God had given me dreams and revealed a message from Jesus that I should take to Tunisia. The *Imam* maintained his solemn expression. I felt so inadequate, and his unwavering stare made me think that I might be as crazy as everybody said I was.

Not being very successful at words, I finally decided just to show him the painting. I unveiled it, and the Imam's face changed. It suddenly glowed to match the sunny yellow tunic he wore, and a gentle smile erased the intense stare. *"Tihib hada?"* ("Do you like it?") I asked. He answered simply by placing the palm of his hand over his heart.

I explained the painting that showed the Great Okba Mosque in the background. God is symbolized as a lamp, and out of the light is a shooting star. The star symbolizes a repentant person who has received New Life by the power of God's Spirit. The tail of the star is made of three bands of color that represent mind, body, and soul.

I gave the *Imam* the translation of the message, and he read every word aloud:

> Allah is symbolized as brilliant light from a lamp of luminous oil (Al Noor 24:35). Like a new star bursting into existence, a lost soul can be ignited and changed by Allah's eternal power. In the Gospel, Jesus (Peace!) invited sinners to experience New Life: "You must be born again—not physically, but by the Spirit of Allah."
>
> ...Allah will change the evil of such persons into good... (Al Furqan 25: 70)
>
> The soul is purified and colored by the Spirit of Allah filling the believer like sweet incense. To experience a spiritual transformation is to receive the full measure of Allah's amazing grace and to know His magnificent power to instill peace, joy, and love.
>
> Muhammad (Peace!) taught, "To go out in the morning in the way of Allah and to go out at dusk in the way of Allah is better than the whole world and all it contains." Such a close walk with Allah requires that each believer submit the whole self—mind, body, and soul—and our lives should reveal what is righteous and holy.
>
> As People of the Light in a dark world, we must peacefully and gently proclaim, Allah "...will provide a Light so you may walk on the Straight Way, and He will forgive you of your sins..." (Al Hadeed 57:28).
>
> In the Name of Allah, Most Gracious, Most Merciful. May Allah's grace embrace you so that your soul is daily refreshed. Most assuredly Allah loves you!

The *Imam* told his son to escort us to the mosque the next day, so that I could deliver the message to another *Imam*, the Grand *Imam* Supreme.

AT THE GREAT OKBA MOSQUE: Thomas "TaHa" with Tana and "iLham"

As we approached the mosque the next

evening, hundreds of people began arriving by foot, motor scooters, bicycles, and donkeys. Some came from nearby homes in the city; others came from the distant hills and deserts and had traveled most of the hot, dusty day to come to the service. I had not realized, however, that I was going to a service; I thought I was just going to meet the *Imam*.

The Great Okba Mosque began in 670 by Okba ibn Nafaa and is considered the fourth holiest site in Islam. Surrounded by massive walls, the main arena of the mosque is an outdoor court in which the floors are laid with white marble. As we sat on grass mats, everyone participated in *Qur'an* readings. The words were read, or recited from memory, loudly and vigorously – every syllable pronounced distinctly. Everyone was in perfect synchronization, and a symphony of voices combined into one huge spiral of praise rising into the night. I looked into the star-specked sky and expected it to peel away to reveal angels ushering the spiral into Heaven. It was truly magnificent.

As my heart pounded with the rhythm of the *Qur'an*, I finally took time to gaze at the tower guarding the mosque. It was the minaret from my painting, and the crescent moon nestled behind it just as it did in my art. I was sure there must have been guardian angels standing on its corners.

Finally, I was told it was time to...speak to the *Imam?* Well, yes...and to the nearly one thousand Muslims waiting for me to present the message.

"What!" I was terrified. That's the way it happened in my dream, but I thought God was only joking. I didn't think He would actually let things go this far.

"First," the young lady said, "you must say *Shahadah*."

"Noooo! Huh-uh! No way, Jose!"

"You must," she insisted.

"I can't," I insisted more.

"You have to! *Imam* say. You must do what *Imam* say."

"I can't speak Arabic," I protested.

"You learn," she ordered as she gently peeled my fingers from the pillar to which I clung. Then, she escorted me to the front.

Of course, I had finally come to believe that Muhammad was indeed called by God and that the *Qur'an* was truly revealed. I did not feel that accepting Islam would negate my belief in Jesus. In becoming a Muslim, I would not stop being a Christian; I would simply add layers of Light to the Light I already had. I wanted to say the *Shahadah* (the Muslim confession of faith), but, leapin' lizards!, I never expected to say it in front of a thousand people! Mama!

As I walked in a daze toward the front, I heard a familiar voice echo across the open court. It was Tom's! He was saying the *Shahadah*! Did they wrestle him down, too?

Finally, I was standing beside the Grand Imam Supreme with hundreds of people staring at me with such awestruck silence that I thought there must have been lobsters crawling out of my ears. Finally, I heard words slowly evolving. Were they coming out of my mouth? "*La Illaha Illa Allah; Muhammad Rusul Allah*" (or something like that). After I had stumbled through my hillbilly Arabic, everyone sighed a long-held breath of relief. Hey, I did it!

Now everyone was staring at me again. Why? One of the lobsters crawling out of my ears whispered, "Show them the painting, stupid." Oh, yeah.

I lifted the veil from my art, and the crowd responded with a collective "Ahhhhhh."

I handed the *Imam* the translated message, and he read it aloud. Eyes filled with tears, and many voices praised God.

The *Imam*, who spoke no English, took my hand and slowly said a well-rehearsed, "God bless you."

The painting was hung in the mosque where it remains today.

Considering the lack of religious freedom in many countries, being a Muslim in America is not so difficult. Despite the frays and tears in our society's moral and ethical fabric, there is much about the United States that is like the Islamic ideal. Humanity, for example, was given the responsibility of caring for God's creation, and the United States does more toward ecology and preservation of wildlife than probably any other country on the earth. The *Qur'an* stresses the importance of charity and good deeds. Despite widespread greed and materialism in our country, the people of the United States give more to charities than probably any other country, and our government is always coming up with new plans to improve economy, welfare, and civil rights. Although you won't hear about it on the evening news, the United States military is always involved in performing good deeds; i.e., building roads and schools in poverty-stricken countries, and air dropping medicine and food into disaster areas all over the world. Think how different our world would be if all countries' military forces were so busy performing good deeds that they didn't have time to fight.

We hope for the new creation in which there will be no more pain and grief. Jews believe that if we make our world more like God's plan for us, He will reward us by establishing the Messianic Age sooner than He intended. The United States is a world leader in research yielding new medicines, products, and techniques that improve the quality of life so there will be less pain and grief. Our safety standards may be the highest in the world, and our justice system, though far from perfect, excels in seeking truth and protecting the innocent.

Islam stresses the importance of knowledge. The United States offers public education to every person, regardless of gender, race, religion, national origin, or economic status. This is not true in many countries, including some so-called Islamic countries.

The United States was founded by people seeking refuge from religious persecution, but the Europeans only wanted freedom for those who agreed with them. Quakers, for example, were beaten, and their ears were lopped off. Anyone espousing complete separation of the Church of England and government was in danger of execution.

The *Qur'an* says, "Let there be no compulsion in religion..." (*Qur'an* 2: 256). Despite the Crusader tactics of many of our nation's founders, the United States has evolved into a nation of increasing religious tolerance, and tolerance is slowly giving way to sincere understanding and accommodation of religious diversity. We still have a long way to go, but more and more people are joining the effort to respect and support religious freedom for everyone.

Our history books must truthfully relate the acts of terrorism and exploitation on which our country was founded—from the massacres of the indigenous American-Indian peoples, to the enslavement and oppression of black Africans, to the atomic bombing of the civilians of Hiroshima and Nagasaki. Repentance has not been a virtue of our United States, and restitution has been slow and imperfect; however, we have become a people of which a majority seeks to improve the world around us. We still make mistakes, and our government does not always follow the will of the people and certainly not the will of God, but America is a great nation of great people. All people of Light—Jews, Christians, and Muslims—must take an active role in improving the morality and quality of our nation.

On the Day of Judgment, nations as well as individuals will be judged (*Joel* 3: 2). It is incumbent upon every American citizen to make America a nation deserving of God's favor. According to John Adams, "Our Constitution was made only for a moral and religious people. It is wholly inadequate for the government of any other." The majority of problems in America today stem from the lack of morality and the decline of religious influence on society. Many

Americans do not have the moral integrity required to responsibly use the freedoms and rights that we have. Freedom without integrity makes us slaves of our own evil inclinations. We see this each time, for examples, pornography is defended as a First Amendment right, people are denied the right to voluntarily congregate for prayer in public (i.e., because it is "too dangerous to permit" according to Brandon vs. Guilderland, 1981), or the criminal's rights are greater than the victim's. Justice Oliver Wendell Holmes stated, "A page of history is worth a volume of logic." May the mistakes of our past help us improve our nation and our world today.

In my opinion, there are three things that impede the growth of Islam in America. Third on my list is the lies told by Crusadists. Dr. Saleem Almahdy is one of the leading enemies of Islam in America. He has a wide audience and convinces Christians of such distortions as, "The Koran legalizes unlimited lust for its author's followers" (*The Voice of the Martyrs,* April, 2002, p. 9). Muslims must take these attacks as a challenge to peacefully but emphatically proclaim the truth of Islam.

The second greatest danger to Islam is the incorrect, and often insensitive, reporting by the media. I think many of the major news reporters want to do the right thing, but they need to be educated about the truth of Islam. They should be advised that the use of the word *Jihad* (struggle) is, as described by James Reston, Jr. (*the Washington Post Company*), "a gift to (Osama) bin Laden" and other such deluded mis-followers of Islam. Reporters should be encouraged to use the word *Irhab* (terrorism) instead. It is the job and duty of journalists to faithfully report current events, and, when the news involves terrorists' actions, the reporters need to be able to identify which terrorists. Every year, dozens of new words and new meanings for existing words are added to the English dictionary. Most of these are invented by news reporters. Surely they can come up with appropriate words to identify terrorists linked to specific religious systems. For example, instead of Islamic extremist or terrorist, how about Mislamist? (The prefix 'mis' means not.) For other religious mis-followers, how about terms like Zionazi, Crusadist, and Hindite? If we Muslims use more accurate words ourselves, maybe the rest of the world will eventually catch up!

I feel the number one threat to the growth of Islam in America is the pharisees. In Jesus' time, the Pharisees were a group of Jews insisting on obedience to strict rules added to the *Torah*. Jesus said, "They burden the worshipers with doctrine too difficult to follow, then won't help them with their real spiritual struggles." Sadly, there are pharisaic Muslims who criticize other Muslims for such things as their clothes, certain occupations (i.e., photography), the times of their prayers, and even for wearing socks during prayers. One Islamic center had to have two services the same because the men could not agree on the correct time. One Muslim remarked, "At least it gave the Christians something to laugh about."

After having been treated with such respect in Tunisia, I was disappointed with the reception I received from some Islamic centers here, which are an hour or more away from my home. I went to one where I was not even allowed to pray, because some women objected to my not being a member of their group. At another center, only men attended, no one would speak to me, and the *Imam* told my husband, "Only men should come to the mosque; women should stay home to pray." Muhammad, however, said that women should never be discouraged from entering the mosque.

Another Islamic center recently placed a new rule on the front door: "Women must enter through the back door" (instead of the main entrance/lobby that leads to both men's and women's prayer rooms). This reminds me of the fifties when black Americans were discriminated against by restaurant owners in the South who placed front door signs making such statements as, "Coloreds served at back door," and "Whites only. N—s and dogs not allowed."

Ninety-five percent of the time, I wear a scarf in public places, but I get criticized for the few occasions in which I wear a cap or hat or simply wear flowers in my hair. If I am working in my overalls, for example, and run out to the garden supply store for a sack of fertilizer, I don't feel compelled to put on a scarf. There are times when a scarf is too uncomfortable and cumbersome (i.e., while engaging in sports), a safety factor (i.e., while operating a printing press in which the rollers could grab an end of the scarf), or inappropriate (i.e., when an organization mandates a dress code or uniform). Everyone must follow her own heart in accordance with God's will and how His laws apply to her unique lifestyle. Allah gave us rules by which to live, but first He gave us common sense! If He hadn't, Muslims living north of the Arctic Circle couldn't compensate during *Ramadan.*

The Muslim woman's scarf is a sign of her submission to God, but when more importance is placed on the symbol itself than on the spiritual quality that makes the symbol significant, then the symbol becomes a type of idol, and God's grace is devalued. Jibran Khalil Jibran (Khalil Gibran) felt that uncompromising adherence to rules was a form of spiritual slavery. The Arab-American artist/poet wrote in "Slavery" that beside humanity's "footprints in the sand" are always the "marks of dragging chains." In "The Storm," Gibran's character, Yusef el Fakhri, explains that he sought solitude in order to be free from others' insistence on strict, inflexible adherence to rules; such uncompromising demands prevented him from being able to seek God unencumbered. I seldom go to Islamic centers because of the pharisaic enslavement I feel there and the lack of true spiritual guidance. My stance may be unpopular, but consider this: almost every Muslim woman I have met has counseled me to always wear the scarf, but no Muslim has ever offered to help me learn the required prayers. Similar to Jesus' question about the temple gold (*Matthew* 23: 16-17), which is more important: the scarf or the submission that makes the scarf holy?

My family prays together and studies the *Qur'an* and *Bible* at home. Sometimes we are joined by other Muslims who are also uncomfortable with the cultural and doctrinal clashes within the local centers. It has been my experience that some immigrants seem insensitive to the needs, perspectives, and traditions of native-born Americans. According to 'Abdullah Yusuf 'Ali, some people believe in too much formalism, and some believe in no restrictions at all. He wrote "Islam follows the Golden Mean," and he explained that each society should have its own reasonable regulations, and those regulations should reflect what is lawful in that given society (*The Meaning of the Holy Qur'an*; Amana Publications; Beltsville, MD; 1989; p. 67, note #169). In my opinion, American Muslims do not have to reflect the cultures of Middle Eastern Muslims, but Islam in America should be allowed to grow with a natural harmony according to God's will as Islam begins to reflect, within the bounds of reasonable interpretation of the *Qur'an*, the culture and spirit of the American people.

Relative to Judaism and Christianity, Islam, as an organized institution, is modern and is especially new to America. There is much that Muslims can learn from the successes and errors of Jews and Christians in America. How have Jews made the synagogues user-friendly to non-Hebrew-speaking people? How have the Jewish congregations incorporated American customs and traditions into the Judaic religious heritage? How do churches attract new members? How do Christians win non-believers into the faith? How have some Jewish groups alienated themselves from mainstream America? How have Christians earned resentment because of their proselytizing? We need to look at the experiences of the other two Abrahamic faiths and discover what has contributed to their growth and what has been their weaknesses, then apply what we learn to accelerate the growth of Islam in America.

We must try to get to a point where Islam can no longer be called "the most misunderstood religion in the world" (as stated by Dr. Shakur Ahmed, "United Efforts Lead to Prosperity," *The Islamic Voice,* September, 1998). I recently read a report of an Islamic non-alcoholic bar and social club where Muslims could "introduce their friends to Islam in a way that doesn't scare them" like the Islamic centers do. Instead of building bars and clubs, shouldn't we be asking ourselves how to make the Islamic centers less frightening? Any house of worship should have an atmosphere of peace and friendship. If our friends have to go to a bar to find such an atmosphere, something is definitely wrong!

My son, Duston, has the hope, *Insha'Allah,* of someday opening a mosque specifically designed for native-born Americans unfamiliar with the language and religion of Islam. It would accommodate first-time visitors who only want to observe and learn (i.e., seats in the back and printed programs explaining what's happening), new believers who have not learned the Arabic prayers and *Qur'an* (i.e., one line of Arabic immediately echoed by the same line in English), and Christian-to-Muslim believers who still treasure some Christian traditions (i.e, songs of praise and worship). Dusty has discussed some of his plans via E-mail with a wealthy Sheykh who has offered to pay for such a mosque if Dusty will study, at the Sheykh's expense, in Saudi Arabia. I think it is too dangerous for Americans—especially fair-skinned, blue-eyed blondes—to live in the Middle East at this time; but, he is young, and things change in Allah's good time.

Just prior to my trip to Tunisia, I had a vision of a yellow rose on desert sand. I wasn't sure what it meant, but the *Bible* mentions a desert rose in reference to a woman. While I was at the hotel, a young woman came to see me with a message that she and the two men with her had individually received from the Holy Spirit as they had participated in afternoon prayers at the mosque. (In Islam, "Holy Spirit" is used to refer to an angel, usually Gabriel, but can also be used in more general terms to refer to the power of God transmitted to an individual; i.e., as inspiration.) As soon as I saw her, I realized that she was my yellow rose. I did not tell anyone about this sign, but later, after arriving home, I received a postcard from another young Tunisian woman. The picture on her postcard was a yellow rose with a background resembling sand. I now associate the yellow rose with all Muslim women.

When spring awakens the rose bush, the fresh, green leaves give us hope as we await the beauty of the season. A woman's advice and guidance offer hope to those who depend on her silent strength as they await the day-by-day unfolding of life's challenges and rewards. The wisdom of women was created as a unique and wonderful source, from which the world can gain perceptions and insights that complement the acumen of men. Some estimates indicate that almost twice as many women as men are entering Islam. Women should accept the responsibility of taking a greater role in the development of Islam in America and the world. It is important that women accept the equality that Islam espouses and use that equality, not for self-serving vanities, but for God's glory.

An old *Imam* taught that men have to learn to be fathers, but every female is born a mother; whether she has children of her own or not, she has the responsibility of motherhood to every person who seeks her wisdom. The *Imam* explained that Woman was created from Man's rib as a sign that she is the protector of family and community, just as the rib cage protects the heart and lungs. As the rose bush's thorns protect it from damage by animals, women's prayers are the thorns against the beasts that threaten our families and communities. Women must be prayer warriors as they daily stand in service to the Divine Guardian who has given women a special role in His spiritual army.

"Peace" is the name given to a specific yellow rose blushed with feminine pink. Yellow is the color of happiness, and God's peace grants joy to all who truly submit to Him. It is the responsibility of Muslim women to reflect God's peace in the kind, gentle way in which they live.

When roses fade, they leave behind a fruit called *rose hips*. The fruit makes a pretty, red tea that has a calming effect when drunk, and I add the tea to my homemade soap for the therapeutic value of the essential oil. Women of faith affect the world as they dispense mental and spiritual nourishment and leave behind legacies of good will, harmony, and inspiration. A woman's gentle strength will always be remembered by the people touched by her life.

Being a sincere Muslim woman is like being pregnant; either you are or you're not. You can't be semi-submissive to God; every woman must submit her whole self to Allah in order to become all that He created her to be. A woman may be many things – daughter, sister, wife, mother, student, teacher, community leader, employee, business leader, friend – but only God's Wisdom can insure that she fulfill each facet of her life with integrity and success.

As women of faith, we must not walk in shadow so that Allah's Light is encumbered by oppression, and we must not walk in brilliance so that Allah's Light is drowned out by the lack of humility. We must stand firm in our proper places and fulfill the destinies Allah has planned for us. Only then can we fill the world with the yellow roses of peace, faith, hope, and charity.

Note: Anyone wanting to receive a free 5 x 7 art print of the painting hung in the Great Okba Mosque should send two first-class stamps (without an envelope) and a neatly-prepared pre-addressed label (sticky or plain paper) with a written request to: PAPER WINGS; 3806 Grady Wms; Maiden, NC 28650-9535.

Walkin'
The Walk

Debra L. Dirks

I was born the third of seven children, entered the world on March 17, 1952, and was named Debra Lea Stucky. However, given the consciousness of tradition that so permeated my Swiss-German and Mennonite heritage, it may be fairly stated that my identity started to be formed by Mennonite traditions that began many centuries before my birth. Perhaps, the story of my journey to Islam should commence with those traditions.

The Mennonites were and are a very conservative sect of Christianity that grew out of the Anabaptist movement in 16th century Switzerland and Holland. They were part of the church reformation that came as much of Europe was breaking away from the Roman Catholic Church and as the Protestant churches started forming. As most countries at that time officially maintained the Roman Catholic Church as "the State Church," those who spoke out against it were considered to be traitors and heretics. The Anabaptist movement claimed that it was necessary for a person to be of an age

of reason, so that one could choose one's religion before being baptized. As this position was contrary to the Roman Catholic Church's
propagation of infant baptism, and as the Roman Catholic Church
was the state church, the Anabaptist movement was perceived to be
a threat to the state in most European countries. Any person who was
baptized twice (an adult Anabaptist baptism being superimposed on a
Roman Catholic infant baptism) was deemed a traitor and heretic.
As such, the 16th century European states deployed groups of
Anabaptist hunters to identify and capture Anabaptists. Once caught,
the Anabaptists were typically put on the rack for torture, and then
tied to a stake and burned. However, if they recanted their religion
during torture, they were mercifully beheaded or had a packet of
gunpowder hung from their neck to make death come faster when
they were burned at the stake.

It was in this climate that Menno Simons was ordained as an
Anabaptist minister, having previously been a Roman Catholic
priest, and started his mission in the early 1500's. His followers were
eventually termed Mennonites. Naturally, in this kind of hostile environment, these initial groups of Mennonites were migratory as they
fled from the Anabaptist hunters. However, there was a second issue
about which the Mennonites differed from mainline Christianity.
They believed that it was a sin to fight or kill anyone, and that included participating in any form of military service. As committed
and absolute pacifists, they moved their farming communities from
country to country across Europe and Asia as they fled from army
conscription. Finally, in the latter part of the 18th century, Catherine
the Great of Russia granted the Mennonites farmland for colonies,
and she promised them they would never have to serve in the Russian
military. As such, many colonies of Mennonites moved to Russia
starting as early as 1780. However, almost 100 years later, this exemp-
tion from military service was revoked, and the Mennonites in Russia

learned that they would be subject to military conscription starting in 1880. Many of the Mennonite colonies in Russia packed up and left Russia for America between 1870 and 1880. While groups of Mennonites had been coming to North America in search of religious freedom since 1683, the numbers increased dramatically in the 1870's as 18,000 Mennonites left Russia and eventually made it to America. My own ancestors came over from Russia in 1874 and immigrated to Kansas.

While I did not know all the names and dates, this ancestral and religious history was impressed on me before I can remember. This general history was just there, an imprint on my core identity. I do not recall that any part of it was ever formally taught to me. It was just always there, being referred to with the assumption that I should know it. I knew that the Mennonites had suffered, been burned at the stake, been tortured, and had moved all around Europe before coming over from Russia, so that we could have the religious freedom to practice our Mennonite beliefs and heritage. More specifically, I knew that my great great grandfather, Elder Jacob Stucky, had led the Swiss-German Mennonites out of the Russian province of Volhynia to the United States. I was never to forget that I was his descendant, and that I was always expected to live up to his religious legacy. (In the attic and upstairs' closets of our farmhouse were the trunks my ancestors had used in traveling from Russia. During our childhood, those trunks provided splendid hiding places for my sisters and me during games of hide and go seek.)

Debra Lea Stucky
... during her Second Grade
schooldays

Despite my religious and family heritage, and despite the expectations of my elders in the rural Mennonite enclave of my childhood, the lessons I remember from Sunday school were not always those my instructors were trying to teach me. For me, Sunday school was the source of many untruths which were steeped in longstanding, tradition. From the time I was two or three years old, I was attending Sunday school and giving my pennies to the "heathens from India". I had no idea who the "heathens from India" were, what they had done, or even why they needed my pennies. I only knew that they were bad and needed my pennies, or God would not take care of them. For me, India was not a country but was just some place where God needed my pennies to help those bad "heathens." ("Good" and "kind" were equivalent with being a Christian, and being a Christian meant being a Mennonite.)

I remember a church discussion that took place when I was about seven. It was the Christmas season, and we were getting ready to deliver Christmas baskets to the needy members of the local church. These Christmas baskets were filled with practical items like food, towels, and warm socks. They always seemed to include oranges and peanuts. During the discussion, a disagreement arose about giving a basket to a family who lived in Moundridge, the nearest small town to our country church. In this family, the father was out of work, the mother was in the hospital, and there were five or six kids. Along with my father, I had several uncles that were on the church board of elders. All of the other children were playing in the aisles of the church, waiting for the meeting to be done so that we could go home. I think I had gotten into some sort of trouble and had been made to sit next to my mother on the church pew. As I sat there, I started to listen to the "grownup talk." My uncle must have noticed that I was listening. All of the sudden, he turned to me, and asked me if I thought that we ought to give a basket to these people even though they were not Mennonites, but were Methodists. I thought for a moment and asked, "Are the Methodists worse than the 'heathens'?" "No," came the surprised answer. Then I pronounced my best bit of seven-year-old reasoning: "Then why can't we give the Methodists a basket if I can give my pennies to the 'heathens'?" As this did not support the side of the argument that my uncle was propagating, he quickly dismissed my statement as childish thoughts, but the Methodist family received a basket that Christmas.

Sometime later, I was surprised to discover that I knew this Methodist family. I did not know that I knew anyone of another religion. (In reality, Mennonites and Methodists are merely two different denominations of the same religion, i.e. Christianity, and not two different religions. However, it was symptomatic of the religious heritage in which I was raised that I then thought of them as two different religions.) This Methodist family lived next door to my maternal grandmother, and I had played with the children several times. They did not have horns, and they seemed fairly normal to me. This was a real revelation to me, and I would never have known they were so "different," if I had not overheard the "grownup talk" at church.

As I look back at my childhood, it seems that I grew up in a small, quaint community that was totally permeated by the traditions and teachings of the Mennonite Church. However, as I lived it then, it was my whole world. I had no concept that the rest of the world was really quite different than the one I was experiencing. Everywhere I went was part of the Mennonite community, and almost everyone I knew was a Mennonite. In the middle of Kansas there were several German-speaking, Mennonite communities huddled together in an almost monastic retreat from the rest of the world.

The Mennonite faith and traditions were all encompassing in my life. My family, my church, my relatives, my community, my public elementary school were all Mennonite. While the public school did not have Mennonite in the name or in the curriculum, almost all of its employees and all of its students were Mennonites.

There are several different sub-sects within the Mennonite tradition, ranging from the Amish, which is the most conservative, to the General Conference, which is the most liberal. I was raised within the General Conference Mennonite Church. However, by almost any standard other than Mennonite, that made us anything but liberal. It meant that we drove cars and tractors, rather than the horse and buggy used by the Amish Mennonites. We, that is the women, did not wear "prayer bonnets", as did the Old Mennonites, Holdemans, and Amish. We also did not leave our hair uncut and braided from childhood, as did the Amish and Holdeman women.

Showing skin was another thing that varied across the Mennonite groups. Grandpa Stucky never wore anything but long-sleeved shirts, buttoned at the wrist and collar, even in the hottest weather, and Grandma Stucky's skirts were, at most, ten inches off the ground. However, my dad wore short-sleeved shirts, and my mom wore skirts that were around five inches below her knees. As children, we wore skirts that ranged in length from mid-calf to just below the knees. Our shorts went to the knees and were mainly worn under dresses, so that we could play without worrying about showing "too much" if we were swinging and jumping.

We attended church, Sunday school, Wednesday evening services, *Bible* school (for two weeks every summer), and school. As our church was on the half-section adjoining our farm from the south, one did not stray very far from home. Because it was such a closed community, my school friends were my church friends, and almost all of them were at least my second or third cousins. Everyone within the community could be pigeonholed with a, "Oh, so your mother is my father's aunt's granddaughter!" or some such other relationship. It was not used as much by my generation as by the grownups, but one always had it to fall back on if one actually managed to meet someone new, which was not often.

Church was an ever-present part of life. When I was real young, we all attended church regularly, and our social and cultural lives revolved around the church. Dad was a leader in the church, the adult Sunday school teacher, and the one who normally "filled the pulpit" if the regular minister was unavailable. Mom filled Christmas baskets, was part of the Ladies' Aide group, played piano during the church services, and was Sunday school superintendent.

While my mother was busy teaching me the New Testament maxim, "Judge not lest ye be judged," the rest of the community and church seemed to be stuck in a "holier than thou" mode. This mode can best be illustrated by considering gossip. Gossip was evil, and we all knew it was evil. However, if it were stated in a way as to "instruct one's listeners to a better Christian life," who could say it was wrong? Naturally, the finer aspects of this were soon forgotten, and gossip was gossip. The attraction of this gossip was that it never failed to make the speaker feel superior to whomever he or she was speaking about. In other words, "holier than thou." Enough "holier than thou," especially if one always feels like the "thou," and one becomes rebellious. By the time I was starting high school, I was feeling tired of the small and narrow-minded opinions of the "holier," and of trying to justify being part of the "thou."

Grandfather Stucky not only refused to wear short sleeves, because it exposed too much flesh, he insisted that the skirts of us girls be long, i.e., to the ankle. But when Grandpa was not there, skirts were normally mid-calf, and we even wore shorts to do work on the farm, but not out in public. In public, we were not allowed to wear jeans or pants unless it was to play, and then they were under our skirts or dresses. However, even in my rural Mennonite community, the hemlines were beginning to creep up. By the time, Grandpa passed on, mine and my sister's hemlines also started heading upwards. During my high school days, hemlines were a constant source of conversation among the "holier" on how high the "thou" had let the hemline go. Makeup was viewed as okay in moderation, but, according to the "holier," the "thou" had applied it too liberally.

Pacifism was taught throughout the community. Perhaps it was stressed even more stringently within my own family as my father took an uncompromising and absolute stance against American involvement in WWII. He felt it was wrong, not only to serve in the army, but also to perform alternative, conscientious objector service. As such, he refused to comply with the directives of his local draft board. His stance against the Selective Service Act of 1940 was so extreme that he eventually was sentenced to two years in a federal penitentiary, of which he served nine months before being paroled.

While I was unaware of Dad's jail time until much later in my childhood, I cannot remember a time of not knowing that to fight was wrong. We were taught that God said, "Thou shall not kill," and He did not say, "Unless some government of men said you may." If God had meant that, God would have said it! This not only meant no military service, but it also meant that no violence was allowed. In general, violence of any kind in one's nature was seen as evil. Thus, hitting was seen as an evil deed and was banned. As children, we broke the rule, but not often, and it was considered a very big deal when that happened. Not only was violence evil, but it showed a lack of "Christian character."

The farm on which I grew up was also the farm where my father had been raised. I can't remember not knowing in which upstairs room my father had been born, where the church was, or that if one went to the local grocery store, Mr. Penner would give one a penny candy.

My "day in and day out" playmates were my sisters. My only brother was seven years younger than I, so he was not really a playmate. My first cousins were next on my social agenda as we saw them just about every Sunday. Sundays were our social time. After church, we went to Grandma and Grandpa Stucky's, then home to "chore" (take care of the animals), and then on to Grandma Schrag's, or vice versa. Other than that, there were get-togethers with a couple of other families maybe once a month.

Summers were times of isolation on the farm. There was neither school nor get-togethers during the summer, as farmers do much of their fieldwork at that time. However, summer did bring the family gathering. These happened two or three times each summer and would have up to 250 people who walked around and said, "Oh, so you are Carl's girls," or said, "Oh, so you are Deloris's girls," depending upon whose family was gathering. Some of the people I would recognize, some I did not know, some I would avoid, but most of the time I found someone I knew, with whom I could play.

Our farm, which was a combination grain and animal farm, had a variety of farm animals and was a wonder to me when I was a young child. Everything from chickens to goats came and went over the years, but having about 300 head of sheep and about 150 head of cattle was fairly constant. While there was a short period of time when we did not have a horse when I was very young, by the time I married and left home, there were about forty horses in our herd. I can just barely remember the time when the farm was a dairy, but that changed when I was three. While we always had a milk cow or two, the cattle emphasis switched from dairy to beef when I was still fairly young.

In spite of the fact that there always seemed to be more work than time, I loved the farm. Taking care of the farm animals, including feeding, watering, milking, etc., had to be done everyday, twice a day. Such tasks were simply part of the daily farm routine that fell under the heading of chores. In addition, I started driving a tractor at the age of six, and spent many hours in the fields over the next eleven years.

I was always an animal lover, and, in particular, I loved the horses. I trained my first horse, Goldie, when I was seven, and she was five. It was truly a love match. During the time that I was becoming proficient at riding, training, and competing on horses, Goldie remained my constant companion and confidante. Riding always gave me the feeling of freedom, and it promoted contemplation of God and the world. The only one who ever rivaled her in my affections was Jem, whom I trained for racing, barrels, reigning, etc. Jem and I competed and took ribbons at everything from the county fair to the state fair, and on to The American Royal Livestock and Horse Show in Kansas City. During the summer, he was ridden on the local racetrack on Sunday afternoons. I trained Jem when I was fifteen and he was four, and, from then on, I talked incessantly to both Jem and Goldie.

There was always an oversupply of work, but we also played. We slid down the barn roofs, and swung and tightrope-walked on the bars in the grain elevator. We made mud pies, and played tag, fox and goose, hide and seek, and farm. As we got a bit older, we told horrible ghost stories to each other, played cards (mainly Rook), and rode horses. I remember, along about this time in my young life being at the county 4-H fair and doing very well with a beef calf. However, this calf weighed about 1200 pounds, and he stepped on my foot. It was the first time that I can remember actually using a real swear word. I said, "G---d----it!" I was not allowed to show the calf in the championship class. Instead, after being spanked, I was made to sit in the car while my sister showed the calf.

We children did use what we considered to be not-real swear words like darn, shucks, dag-nab-it, ding-dang-it, etc. However, even that was looked down upon. I remember one of my uncles stopped his car as he was leaving our farm, because he heard me say the word "cotton-pickin'." He told me that while it was not a bad word, I was saying it in a bad way.

When I started school, Dad was on the school board of our local elementary school, Cloverleaf. Cloverleaf was located only about a half mile away from the far end of our farm, and was a country school of about 75 students. In those days, there was no preschool or kindergarten in our rural community. Without exception, every child in my school went either to Hopefield Mennonite Church (as I did), or to Eden Mennonite Church, which was a country church less than two miles away from Hopefield. Furthermore, the children who were my classmates in the first grade were still my classmates in the eighth grade. After the eighth grade, it was off to high school, which was a consolidated rural high school and which included students from all the small, rural grade schools around Moundridge, as well as from the town itself.

Beyond being active in the church and community, my mother provided an excellent example of generosity. She was always ready to help anyone who needed a hand. She was the first one there when the neighbor was sick, and she took care of the cousins when a new addition was made to their family. However, as I grew older, her health seemed to fail in stages. She had a car accident when I was five and quit driving thereafter. (My oldest sister, LeAnn, was nine, and she started to drive into town for groceries and supplies during that summer's harvest in order to compensate for Mom's not driving anymore. Dad was busy farming, and there was no one else to drive. I started driving tractors when I was six and started driving into town on farm errands when I was eight or nine.) It seems that we always knew that something was wrong with Mom's health, because she fell so often. I do not recall there being any diagnosis until after she fell and broke her hip. At that time, I was thirteen, and my youngest sister was six weeks old. Mom never walked again and was diagnosed with multiple sclerosis.

While I do not remember the day we purchased it, the addition of a television set was an altering event in my personal world. Although our TV time was closely controlled and supervised, my sisters and I learned many things through this medium. As I grew up, I knew no one who drank, smoked, or swore. I had no concept of what a drunk was until I watched Red Skelton stumble around on TV as if he were drunk. I did not know what beer was and did not even know the word until TV ads brought it to my attention. I knew that wine was what we did not drink, even though the *Bible* said that Jesus (peace be upon him) performed a miracle by turning water into wine. Our Sunday school teachers were always busy telling us kids that it really just meant grape juice, but there wasn't a word for grape juice when the *Bible* was written. I was told that so often that I didn't really question it until my teen years.

We had purchased our first TV sometime in 1960 when television was still a black and white medium. I can remember not being allowed to watch variety shows, because, when the women danced, their skirts would billow up, and we could see their tights or even their under-wear. In general, movies, television, and Hollywood were seen as the devil's tools. However, once when I was around nine or ten years old, my parents took us to see a movie at a theater in a small city about thirty miles away from our farm. I am not sure what the second movie was, or if there was an accompanying cartoon. The movie I do remember was called "(something) Champion," or just "Champion." It was the story of a young girl who loved a little, black calf. The calf was sick, and the girl stayed out in a blizzard to save it. Then, the girl got sick. When she got better, they won the championship at the fair. I did not get to see another movie until I was 13 years old. Then, my two older sisters took me with them to see "Tickle Me" starring Elvis Presley.

As I look back, it seems that moving into my teen years brought a lot of changes. The biggest one was when I was thirteen, and involved changes within the family structure. With Mom's not walking, LeAnn, my oldest sister, did the housework, and Leona, my next older sister, and I did almost all the outside chores. LeAnn left home that fall, leaving Leona and I to do both the inside and outside chores. Later, during the summer after I turned fourteen, I began dating—just double dates with Leona and her boyfriend. The following fall, I entered high school, which was a big step for me, as I went from having a class of ten to a class of eighty. At that time, Moundridge Rural High School had just over 200 students. Instead of two grades per teacher and per classroom, as was the case in my grade school, the high school offered several classes on each topic, in order to allow all the students to get their proper courses.

Among the changes that came in my early teen years, I began to experience a searing anger at God. I was totally furious that He would allow such a thing as multiple sclerosis to happen to Mom, who was the epitome of a good Christian. When I finally got the nerve to express some of this anger, it was my mother who took me to task for it. She rolled her wheelchair over to me, and said, "Debbie, I may be able to witness better from a wheelchair than standing on my own two feet. It will work out. You will see." I was not only speechless, but felt guilty.

Despite feeling guilty, I began to rebel, albeit in a very controlled manner. For example, I could not actually bring myself to drink beer as it smelled so badly. Likewise, I could not smoke as I would cough my head off. However, the community did not need to know that. I can clearly remember walking down the main street in Moundridge and carrying in one hand an empty beer can that I had found and a lit cigarette, which I had "bummed" from a friend, in the other hand. I was making a statement. It was not my statement, but I did not know that at the time.

At age seventeen, I married my husband, Jerry. Jerry and I had attended Moundridge High School together. He was a senior and the student council president when I was a freshman. I had a crush on him even back then, but we did not really get together until two years later. Jerry was a Methodist and already a lay minister at the time we wed. He was nineteen years old and was ready to start his junior year at Harvard University. I was between my junior and senior years in high school. We agreed that he would finish college and graduate school, and then I would see what training I wanted. Finances dictated that one of us needed to work full-time. Jerry worked long hours during the summers and also worked part-time during the school year. I worked full-time until after I had my first miscarriage at age nineteen. Then I quit working long enough to make it through a difficult pregnancy and have our son, Sean, when I was twenty years old.

Jerry and I had lived in the Boston area from the time of our marriage in 1969 until he had completed seminary at Harvard in 1974. For me, this was an expanding and educational experience. Not only did I get the opportunity to audit some of Jerry's classes unofficially, but I was able to be part of the whole culture at Harvard. It was severe cultural shock for a farm girl from Kansas; however, I loved it. I grew in more ways than can possibly be explained in this short chapter. Conversations were intellectual exercises. Discussions were based on fact and research. For the first time in my life, my curiosity was being satisfied, and part of that process included gaining some insight about the *Bible*.

I had previously used only the King James Version of the *Bible*. Everything that I had memorized in all those years of Sunday school etc. was from that version. Now, I was learning about how the *Bible* was really made and who really wrote what books. I learned the value of documenting and knowing not only the canonical books of the *Bible*, but also the various books that were abolished and systematically destroyed by some of the powers that were in control of the early church. I learned that each of the various communities of Christians had its own set of recognized scripture and that these various sets of scripture were not identical with each other. In just a few short years, I had joined the ranks of the "educated Christians." I had discovered that there were many inconsistencies and errors in the *Bible*. Like so many other "educated Christians, I no longer believed in the deification and crucifixion of Jesus," and questioned the story of the virgin birth. While I considered most of the Pauline writings to be dubious at best, I still called myself a Christian and was active in the Methodist church for many years thereafter.

When I was twenty-two years old, we spent an eventful summer back in Kansas, before moving on to Denver, where Jerry completed his M.A. and Psy.D. in clinical psychology. That summer, Jerry served as the pastor of two small churches in rural Kansas. Between youth groups, visitation and ladies groups, I put in over thirty-five hours a week. Jerry was easily working over sixty hours and still we did not accomplish all our goals. In spite of our putting in long hours, it was a comfortable life style for us. We enjoyed both the challenges and the people. The people there also enjoyed us and formally requested that we stay and take the position permanently.

That summer, we lived only about an hour away from where both Jerry's and my parents lived. We had planned to enjoy time with our parents and families of origin. However, on the morning of July 13, 1974, my parents' farmhouse exploded when Dad tried to light the hot water heater. My two youngest sisters and my brother, as well as my father and mother, were in the house at the time. They all got out alive and unburned, except for my father. He was severely burned and lived one month in a hospital burn unit. He died on August 13th. My mother was unburned, but had been bedfast for several years prior to the fire, due to her multiple sclerosis. All of her medication and most of her physical care had been managed by Dad. For the first month and a half after the fire, she was hospitalized. Then, at about the time we moved to Denver, she was moved to a nursing home where her medical and physical needs could be met. We went back and forth from Denver very frequently that fall and visited her often during Christmas break. On January 2, 1975, we saw her for the last time. She chatted cheerfully and shared stories from her past. At one point, tears of laughter rolled down her face as she shared a particularly humorous incident. As we later drove back to Denver, Jerry and I discussed how she had told us good-bye. On the ninth of January, she passed away.

Sean was two when my parents passed away and was already an inquisitive child with an active mind and imagination. Prior to becoming four years old, he started asking questions like, "If Superman were combined with the Six Million Dollar Man, would they be stronger than a combination of the Incredible Hulk and Wonder Woman?". These were easily answered with, "They are all pretend, so you can pretend what you want." However, these questions quickly escalated to, "If you combined all four, would they be stronger than God?" "No, God is stronger," was the easy answer. However, when they grew into, "Can God make a wall so tall that God cannot jump it?" I sent Sean to see his father for an answer. When Sean was still three and four, his questions grew, and included, "Is Santa Claus real?" As I did not want to lie to him, I asked him to pretend however he wanted. He found this answer very unsatisfactory, so I told him, "No, Santa was not real." The very next day, he arrived home from pre-school to inform me, "Santa Claus is too real!" When I inquired how he knew that, he stated emphatically that the kids at his school had told him.

Thus, when he asked if Jesus were really a god or not, I took my time to answer. I also checked on why he was asking. It turned out that he was asking, because he could not make sense out of his Sunday school lessons. Complicating matters, he was playing the part of one of the wise men in the church Christmas pageant, and I was directing this same pageant. I told him that Jesus was a very good man who had lived long ago, and that many people had benefited from trying to live their lives like Jesus had lived his life. (I did not give in to the impulse to tell him not to mention it to anyone, but hoped he would not make an announcement to his Sunday school class or at the pageant practice.) I could not hand out the Trinity theory to him. How does one explain that God, who is complete in Himself, and who can be, do, and create anything, decides that He wants a son, impregnates an earth woman and has a child out of her. Then, for some unknown reason, God cannot forgive humans for their sins unless God's son dies a very painful death. It sounds as if one sins against Him and if one wants forgiveness, one just has to go kill His son. That is very twisted logic, and I could not tell my son that it was the truth. Nor could I explain to myself, let alone to a four year old, the three-in-one theory of the Trinity.

In spite of obvious difficulties, I continued attending church, and saw to it that Sean participated in church activities. Jerry had a much more difficult time with church. While I elected to hunt through any sermon for the one nugget that spoke somehow to my life, and to take what inspiration and comfort that I could from those sermons, Jerry had another way of listening to the sermons. He would grit his teeth at the incorrect information given out from the pulpit, and worried that his silence was misleading people. Yet, he was wise enough to know that if he said anything, it would only make the congregants angry with him. It wore on him. He felt angry and dirty after a misleading sermon, with the end result that he very seldom attended church.

Throughout the time that Jerry was going to graduate school, I continued to work. I also finally found the time and initiative to get my GED, and then took several courses from Denver University. As a result of one of those courses, I was granted a full scholarship to the Institute of Psychodrama in Denver. However, attending would have meant stopping work, and my work was paying most of the day-to-day expenses. Needless to say, I had to pass up the scholarship.

In 1978, our lives changed dramatically, as Jerry finally received his doctorate in psychology. We moved out from Denver to a small, farming community, where Sean would not have to attend the Denver Public Schools. Sean had completed his kindergarten at his pre-school, and was now ready for the first grade. That summer, I settled into gardening and into having animals again. Beyond a dog and some cats, I had not had animals around since I had married. Now, we purchased some pigs, a milk cow, chickens, and a horse named Reggie, on which I could teach both Sean and Jerry the finer points of riding. I chafed a bit at not riding Reggie, but I knew that if I did, my bond with Reggie was likely to be stronger than Sean's bond with him. As he was technically Sean's horse, I was unwilling to do that.

The following spring, Jerry noticed a classified ad in the local paper for a half-Arabian mare for sale. He mentioned how much he liked Arabians, and so we went to have a look. We bought the mare, Kelan, and I set about training her. Then, a whole new area opened up for me very unexpectedly when I went to find a stallion to sire Kelan's first foal. I hunted high and low for an Arabian stallion that looked like an Arabian, and I kept finding Arabian stallions that looked like Saddlebreds to me. When I finally found one that looked like an Arabian, I asked the owner why this was the case. As he explained that the stallion was totally descended from Arabian horses imported from Syria in 1906 by Homer Davenport, I began to find that new interest for which I had been searching. I went home, having not only contracted to use his stallion on my half-Arabian mare, but also leasing one of his mares. Then, it was time to convince Jerry that this was the way to go.

After viewing this gentleman's Davenport Arabian horses and some film footage of other horses of the same bloodlines, Jerry and I were convinced. We later sold Reggie, Kelan, and her foal, and purchased our first Davenport Arabian horse. More importantly, we became dedicated to finding out more on the history of these horses. Over the next several years, we acquired more Davenport Arabian horses, and had several foals born at our place. We studied the history of these horses in America since their importation, and began to research their history in the Middle East. By 1985, we were starting to publish articles about the history of the Davenport Arabians in America, and I was involved in organizing an educational meeting and national conference for Al Khamsa, Inc., an Arabian horse organization devoted to those Arabian horses whose extended pedigrees can be traced in all lines to Arabian horses in the Middle East – only about 02% of all registered Arabian horses actually meet Al Khamsa's standards.

In 1985, my family experienced another tragedy. My oldest sister, LeAnn, died at the tender age of thirty-six. She was survived by her husband and her two young children. It seemed almost unbelievable that we had already lost Mom, Dad, and LeAnn.

In 1986, Sean graduated from the eighth grade, and we decided that our tiny five-acre farm was too small. That summer we moved to a thirty-five acre farm within commuting distance of Jerry's work in Denver. Sean started high school in a new school system, and I became a member of the board of directors of Al Khamsa, Inc. I was running a horse breeding operation that ranged from twelve to twenty-seven horses. Together, Jerry and I were gaining expertise in the history of the Arabian horse—not only about our own horses' history, but also about some of the other groups within the designated Al Khamsa bloodlines. I was digging through information that had been housed at the US National Archives for eighty to a hundred years, finding bits and nuggets to fill in the history of how some of the Arabian horses had come into this country, and was discovering some documents pertaining to the history and pedigree of some of the original Arabian imports to the United States.

Sean was participating locally in the church youth group, was a member of the church's drama group (even though he was the only minor participating), and participated in most of the high school sports scene. During that time, we attended the only "mainstream" church that was locally available. While the first two ministers that served that church were only mildly objectionable, the third minister had me gritting my teeth through the sermons. Sean was by now a senior in high school, and I felt responsible for him and his school-mates getting correct information from the pulpit. I guess I had final-ly begun to experience the responsibility that Jerry had been feeling. I also recognized how important it was for me, as well as for Jerry, to be able to celebrate our God together, and realized that was not going to happen in that church. I was so tired of the constant, inner speech that negated over half of what was being preached. During one of those particularly teeth-gritting sermons, I sat in the church pew and silently prayed to God. "Please God, give us a way for Jerry and I to share our religious experiences and to do so honestly and openly." I was concerned about my being able to continue to attend church, and I knew Jerry would not attend with that minister in the pulpit. It was several years before I reflected back on that prayer and realized that God had almost immediately given me a response.

By September of 1990, Sean was off to college. (He would marry in 1992, and has since given us two wonderful grandchildren.) I was busy handling the horse operation all on my own, without the benefit of Sean's help with the heavier work. Jerry was working lots of hours in Denver, and Jerry and I were co-authoring articles on Arabian horse history. By late 1990, we had thirty-five articles in print in a variety of Arabian horse magazines.

Another activity in which I had become involved was the Elbert County Republican Forum. George, an elderly gentleman who spent most of his retirement raising goats, had originated the idea for the group. He and I had managed to get the organization started and registered with the State of Colorado. Before one of those meetings, as George and I set up the chairs for a discussion group, I mentioned to George a theory of mine pertaining to Arabian horse history. (I was so enthusiastic about finding information pertaining to Arabian horse history that it was always on my mind. I was constantly sharing ideas about it and was always exploring new ideas and perspectives.) I was hypothesizing that there were two prominent men in Egyptian history, whose life stories were being incorrectly woven together into one person in the Arabian horse literature. However, I had searched through numerous tomes of Egyptian history and could not find enough information to separate the two lives out with authority. As George was an ex-history professor and was in the process of reading a new, authoritative work on Middle Eastern history, I ran my theory past him. George could not tell me anything about my hypothesis off the top of his head, but he promised to check it out. Almost as an afterthought, George mentioned that several Arab men came out to his farm to butcher goats. He said he would run my theory past them and see if any of them could address my idea.

A couple of months later, long after I had given up on the idea of George being able to help, the phone rang. George told me that he had found someone who knew the difference between the two men whose names I had given to him. He then turned his phone over to Jamal, a young man from Palestine. I briefly explained about owning

Asil Arabian horses and about my theory of the Arabian horse literature merging the identities of two different men in 19th century Egypt. Jamal was polite, but allowed that he had not thought there were any *Asil* Arabian horses in America. He then made arrangements to visit us the following Sunday, to see our horses, and to explain details regarding the two 19th century Egyptians.

When Jamal arrived, we began by showing our horses to him. After being shown the horses, Jamal asked to use our garden hose to make ablution and asked for permission to pray on our front porch. We quickly agreed with his requests, and for the first time observed a Muslim prayer. (It did not occur to me until much later that Jamal was behaviorally witnessing about Islam and about his quiet devotion to it.)

Jamal's prayer completed, we went into the house to discuss my theory of merged identities in the Arabian horse literature which I was pleased to learn had been correct. The conversation then gradually shifted to our horses and their ancestry. As part of that discussion, we showed Jamal a copy of one of the Arabic documents that had accompanied our horses' ancestors in their 1906 journey from Syria to America. As Jamal read it, he translated its contents for us. By the time he was done, he was literally bouncing on the couch, saying, "But these are real Bedouin horses!" Before he left, we made arrangements for him to come back and to translate fully all of the Arabic documents that had accompanied our horses' ancestors to America.

All in all, it had been a very wonderful meeting. Jamal was both friendly and unassuming. He was not only enthusiastic about our *Asil* Arabian horses, but was willing to translate the Arabic documents from 1906. Several other enthusiasts of these horses had previously tried to get the documents translated by professors of college Arabic courses. These professors had not been able to make sense of the horse-specific terminology that was contained in the documents. The professors' confusion often led to misinformation and, at best, an imperfect understanding of the horses' history. In contrast, Jamal was quite conversant with horse terminology in his native Arabic. As such, Jerry and I saw Jamal as a fountain of information on the history of the Arabian horse and as a valuable translator of horse-related documents in Arabic. There was no doubt that he had a great deal of knowledge about the history of the Arabian horse in the Middle East. However, we also recognized that he was the type of individual that we would like to have for a friend.

The next time Jamal visited us, he was accompanied by his sixteen-month-old daughter, Miasar, who charmed me from the moment I met her. As they got ready to leave, I suggested to Jamal that the next time he bring his entire family out to meet us. He was obviously pleased to have the invitation, but commented that it might have to wait a bit as he was expecting his second child in the next few weeks.

Jamal's son, 'Ali, entered the world just about a week after our second meeting. A few weeks later, the entire family came out to our home for a meal. I was aware that Islam had some dietary restrictions and asked Jamal about how to handle that. Only after my absolute insistence that a meal be a part of the invitation, Jamal finally said that baked fish or seafood would be safe for their meal, but that they could not eat meat products from animals that had not been ritually slaughtered. I do not now recall what all we had that first meal, but I remember that Jerry saved me from making a mistake. I had prepared a Jello salad. Jerry pointed out to me that gelatin was a meat by-product, so I did not serve the salad.

I remember with special fondness my first meeting with Sahar, Jamal's wife, who was also from Palestine. Sahar entered our home wearing not only a *Jilbab* (traditional, loose, outer garment) and *Hijab* (scarf), but also a veil. Jerry asked them to sit in the living room, and I served some lemonade. As Sahar was carefully lifting the veil to drink without exposing her face, I realized that I needed to change the eating arrangements. I asked Sahar if she would like to take 'Ali, who was just starting to fuss, to a back room to feed him, to which she gladly agreed. Once I had her in private, I asked if she normally ate separately from men. She had removed her veil in the back room, and she smiled warmly, as she assured me that she could manage to eat with the veil, and that I should not go to any extra trouble. I told her that it was no trouble and went to move Sahar's and my plates to the kitchen. Unfortunately, my kitchen had two doorways, and neither had a door. I simply tacked a couple of older tablecloths over the doorways, and then invited Sahar into our kitchen to eat with me.

It was easy to talk with Sahar, and I liked having a female friend to ply with questions. She always answered them so earnestly. She would explain in great detail about Islamic customs, and about how Islam taught or had influenced this or that. From the very beginning, I loved her approachability and strong belief in God. She would not do anything that was against her Islamic teachings. She did not set aside her beliefs just because they were sometimes inconvenient in our American culture. Even more impressive was her manner of teaching her children. Her firm, but gentle, corrections were heeded. Her serious manner of following each and every rule of Islam totally impressed me. I had lived so long with my own questioning of the Christian faith that it was refreshing to see someone who really could believe in her own faith.

I knew many Christians who adamantly espoused Christian dogma and creed, but most of them knew almost nothing about their religion and its history. Other "Christians" that I knew were living with the outer trapping of their religion, but they could not truly agree with the basic doctrines of Christianity. In my "good old country" terms, Sahar and Jamal not only talked the talk, they walked the walk. The last Christian that I could think of who did that was my mother, who was much better at walkin' the walk from her wheelchair than anyone else I knew. Sahar and Jamal demonstrated this same type of absolute faith, and had the same type of calm adherence to their religious beliefs that I had once seen in my mother. However, they never pushed Islam on us, nor did anything that even vaguely resembled the aggressive proselytizing that many Christians attempt. At first, it did not occur to me that I could believe in Islamic doctrine when I could not believe in the doctrines of Christianity. However, as Jamal and Sahar taught us about the history of the Arabian horse, a topic which constantly overlaps with Islamic history, it became abundantly clear that they were knowledgeable about their religion and that they were living their religion on both an inner and outer level. Viewing them, I found Islam attractive, and I admired their commitment to their faith, but I continued to see Islam as being somehow foreign and as being their religion.

As we continued to work on the publication of Jamal's translation of Arabian horse documents, we deepened our friendship with Jamal and Sahar. Before long, we started to meet some of their friends. Among these people were other excellent examples of Islam. Khalid Al-Nabhani and his family were among the first ones we met. His father was originally from Oman, but was then living in Saudi Arabia. His wife, Sharifa, did not speak English. Our relationship was my first experience of going through a translator to communicate with someone. However, with Sahar's aid, we managed to form a friendship, and to share experiences and ideas. We also met the families of two brothers from Jordan, Abu Hasan and Abu Omar. Abu Hasan and his very kind wife, Um Hasan, were like a breath of fresh air. Like Jamal's and Khalid's families, they also adhered strictly to Islam. Just being in the company of such people made me feel privileged to be a part of this wonderful group.

As we gathered knowledge on the horses from each of them, and as we learned to understand the Islamic influence on the Arabian horse documents, we became more and more familiar with Islamic thought and its differences from Western teachings. It was a time of exciting discoveries and of self-awakening. It was also a little intimidating and frightening.

Gradually, Jerry and I began to fantasize about going overseas and finding some new information about Davenport's 1906 trip and the history of the horses that he brought to America. As 1991 turned into 1992, we continued researching Arabian horse history and began to co-author a series of articles with Jamal. Somewhere in there, Jamal started to tell Jerry and me that we ought to go to the Middle East and see what all we could discover. I especially remember an occasion when Jerry was joking with Jamal just as Jamal and his family were getting ready to end a visit at our home. Jerry said that he would have to be the one to go to the Middle East, and that I would have to stay home and care for the horses, as Jerry could move around in the Middle East, while I, as a woman in the Middle East, would have more restrictions placed on my movements. Jamal, ever quick on his feet, immediately informed Jerry that he did not understand. It was I who could go everywhere, not Jerry. I, as an American woman, could go in with the women and in with the men, in order to find out horse information! Jerry could go in with the men, but could not go in among the women.

It was at about this point that I became aware that Jerry had taken down from the bookshelf his English translations of the *Qur'an*, which he had used many years before in his comparative religions course. I watched as he started studying and looking at Islam beyond the horses. At that point, I had a choice. I could start to figure it out for myself, or close my eyes as tightly as I could and pretend that

Islam was not there. I propped one eye open and started my journey. I had always believed that truth was what one should follow, and the more I learned about Islam, the more I could hear its ring of truth. Like the clear sound of silver tapping crystal, Islam pierced through the cacophony of noise formed by the religious teachings of my youth, with the melodic ring of *La Ilaha Illa Allah* – there is no god but God.

Jerry and I had now been married for over twenty-two years, and sharing was a way of life for us. We shared our joys, sorrows, discoveries, daily trials, exasperations, oddities and all aspects of our lives. Thus, Jerry and I shared the discovery of Islam with each other, using each other as sounding boards, and enjoying the new discoveries together. However, questions such as "Could Muhammad (peace be upon him) be a prophet and was the *Qur'an* scripture" were still hard hurdles for me. I did not want to accept a new religion only to have more questions than I had before. At the same time, I started to realize that Islam taught a great deal that I had come to believe anyway. Islam taught that Jesus was a prophet, and that all prophets were fully human and not divine. Adam, Noah, Moses, Aaron, Abraham, Lot, Ishmael, Isaac, Joseph, David, Solomon, John the Baptist, and Jesus (peace be upon them all) were among the prophets who are mentioned in the *Qur'an*. My Christian background gave me some familiarity with the Biblical stories about these prophets of Allah, but the stories about them in the *Qur'an* were clearer and crisper than the ones in the *Bible*. I loved reading these stories from the *Qur'an*, and found them refreshing.

However, in many ways, it was the scientific knowledge within the *Qur'an* that I found most irresistible. As an example, I wrestled with the following: The *Qur'an* was received by Prophet Muhammad in the early seventh century. So, just how did Muhammad know that the shape of the earth was a slightly ovoid sphere, similar to the shape of an egg? Yet, such a statement appears in *Qur'an* 79: 30. Although most English translations of *Qur'an* 79:30 translate the relevant Arabic word Dahaha as "spread" or "expanded," a more literal translation would include the concept of being egg-like. How did Prophet Muhammad know in the early seventh century that the earth was spheroid? More specifically, how could he have known that our planetary sphere had been pulled into a slightly ovoid shape by the gravitational forces of the cosmos, when science had not discovered that fact until the latter half of the twentieth century? How could Muhammad have known that? Only God could have known that in the early seventh century. Other examples of scientific knowledge found in the *Qur'an* centuries before science discovered these facts have to do with celestial orbits, the moon's reflection of the sun's light, ocean tides, and the stages of development of a fetus in the womb. While these issues raised intriguing, but disturbing, questions for me, I was hardly ready to make any announcement of conversion.

I slowly came to accept that Islam had the answers for which I was looking, without realizing that I was looking. After all, it's hard to search for something that one doesn't believe exists. I didn't look for a religion that would answer my questions, confirm my truths, and soothe my spirit, as I did not think that one existed. Now, I was inconveniently confronted with one. It seems crazy to call a religion that does all that "inconvenient." However, I did not want to deal with the consequences of Islam's being the answer to my questions. My life was fairly set, or so I thought. I was busy raising horses, helping organizations that dealt with the horses, and writing articles, and I had my little group of friends. I did not welcome the change that Islam would bring, so I resisted.

I finally recognized that I did believe that Muhammad was a prophet, but I did not proclaim myself to be a Muslim. I figured that I could keep this knowledge a secret, just like many of my other beliefs had been a secret for many years. There was no reason for the little community in which we lived, for my family, or for the horse community to be aware of my developing appreciation for Islam. Believing in the message of the *Qur'an* was an even bigger step for me than was believing that Muhammad was a prophet. However, even after achieving this level of belief, I did not think any conversion announcement was necessary. Slowly, I started picking up some of the sayings and teachings of Islam, but I still resisted change and continued clinging to my old Christian identity. Couldn't I stay a Christian, or at least something close to it, and just privately know that I thought Islam was correct? I was used to hiding my thinking about Christianity, so why couldn't this just be an extension of that? Why should I give up all the nostalgic Sunday school songs and Christmas carols of my youth? Why should I part with my religious terminology? Why should I abandon all the "word equations" of my native language and religious heritage? After all, almost any positive adjective that one can be, had been linked in my education and training with the term "Christian." One had a "good Christian heart," performed a "good Christian deed," did things in a "gentle Christian manner", and aimed to be an "upright, straightforward, and honest Christian." Concepts such as these were not only part of my own personal upbringing, but were woven into the everyday fabric of my American culture.

With the dawn of 1993, our fantasized trip to the Middle East was on the verge of becoming a reality, and Jerry and I enlisted Carol, a fellow student of Arabian horse history, to accompany us. The three of us, all of whom were at least nominally American Christians, decided that out of respect for the Islamic culture of the Middle East, we would observe the local customs of behavior and dress. This meant fasting during *Ramadan*, and wearing appropriately modest dress. Most notably, long sleeves, long skirts, and scarves were needed for Carol and myself. Both Carol and I spent time locating appropriate clothing prior to the five-week trip. I spent Tuesday mornings with Sahar, who taught me some of the basics of Arabic and the pronunciation of a few simple Arabic phrases.

Our trip was scheduled for March and April of 1993. We planned to make Jordan our home base during our trip, using it to travel to and from Oman, Palestine, and Syria. We would arrive in Jordan during *Ramadan*, and would arrive back home on April 11th, Easter Sunday, just one week before the foaling season was due to start.

The night before we left for the Middle East, Jerry and I spent the evening at the home of Jamal and Sahar. They had a big gathering of friends at their home that night. Among them was Hani, a visitor from Jordan, who was returning to Jordan in a day or two. Hani offered to host us during our stay in Jordan and to assist us if we should encounter any difficulty. Also present there that night was Abu Hasan, a person from Jordan that we had met once before. As soon as he learned that we were leaving for Jordan the next day, he insisted that we stay at his parents' home. His parents were currently in Denver for a visit, but he promised to phone back to Jordan to arrange for his brothers and for his aunt and uncle to meet us at the airport in 'Amman. As we had thought we were going to be on our own in finding lodging upon arriving in Jordan, his offer was most welcome and generous beyond all words. However, the next morning, as we prepared to leave North America for the first time, we weren't at all sure that we still wouldn't be on our own when we arrived at the 'Amman airport Upon our arrival in Jordan,

During a trip to Syria in 1993: Jerry and Debra with their generous hosts, Brother Mohammad 'Ali Al-Hafez and Brother Mustafa Al-Jabri

we were greeted by Maher and 'Awad, Abu Hasan's brother and uncle, respectively. They were holding up a sign with "Devra Dirk" written on it in large English letters. All three of us (Carol included) greeted them, then piled our luggage into their car, and began our journey to their home. It was raining as the five of us made our way through the 'Amman streets, but when we arrived at their home, everything was warm and welcoming. They showed us to our apartment within their home. It had a bedroom, bathroom, and a living room, the last of which was immediately refurnished to make a second bedroom, as they had not been expecting Carol. This fantastic greeting from friends, whom we had never met before, was heartwarming. We felt like long-lost family in this land so far from home. From the moment we arrived, our every need was anticipated and met.

Shortly after we arrived, *Adhan*, the Muslim call to prayer, sounded from a nearby mosque. I had previously heard parts of the *Adhan* only on movies or TV and was unprepared for its beauty. I sat almost wanting to hold my breath, as I listened. It was both uplifting and somehow personally summoning with its beautiful, melodic sound.

There were many things that happened during this trip to the Middle East that helped me over the hurdle in proclaiming myself to be a Muslim. In general, the acceptance of us, as three non-Muslim Americans, into the homes and lives of the people there was beyond amazing. There was the gentle witnessing of so many that I cannot possibly mention all the incidents. However, I will try to give a brief overview of some of the events that propelled me forward into Islam.

The two young men of the household, Maher and Rami, both spoke excellent English, although Uncle 'Awad and Aunt Seham (they have forever afterwards been, and to this day remain my aunt and uncle) spoke only Arabic. As both Maher and Rami were gone during the day to work and school respectively, that meant that we

Americans needed to communicate in Arabic, in sign language and pantomime, or in a mixed-up combination of the two. We did just fine figuring it out, although occasionally we waited for Maher and Rami to translate something at night.

I was genuinely touched and affected by the generosity and care of Uncle 'Awad and Aunt Seham. Uncle 'Awad took time out of his busy *Ramadan* schedule to take us to many historical sites around 'Amman, plus he arranged and accompanied us on two large excursions during our time in Jordan. The first included Petra, an ancient city carved out of mountainsides, which was the site of the death and tomb of Aaron, the brother of Moses. The second was to the north, where we were able to look out over Lake Tiberias, the Sea of Galilee, from the ruins of Um Qais. Looking across the expanse of the Sea of Galilee made the Biblical story of Jesus' calming the sea seem so close and real. It was like I could reach out and almost touch that history just beyond the end of my fingertips. On one of the shorter excursions, he took us to see Mt. Nebo where Moses looked across the River Jordan and saw the Promised Land. Being that close to the site of so many significant religious events from the shared religious history of Judaism, Christianity, and Islam began to turn my thoughts in a more spiritual direction. Just being there was changing me.

However, it was not the many historical sites, but Aunt Seham that was having the greatest effect on me. With the language barrier between us, we could not verbally discuss Islam, but her every deed was an example of religious contentment. The thought and care that she gave to everyone around her, her quiet offering of her prayers, and her obvious devotion to Islam were like a beacon of light slowly bringing me into her realm and showing me the true meaning of Islam in her daily life.

As it was *Ramadan*, Aunt Seham was busy preparing big meals for breaking our fasts at sundown. Whenever we were at the 'Awad home in the afternoon, I would go to the kitchen and try to help her. She would set me up at the table, and then go about her business, always smiling at me. Sometimes, she would let me chop the tomatoes or cucumbers for a salad. Before letting me help in this manner, she would demonstrate, so that I knew how large the pieces were to be, and then she would hand me the knife. I would try out my limited Arabic on her at these times, but I still have no idea what I must have actually been saying half the time! However, from the look on her kind face, it was not always what I intended.

I recall one time in particular. I was heading into the kitchen area, intent on offering any help that I could, and I found her praying. The look of peace on her face was so serene. I knew that I wanted to find that same kind of peace and tranquility that Aunt Sehim found in her five daily prayers.

My first opportunity to join her in prayer was the first Friday that we were in Jordan. We were asked if we would like to witness the Friday noon prayer service, and we quickly accepted. We were taken to the King 'Abdullah Mosque in the middle of 'Amman. Jerry, Carol, and I had never been to a mosque for prayers. Rami, Uncle 'Awad, and Jerry headed for the men's entrance, while Aunt Seham, Carol, and I went to the women's area. Just after I entered the mosque, a policewoman took my purse and left with it. In that little purse was my passport, several thousand dollars in cash, and all my other identification papers. I tried to ask Aunt Seham if it was normal or okay, but my Arabic was not up to the task. Aunt Seham just smiled and motioned for Carol and me to sit down. Our presence caused a bit of a stir as those around us figured out that we were "Americani." I decided to put my faith in God, try not to worry about the missing purse, and just enjoy the experience. I did not know that the security was because Queen Noor was in attendance for the Friday prayers. The *Khutbah* or sermon was relatively short, and, as we were in an

Arab country, the *Khutbah* was given in Arabic, which did little for my comprehension of its message. Once the *Khutbah* was finished, we all stood to pray. I had no idea what I was doing, although I went through the motions of copying what everyone else was doing, as best as I could.

It was an unusual way for me to pray, but I still experienced it as being both inspirational and moving in its beauty. I found myself caught up in a communal unity of worship with all the other congregants in a way that I had never before experienced in any communal prayer in any Christian church service. There was something different here, and I was surprised to find it personally meaningful to join in a prayer when I could not understand the language in which it was being prayed.

With the prayer completed, people were moving to the doors, and I made a determined effort to find the policewoman who had taken my purse. As English is the second language in Jordan, I had no trouble finding someone who could understand my question about where I was to pick up my purse. However, when I got there, the policewoman was not there and neither was my purse. Just as my newly reinforced faith was about to desert me, a lady took my arm and pointed out the policewoman who was busy trying to find me to return my purse to me. The policewoman was happy to find me and looked as relieved at being able to return my purse to me as I was at having it back in my care. I resisted the impulse to look inside the purse and went to locate my shoes, so that we could leave. Naturally, everything was in the purse and just as I had left it. I wasn't at all sure that would have been the case back home, and the contrast left its impression.

The issue of prayer was raised again a few evenings later when visitors came to the 'Awad home to share in breaking the *Ramadan* fast. Among the visitors was an 'Awad cousin, his wife, and their lovely daughters. The earnest questions from these young ladies further advanced me on my journey into Islam in two different ways. Firstly, the fact that one of them was a nurse, one was a teacher, and one had a degree in agriculture made me realize that I could fit into an Islamic society. Secondly, being curious about my life in America, they asked me about my manner of praying. "We pray five times a day; how often do you pray?" My immediate, unspoken reply was, "It depends on how many times I misplaced my keys that day!" While I did not mean that literally, I suddenly realized that my prayers should not be contingent upon external circumstances. Their innocent question had really struck home. Was I really worshiping God, or merely begging for a handout when things were going wrong?

Later, these same young ladies started my instruction in prayer. They explained to me some of the intricacies of the prayer that I had previously tried to pray at the King 'Abdullah Mosque. They patiently and repeatedly went over the Arabic words of the prayer and explained their meaning, so I had at least a vague idea of what I was mouthing. Their generosity and kindness in allowing me to mispronounce the same word dozens of times were beautiful examples of Islamic values and etiquette.

Another influential person on my understanding of Islam and its customs was Hanadi. She was the wife of Hani whom Jerry had met at Jamal's the evening before we left for Jordan. Hanadi took the time to answer my many questions which had been piling up while waiting for a female ear attuned to English. She explained with clarity the need for modest dress and its significance. Until meeting Hanadi, I was not keen on wearing a *Hijab* (scarf), which did not want to stay on my head, and was questioning why someone would ever choose to wear a veil. Hanadi's explanations helped me to recognize that it was an honor and a privilege to serve Allah in this manner, and that this was something one chose to do "for the sake of Allah."

Once again, I took advantage of having an English-speaking Muslim to guide me in my prayers. I was beginning to look forward to coming home to America and to sharing prayers with Sahar.

My experience of Islam continued as we began to make excursions out from our base in Jordan. Our first excursion was to Palestine. This border crossing was enlightening in more ways than one. Firstly, I was shocked upon initially seeing the River Jordan. All of my life, I had been reading about and seeing paintings of the River Jordan, and not once had I imagined it looking anything like what I crossed over to get into Israel/Palestine. I had always visualized a broad expanse of river with sloping banks. When I actually saw the River Jordan, I assumed it was merely one of those little spillways to prevent flooding, like one finds by the Mississippi River. The River Jordan looked like an Illinois irrigation canal! There was nothing regal or picturesque about it. Just a small, slowly moving, drainage ditch was the River Jordan. It was a huge disappointment and really drove home the misrepresenting imagery that had lingered in the Christian-trained nooks and crannies of my mind. Then came the next shock. When we were ready to get off the bus that had taken us to the Israeli-controlled areas, it was like entering a prison. I noticed that everyone moved forward in line with very little being said, and that most people automatically hung their heads. The other entrants here were not Palestinians, as they had to go through a much more rigorous interrogation at another boarder facility. These were other travelers like ourselves. For the first time, I really appreciated how oppressive an occupation actually is. It dampened our enthusiasm and permeated our mood—all without any untoward incident.

Once inside the country, we spent several days being shown Jerusalem, Bethlehem, and the surrounding area, while evenings were spent being spoiled and pampered in the homes of Jamal's and Sahar's families. One evening that particularly touched my heart was at the home of Jamal's sister, Hanan. However, before detailing the events of that evening, it is important to digress for a moment.

Earlier that day, Hanan's eldest son, Ahmad, had spent the day giving us a tour of Jerusalem. Despite the fact that Ahmad was a Muslim and that Jerry and I were still nominally Christians, albeit Christians who were now joining in Muslim prayers and fasting during *Ramadan*, Ahmad went out of his way to show us various sites of special interest to Christians, including the Via Dolorosa (the path along which Jesus allegedly carried his cross), the Basilica of the Holy Sepulchre (the place at which the Roman Catholic Church alleges that Jesus was crucified and buried), the Garden of Gethsemane, the Mount of Olives, etc. Although these places had no religious significance for him, as Muslims deny the literal crucifixion of Jesus, his Islamic need to care for others led him to show these sites to us, and especially to Carol, who remained a Christian in more than just a nominal manner. However, despite Ahmad's thoughtfulness, these sites were not moving me spiritually in the same way that I was experiencing more traditionally Islamic sites.

That night, after a delicious feast at his parents' home, Ahmad showed us a video of him and some of his friends doing the traditional dances of their Bedouin heritage. As much as I loved the dances and the beauty of these songs, they weren't what touched me. Ahmad sat and quietly pointed to this friend or that one, giving us their names and current status. It broke my heart that he did not seem to think it was unusual or odd to be saying: "They put that one in jail...they killed that one...they took that one, and we have never seen him again." These were the friends of a sixteen-year-old boy. It was simply a fact of life. (Regardless of the difficulty I would later encounter in being a Muslim in America, such difficulties were nothing compared to the trials of this young man.)

Another special contact that had long lasting effects on me was that of Um Bilal, Sahar's sister. Her bright and cheery manner was only outshone by her earnest endeavor to do Allah's will. Her English was excellent and she helped me understand some of the expressions that you hear Muslims use repeatedly. She told me that Muslims were to "moisten their lips with the name of Allah." If one considers the arid country in which we were, that meant that Allah was not only to be continuously in our minds and hearts, but also to be constantly on our lips.

It was on the last day of our visit to Palestine that we went to Al-Aqsa Mosque and the Dome of the Rock. I was fascinated by the beauty and grandeur of the Dome of the Rock. I experienced being sucked into it, as if I had a fifty-mile an hour wind at my back. The Arabic calligraphy was exquisite, and the dome glistened. However, it was at Al Aqsa that I finally got my answer. As we entered, there was a little area where some women were praying. I smiled at them and did my own two *Rakah* (units of prayer), not because it was customary or because someone expected it, but because I sensed that I was in a holy place and because I desired to feel closer to God. I could feel the millions who have gone before me to that spot praying with me, and could only hope that Allah would allow me to return there often. I now knew that to do anything other than openly devoting myself to Islam would be to violate my true, inner self. My search for God had brought me to this point, and I had finally managed to let go of my Christian trappings and identity. The questioning was gone, as well as the hesitation that had previously held me back.

Now that my path was set, I had only a couple of weeks left to be in an Islamic society before going home to try to stand, with the help of Allah, on my own two feet. I needed to learn from my sisters and brothers in Islam as much as I could. That education began as we returned to the 'Awad family in Jordan by *Eid*, the three-day holiday marking the end of *Ramadan*. We spent our very first *Eid* in 'Amman.

It was a beautiful way to learn the traditions and blessings of *Eid*.

Shortly thereafter, we went to Oman. Khalid Al-Nabhani, who had become our friend back in Denver, had arranged to have a friend of his greet us, guide us around Muscat (the capital city), and provide horse information and tours. Our second day in Oman started with a short visit to the beach. Later, as our host was driving, he said he was going to show us some "Omani magic." He then turned into a driveway and informed us that we were at the home of Khalid's brother. When we entered, it was Khalid who greeted us. He had flown in from America to be able to show us his country! His extraordinary generosity and kindness were further examples of what it meant to practice Islam in daily life!

The next day, Brother Khalid took us deep into the interior of Oman to show us some ancient rock drawings. As we neared the site, he stopped to speak to a young gentleman, in order to get better directions. Instead of just giving us the directions we needed, the young man volunteered to come with us and personally show us the paintings—yet another example of what it meant to live an Islamic life. After about a quarter mile of walking on lava rock, we found the rock paintings. The drawings were dated and included camels, lions, gazelles, horses, etc. that the ancient artist was afraid would disappear from the area. These were out in the middle of nowhere, with no markings and no signs that anyone else had ever seen them.

Having seen the rock drawings, our newfound brother insisted that we stop at his humble home for refreshments. Carol and I were escorted to the women's side of the yard where we were greeted by the wife and children of the household. While there was no one to act as translator for us, we truly did not need one. The Islamic kindness and generosity of our hostess needed no words of translation, and we were very grateful for the wonderfully delicious fruit and refreshing water of our repast. With my limited Arabic, I managed to sort out the relationships of the family with our hostess (my new-found sister-in-Islam). Among her young daughters was a five-year-old who was one of the most beautiful children I had ever seen. There I sat, wanting to comment on the unique beauty of this child and afraid to try to say the words in Arabic. I knew that the Arabic for camel was *Jamel*, and that the Arabic for beautiful was *Jamil*. I was terrified that I would end up telling my sister-in-Islam that her daughter looked like a camel. My fear kept my mouth shut. Finally, as we were leaving, I took the young child's face in my hand, and said *Quwayis*, which means good. The mother beamed at my compliment, obviously pleased with the compliment beyond the significance of the simple word I had finally uttered. She smiled as she thanked me and bid me "*Ma Salamah*" or "peace be upon you."

During a trip to Jordan in 1993:
Debra and her husband Jerry with their friends in a typical Bedouin style pose. Seen in the picture (L to R) are Carol, Jerry, Debra and Sister Dalal

A few days later, we were in Syria where we were on our own until we could link up with the government officials with whom we had previously been in contact about seeing the Arabian horses of Syria. We had taken a taxi from 'Amman to Damascus. When we stopped at the boarder to fill out forms to enter Syria, we were given a new example of the extreme thoughtfulness, generosity, and kindness that are the duty of Muslims. There was a very long line of Arabs waiting to get to the window to get their passports stamped so they could cross the border. This line was for Syrians and for other Arabs. There was also a window for foreigners that were not Arabs. This line just had the three of us. However, the forms that we were required to fill out were written in Arabic only. I could make out where to put our names, but about the rest I had not a clue.

At that same time, a young Syrian couple was almost all the way to the window of that long line for Arabs when they realized the difficulty we were having. They immediately left their own line, losing the turn for which they must have waited the better part of an hour. They approached us with smiles on their faces and greeted us in English. They translated the questions for us, and then filled in our answers in Arabic. Not content with having helped us with our forms, they gave us their phone number in Damascus so that we could reach them if we had any difficulties during our stay there. They then returned to the back of their own line and patiently waited to begin their hour-long journey to the front of the line. I marveled at their consideration and benevolence, their regard and concern for three strangers. It was yet another example that Muslims do good deeds as a part of their striving to please Allah, with their only hope of reward being from Allah in the hereafter. This was not like putting spare change in a collection plate; this required real giving of oneself.

After getting our passports stamped, we continued our taxi ride to a circle in Damascus where all Jordanian taxis must deposit their passengers. Here, we were lucky to find a cab with a young Syrian driver who spoke a smidgen of English. He asked us where we wished to go, and we explained that we needed a hotel, perhaps a Sheridan or Holiday Inn. He quickly informed us of the extreme cost of the Sheridan and other American establishments. He asked if we would rather have an Arab hotel that was not nearly so expensive, but was clean and employed desk clerks who spoke English. We readily agreed. We arrived at the hotel and unloaded our luggage which had been multiplying over the course of the trip and which was by now quite a sizable amount. We thanked the taxi driver and start-

ed the process of checking into the hotel. As we waited for the paper-
work to be completed, the clerk had arranged for hot tea to be served
to us, as is the custom in Arab societies.

Then, just as we were heading for the elevators to go to our
rooms, our helpful taxi driver came bounding up the steps into
the lobby. He was out of breath and carrying our video camera case.
Somehow in the middle of unloading bags from the roof of the taxi,
the camera case had gotten left on the taxi floor. The driver had not
noticed it until he was back downtown to pick up another fare. He
had immediately turned his cab around and headed back to the hotel.
His only concern was that we might have missed the case and been
worried. In spite of Jerry's best efforts, he would not accept any
payment, even for the extra cab fare of his driving all that way back
to the hotel. The video camera was purchased especially for this trip
and was obviously brand new. We had paid just over $1,200 for it
just the week before we left, and it was state of the art. Given the
extremely inexpensive cost of living in Syria, the taxi driver could have
easily sold the video camera for enough money to support his whole
family for almost a whole year. However, his honesty and integrity
were such that he had only worried about our being concerned over
the missing camera. The concepts of "for the sake of Allah" and "may
Allah reward you for your good deeds" were fully permeating my
consciousness.

Later, when we ventured out on our own to locate the 'Umayyad
Mosque, the burial site for John the Baptist's head, we became lost.
Spotting a policeman who was directing traffic in the crowded street,
we tried to ask for directions. As he did not speak English, the police-
man started asking every person who passed by if he or she spoke
English. After a few minutes, he found a gentleman who spoke
English. When we explained that we needed directions to the famous
'Umayyad Mosque, this brother-in-Allah insisted on walking with us

to show it to us, even though he had been walking in the opposite direction. Once again, the wonderful kindness and generosity of the Muslim mindset was obvious.

Over the next few days, as we toured the different horse farms in the Aleppo and Damascus areas, the differences between the so-called Christian society of America and the Islamic society of the Middle East repeatedly became evident. Perhaps, two examples will suffice to illustrate those differences.

As a first example, I remember that as we traveled with our host from the Ministry of Agriculture to see and document the Arabian horses of Syria, we three "Americani" kept making sure that the vehicle was locked in order to protect our luggage. Finally, the official, who was also our new found brother-in-Islam, informed us that if we took our luggage out of the vehicle, set it on the sidewalk, and left it there as we went off into a restaurant to eat lunch, all of our luggage would still be there when we got back. No one would touch it, because it wasn't theirs.

The difference was again pointedly obvious a few nights later as we came back to our hotel in Damascus at about two or three o'clock in the morning, following a long conversation with an Arabian horse breeder. Strolling down the street in the unusually hot air were a couple of sisters-in-Islam. As could be seen by a quick glance at their scarves and more than ankle-length outer garments, these were not "streetwalkers," but practicing Muslims who were chatting quietly to each other as they walked. It was a hot night, they had experienced some difficulty sleeping in the heat, and had decided to take a walk to try and catch some breeze. I thought about American society and couldn't help but wonder how safe I would be walking at that time of night in my own hometown where the population was less than 300 people. I sure would not try it in Denver, let alone New York, Chicago, or any other major American city. Damascus is a busy metropolis of several million people, not some sleepy country village. Yet, these two sisters-in-Islam were perfectly safe. What a comfort and delight to be in a Muslim society where rape, child abuse, and violent crime are such a rarity.

As our trip ran down, all my attention was shifting to home. I needed to put into practice everything that I had learned from the examples of my brothers and sisters-in-Islam about Islam as a religion, and about how one lives one's life as a Muslim who submits to Allah and who strives always for the sake of Allah. I thought of the generosity of Jamal and Sahar, Abu Hasan, Khalid, Aunt Seham and Uncle 'Awad, the sisters who gave me my first lesson in Islamic prayer, the couple at the Syrian boarder, the taxi driver, and so very many more Muslims. As we headed home, I was pointedly aware of the path I had chosen and of the difficulty of living up to such beautiful examples of giving of oneself, without expecting any reward but that from Allah. If the transformation that was taking place inside of me was to have any value, I could not just talk the talk, I needed to walk the walk. It was a daunting goal.

As the plane left Jordan and headed home, Carol quickly removed her scarf and was amazed when I elected to keep mine on. For the first time, Jerry and I were working out how we were going to handle being Muslims in America. Somehow, with the help of all our Muslim brothers and sisters, old and new, I had managed to traverse with baby-steps the path from Christian to Muslim identity. That journey had been a pre-numbered, connect-the-dots picture, elegant in its simplicity. Jerry and I had been making these transformations together. Most of the time, he had been a step or two ahead of me, but he never applied any pressure, or even tried to guide me. *Al-Hamdulillah* (all praise to Allah), we made this journey into Islam while sharing our experiences and decisions. I am so very grateful that Allah provided me, not only with a supportive husband, but with one who was willing and able to share these steps with me.

The time had now come for us to transform our identities in America. Our lives would need adjusting in so many ways. What was more, it would start within minutes of our getting off the plane in Denver. The family who had been taking care of our horses was temporarily living in our home. I was sure they would have cooked up one of the hams that I had left in the freezer for our Easter dinner. This was just one of the many decision points that were now confronting us. Just how Muslim were we? The *Qur'an*, like the *Bible*, prohibits the consumption of pork, except in times of dire necessity. While I know of no direct negation of this prohibition in the *Bible*, I knew of no Christian that followed the Biblical prohibition. Pork had always been a staple of our diet as Christians. It was just one of hundreds of items that had to be rethought. We turned down the dinner upon arriving home, and later explained that we would no longer eat pork and that we would no longer be having it in our home.

We elected to embrace Islam wholeheartedly and openly, *Al-Hamdulillah*. I decided that I would cover, i.e. wear *Hijab*, and that I would build my wardrobe around the long dresses and skirts that I had bought for and during our Middle Eastern trip. This was no small feat as I was a working woman. I unloaded the sixty fifty-pound sacks of horse feed when they were delivered, stacked and carried bales of hay, and cared for and worked with horses. These jobs had been accomplished in my old chore clothes – pants and t-shirt in the summer, men's quilted, insulated coveralls during the winter. I was adding a long skirt and scarf? I clearly had some challenges in this regard, but was determined to be dressed modestly at all times.

Another issue was how to continue fitting into our small, farming community. When I began wearing long skirts and *Hijabs* into town to shop, everyone seemed to think that I was just showing off my Middle Eastern attire from the trip. Fortunately, it was foaling season, and that was the busiest time of the year for me. I was too busy to do much socializing until after I had a chance to get over my jet lag, which was topped off with many nights of being up with mares as they foaled. I discovered that pants underneath my long western (and here I mean as in cowgirl style) skirts made the best chore clothes, because there was no impediment to climbing through fences and running after animals. Fortunately, I had spent five weeks overseas adjusting to the look and feel of the *Hijab*, so it no longer seemed foreign to me. My attire did raise the eyebrows of the people who occasionally delivered hay and grain to the farm. However, they treated me with the same respect they always had.

After my adoption of Islam, dealing with friends and family was different than before. In receiving the many acts of Muslim generosity and kindness overseas, I had finally come to understand one of the basic differences between Islam and Christianity. Christianity has a basic pass-fail test, one either accepts Christ as their savior and passes, or one does not and fails. In Islam, there is the constant striving and effort to do everything for the sake or pleasure of Allah. Islam has no pass-fail test, and there is no way to be assured of one's place in Heaven. For me, that meant that my every act was a test of my devotion to Allah, and of whether I was dedicating my every deed to Him. Thus, I strive to make the core of every deed my desire to please Allah. This affects every aspect of my life – always. Not that I always succeed, just that this is my goal.

Within my family, I had an easier time than many of my American counterparts. While I came from a conservative background, most of my siblings were considerably more liberal than I, even prior to my becoming a Muslim. I took care to inform my siblings that I had converted to Islam. One of my sisters – biological, that is – was a liberal Christian minister, and was curious about and fairly open to my conversion to Islam. Another sister made the most negative statement about my conversion when she said, "I am amazed you of all people would become a Muslim, as you were so independent." It gave me an opportunity to explain briefly that the way Muslim women are viewed by the West is not how Muslim women really are. I told her that there was no need for Muslim women to fight for their rights, as they had been granted them in the *Qur'an* clear back in the seventh century. I pointed out that while Europe considered women to be property well into the eigtheenth century, women in Islam had the right of property ownership and self-determination from the time of the Prophet Muhammad. One does not need to fight for what one already has been granted by divine right. Of all of my family, it was my sister-in-law who made the most sense out of my conversion. I was visiting my brother and his family, and we were all sitting at the supper table. My brother asked me about my choice to be Muslim and about how Islam was different from Christianity. (Like myself, he had stayed fairly conservative in his values and outlook.) I sat there explaining, among other things, that Muslims pray directly to God and do not pray through anyone else. My sister-in-law interjected that it sounded a lot closer to what they did as Mennonites than the intercessory prayer practiced by most Roman Catholics who frequently pray to or through a variety of saints etc.

This comment focused me on the people in my extended family and on the differences in their approach to prayer. As children, we had prayed before every meal: "God is great. God is good. Let us thank Him for our food. By His hand, we all are fed. Give us, Lord, our daily bread. Amen." However, some of our cousins had prayed: "Come, Lord Jesus, be our guest. Let this food to us be blessed. Amen." It appeared to me that the families who had prayed the first way always stressed a direct relationship with God, as opposed to a relationship with Jesus. Those who prayed the second way seemed to stress their relationship with Jesus over their relationship with God. I have noticed that the latter family members have much more difficulty relating to me since I chose to be Muslim as well as more difficulty in understanding Islam.

In general, choosing to be a Muslim was viewed as weird by most of the community in which we lived, and some were scandalized by the very idea. I tried to wait to see how people responded when they saw me, and would then go forward from there with whatever relationship was left. When they met me on the street or in a store, some people couldn't decide where to look to avoid seeing me. I always felt sorry for them, but generally let them be. Each person's reaction was different, and the only fair way to handle it was to just let them know that I was Muslim by choice, and then try to move forward if their reaction allowed. This freed me to reevaluate each of my previously close relationships, while most casual ones just went along as before. However, I have to admit that my acceptance of Islam also led to some people simply and absolutely rejecting me.

I became very aware that the minister from the local church that I used to attend would not speak to me, even if I greeted him when we happened to meet in the local post office. He would in no way even acknowledge that I was present. This only changed several years later when he performed the funeral service for one of my Christian friends. I was very close to my friend's daughter and went to the funeral service to be of aid to her. When she and I approached the minister at the end of the service, the minister finally murmured, "Hello, Debra."

Some friends made an attempt to stay friends for a period, thinking I would change back. I can think of one person who had been a close friend for several years. Our sons had been in the same grade in the local high school. That might not be a big connection in some schools, but as there were only twelve students in that class, every student's family knew every other student's family very well. Before we had left on our Middle Eastern trip, this friend had told me how she thought I was crazy to travel to a place where people lived in tents. I had to show her pictures to prove the size and breadth of the cities. After our return, she was dismayed that I was a Muslim. For a time she stayed friendly as I began to hear stories about her brother, who had joined in the peace movement of the 60s, who had experimented with a non-Christian religion for a year or so, but who was now a very "solid" Christian. In all the years that I had known her, she had never mentioned this to me before I became a Muslim. Finally, about a year after our trip, she must have given up on me ever coming back to what she considered "normal," and told me that my Muslim clothes made her skin crawl. She wanted to cut all contact. While this was painful, I tried to respond as a Muslim should. I told her that if she was sure she wanted to do this, I would honor her wishes, but if changed her mind, to just call me. Under the circumstances, it was the most generous thing I could think of to say.

In marked contrast, I was in Kiowa one day when I met up with my neighbor, Stephanie, who took one look at me and became interested. We had shared a back fence between our pastures for over six years, but we had never moved in the same circles. Stephanie asked me about the clothes, and said she wanted to hear all about our trip. It was so healing and so warming to hear this in the midst of all the negative reactions. She came over, I made some *Shai* (Arabic tea), and we sat and talked for hours. In many ways, she was my sunshine, spreading light in the darkness of that community's reactions. I looked forward to seeing her so much that I would remind myself that I might run into Stephanie every time I headed into Kiowa, whether going to the post office, grocery store, or whatever. It took much of the sting out of the disapproving looks, gawks, downright stares, and negative comments of so many others. She was my proof that there were others out there in America who would find my own choice to be a Muslim reasonable, and who would find Islam fascinating. (Sister Stephanie has since converted to Islam, and her story is told in its own chapter.)

There was another interesting reaction from within that community, one that I found both encouraging and sad. Finding anyone who understood anything about what Islam was or why we chose it was usually totally cheering. Just down the road a piece from us was a retired minister and his wife who made a point of inviting us to their home to discuss religion over coffee and dessert. There was no polite way to avoid it, although I was afraid it was probably going to degenerate into a long harangue about "accepting Jesus as our savior." When we arrived, the retired minister began asking Jerry about why we had chosen to accept Islam. Before Jerry could even finish his answer, the retired minister said, "You just couldn't stomach the polytheism anymore, could you." From that moment on, we knew that we were dealing with an "educated Christian." What was so tremendously sad was that he would not personally act on his own understanding. He knew, but was unwilling to embrace and proclaim Islam.

Our horse contacts across the country also reacted. Many responded in the same way as the people in our hometown. However, some of them actually had the nerve to assume that we had converted to Islam to get horse information and to sell horses. Some even had the audacity to say so, which was truly incredible. I was talking on the phone to a man from Maryland about sales of Arabian horses in America and abroad, when he said, "I will never change my religion to sell horses." I bit my lip, clenched my hands, and said as calmly and quietly as I could manage, "Neither would I." He did not seem to be aware that he had said anything untoward or insulting, and went on with the conversation. I was almost struck dumb by the implication of his remark. Only by reminding myself that I should speak gently, in order to try to encourage others to accept Islam, as only Allah decides whom He will guide, did I stop myself from figuratively "taking his head off and handing it to him on a platter!"

However, the negative reactions were totally eclipsed by the reactions of my new sisters and brothers in Islam. Within a couple of days after our return, we went to visit Jamal and Sahar. I could not wait to see my friend, Sahar, who was now also my sister. I had been looking forward to giving her a big hug and watching her face when I told her I had completed my journey into Islam. It made for a beautiful homecoming. Sahar then took me under her wing and helped me in more ways than I could ever list here, although I must mention about her kindnesses in teaching me: the finer points of the prayer; endlessly coaching my pronunciation of Arabic words; giving me *Jilbabs*, *Hijabs*, and prayer clothes, and teaching me how and when to wear them; and listening to my endless questions, and looking up answers to be sure that she was always giving me correct information. She included me in her activities, so that I met more sisters and became more firmly entrenched in the local Muslim community. She also hosted Jerry's and my ceremony of bringing our marriage of twenty-four years under a formal Islamic marriage contract. She even shared her children with me. It was heartwarming and wonderful. We did everything from shopping to cooking together, and were at each other's homes as often as we could possibly manage. Nothing but my horses could keep me away, and then she would come to me.

Quickly, other sisters became a major part of my life. Sister Um Hasan, whom I had met before going overseas and staying with her husband's family in Jordan, now became my wonderful friend. She also gave me of her time, her children, and her knowledge of Islam. At this point, I must digress with a little story to illustrate the unique closeness of these three families.

One day while visiting on our farm, Abu Hasan was teasing his six-year-old son, Hasan about selling him to 'Amo (Uncle) Jerry, since Hasan was always wanting to come and spend time with us on the farm. Jerry quickly inquired as to the asking price, and Abu Hasan told Jerry that he considered five dollars to be a fair price for Hasan. Fearful that this price might negate the possible sale, Hasan immediately protested that the price was too much to ask of 'Amo Jerry, and stated his firm conviction that it should only be two dollars. Abu Hasan agreed, and Jerry immediately gave Abu Hasan the two dollars, which Abu Hasan has kept in his wallet to this day as a loving memento of the day he "sold" Hasan to us. Thus, we had "bought" Hasan. When we next saw Jamal and Sahar, Jerry used the "purchase" of Hasan to maneuver Jamal into a position where his two oldest children would not be happy until he had "sold" them, too. Thus, we "purchased" both 'Ali and Miasar. We adults were having a great deal of fun with this arrangement, but when Abu Hasan's and Um Hasan's younger son, Motasem, learned about it, he cried because we had not bought him. Naturally, we quickly remedied this oversight.

Having "purchased" four children from the two families, we used the situation to have the children out for overnight visits and to do what spoiling of them as we could. This included giving the kids bumpy rides in the pasture in the bed of the pickup and letting the kids drive (with a little help from 'Amo) our car inside the pasture, etc. What a delightful time we had! All the adults encouraged the children so very much in this that it seemed totally natural to them.

During this period, Jerry and I took three of Jamal's and Sahar's kids out to a Baskin Robins ice cream parlor one afternoon. Ahmad was eighteen-months old, and the younger brother of Miasar and 'Ali.

He was just now old enough to participate in this short trip away from home, so we included him in this little adventure. Jerry sat at a table with 'Ali, Miasar and Ahmad, while I went to the counter to put in our order for banana splits.

As I stood in line waiting my turn, an elderly lady came up to me and called me "sister." She was prattling on and was asking me what order I was with? I smiled gently at her, trying not to upset her as I told her I was a Muslim. Her response was, " I did not even know that they had nuns!" I looked on the encounter as a chance to educate someone who did not know anything about Islam. However, she was not listening as I tried to explain that Muslims did not have nuns, but that I was dressed this way for modesty's sake. She just kept talking about nuns, and I was glad that at just that moment the guy behind the counter wanted my order. She wandered off before I was done and could carry the first part of our order to Jerry and the kids. Then, while I stood waiting for the second part of the order to be ready, she approached again, telling me how wonderful it was that we were being so kind to these children. It was obvious that she thought Jerry was some sort of priest, and that we were being kind to disadvantaged or orphaned children. I once again tried to explain, but she was not listening to what I was saying and kept interrupting to tell me how much people today overlook the good deeds of nuns. I finally just told her that the kids had given far more to Jerry and me than we could ever give back, which was a true enough statement. She then wandered off as I gathered together and paid for the remains of our order. As the children were finishing their ice cream, or getting so full that we would carry the rest home to be frozen for a later treat, I went to get a half gallon of ice cream to take home to share with Jamal and Sahar.

When I returned, Jerry was looking very uncomfortable, so I asked why. He told me about how this little old lady (yes, of course, it was the same one!) had come up to tell him how generous he was being, and then commented on how beautiful the children looked. At that point, little 'Ali had loudly informed the elderly lady that we had bought him and his sister. He explained in his best five-year-old fashion that his father had sold them to us, and that was why we had brought them to Baskin Robins for ice cream. The lady had objected, only to have 'Ali assure her that they had been bought and paid for. Jerry and I quickly decided that discretion was the better part of valor, and that it was time to vamoose before social services showed up looking for children that had been purchased by Muslim nuns and priests. To make matters worse, the local media had recently been running an expose on some adoption-for-money exchanges.

This story gives some idea of the wonderful relations shared by these three families. It also points out some of the difficulties experienced by Muslim sisters who dress traditionally and modestly. It was certainly not the only time that I was mistaken for a nun. Several other times, I was addressed as sister, and my interlocutors were not meaning Muslim sister. One day as I was shopping in a Safeway, I had a lady bring up her grandson to me, and ask if he could touch me. I said, "Of course," and turned with a smile to the three-year-old in the shopping cart, took his hand, and then put my hand on his face and tickled his chin. The busy grandmother then took the cart and was in the process of rapidly walking away, when she said over her shoulder that kids today do not even know what a nun looks like. It took a moment for me to digest this, and by then they were gone down another aisle. I did not get a chance to correct her false impression. However, it did leave an impression on me. My smile lasted all day.

Fitting into the American culture as an American Muslim isn't just a matter of repeated encounters with humorous incidents. At times, it requires a good bit of personal adjustment and change. It took repeated surgeries with the old mental scalpel to incise the term "good Christian heart" from my lexicon. However, that was relatively easy compared to the mindless and automatic temptation to sing Christmas songs during December. Those Christmas carols were my greatest affliction. I tried not to go into stores in December, because I'd hear long ago memorized Christmas carols that would get stuck going round and round in my brain. Just like many mothers find themselves humming the Sesame Street theme song or the Barney theme song, even when their children are not present, Christmas carols and some hymns from my childhood were pernicious in their attempt to lurk in and just below my conscious mind. Once the repetitious inner singing began, I would try to replace them with other songs that were not *Haram* (forbidden) in their verbal content.

Even in otherwise innocuous children's songs, there are many hidden messages. Consider Peter Cottontail, which is normally not considered a religious song, but it has "Hippity Hoppity Easter's on its way." Until I became a Muslim, I had not appreciated the extent to which Christianity's terminology had been integrated into mainstream American culture. How many secular movies have Christian holidays as a backdrop for their stories? Everything from "Home Alone" to "Die Hard" had a Christmas theme, usually accompanied by those infectious Christmas carols. I had never even noticed much of this Christian infiltration before becoming a Muslim. If someone had asked me for a movie about Christmas, I would have said "Rudolph the Red Nosed Reindeer," not "Die Hard." Dealing with such issues is, in many ways, just part of living in America. It is one of the burdens carried by Muslims who live in America, and it is a major issue for Muslim families when they consider what movies and TV shows to allow their children to view.

There are other difficulties in being a Muslim in America. Those of us who follow a strict interpretation of Islamic dietary regulations often have difficulty in finding appropriate meals while traveling in

America. Likewise, finding a safe and suitable place for prayer is not always easy when on the road. For those Muslims who do not live in a large American city, attending the Friday noon prayer at a mosque frequently necessitates a lengthy drive. Muslims living in the Middle East do not have to struggle with the same issues, or at least not nearly as frequently, as those Muslims living in America. For these reasons, for the opportunity to live in an Islamic society, for the joy of hearing *Adhan* five times a day, and for the opportunity to continue our relationship with Abu and Um Hasan and their family, we elected to relocate to Jordan as soon as possible after they returned to their native country.

It was just a few months before moving to Jordan in 1999 that I had my most unforgettable spiritual experience, the opportunity to perform the *Hajj*, which is Islam's prescribed pilgrimage to Makkah for those who are physically and financially able to do so. The events leading up to and including our being able to perform *Hajj* deserve a few special words.

In 1999, we had our farm on the market and had been waiting for over two years for it to sell. I was busy with remodeling that was targeted to help the farm sell. Jerry's practice was busy, and we were missing so many of our sisters and brothers who had previously moved overseas. These included both Abu and Um Hasan and their family and Jamal and Sahar and their family. In 1998, Jerry had had the opportunity to do *Hajj* on a special program where he would be the guest of the Saudi government. However, by the time they had let him know that he was selected to do this, he could not undo his work schedule and had to decline. In 1999 we learned that Sheykh Ahmad at the local mosque had again nominated Jerry and had also nominated me to participate in this program for *Hajj*. We were so very honored and pleased. We said prayers asking Allah to show us if this was our course. Once I believed that it was our path, even though there was no answer from Saudi until much later, I bought material and sewed clothes appropriate for *Hajj*, (loose, white, and comfortable for walking in the heat). On faith, we set up everything to accommodate *Hajj* in our schedule. Jerry scheduled no patients during that period. When after two and a half years of waiting, we finally got a contract to sell our farm, we insisted that the closing date be set for after *Hajj* was done, even though this strung out the finalizing of the sale.

With just a week to go, we received our invitation from Saudi Arabia and *Hajj* was on our horizon. I went into Denver, with less than two days of looking, found and rented a condo that would house us after the sale. Then, realizing that we would not have time after *Hajj* to move out of our house and thus satisfy the closing date on the contract, we moved all of our stuff either to a storage unit for later shipping overseas, or to the condo for immediate use. All of this transpired within that last week before *Hajj*. We set off for *Hajj* on the high note of faith and knowledge that we were following Allah's plan for us. All the complications of so quickly joining a group, from getting our passports back from the Saudi Arabian Embassy to finding appropriate seats on a plane to Washington DC where we were to meet the group, just seemed to fall into place. Our passports were hand-delivered to us at the airport, and we were all set to start our *Hajj* pilgrimage, though our journey of faith had started long before actually embarking on the plane.

Like two million other pilgrims, we arrived at the Jeddah airport and started the process of entering Saudi to perform the rites of *Hajj*. This is a colossal endeavor for the Saudi government. There is no other event that happens on the earth that comes close to matching it. Two million people descend on the city of Makkah and then the tiny city of Mina, the latter of which is expanded to house all the pilgrims with the help of thousands upon thousands of tents. From Mina, then pilgrims move on to Mount Arafat, which is literally covered with tents. The amount of humanity is just incredible. As we waited in lines to get our passports stamped and for us to get checked into the country, we continued the process of getting to know our fellow pilgrims that had been started on the plane trip over. Finally, we were suddenly out in the open night air of Saudi. In front of us was a huge banner,which proclaimed in large letters in both Arabic and English, "Welcome to the invited guests of Allah!" I felt so very blessed and honored as I read that sign. An invited guest of Allah! The sign was speaking directly to little, old me.

One of the many beauties of *Hajj* is the clothing. For the men there is no stitching in it at all, just two large pieces of white cloth that are wrapped around them. There is no difference in attire for the millionaire and the pauper. It takes away so many of the societal and worldly distinctions, and reminds us that we are all just people trying to serve Allah. For women, the same effect is achieved by every sister wearing plain, simple, and comfortable clothes.

Everyone had told me to offer a prayer the moment I saw the Ka'bah, the house originally built by Prophets Abraham and Ishmael to worship Allah. I stood still looking at the Ka'bah and whispered my silent prayer. Then did the two *Rakah* prayer, praising Allah and thanking him for being at His house. We then started to do Tawaf (circumambulating the Ka'bah seven times). I had been preparing for and anticipating this moment for six years, and still hadn't even an inkling of the effect it would have on me. It was more exquisite, beautiful, astonishing, extreme, and passionate than my mind was able to imagine prior to coming, and it was so intense that my whole being was forever changed. There was a powerful concentration of the link with Allah, and an incredible closeness of being part of a sea of humanity wrapped in white, all partaking in this worship of Allah. While it was a uniquely personal experience, part of its beauty was doing it with all my fellow pilgrims. It, quite obviously, is beyond anything I can describe in words, but its effect is lasting, as the experience of *Hajj* changes all of us in our inner selves. Being a *Hajjah* gave new responsibility and honor to my Islamic journey.

Over the years that have passed since my conversion to Islam, there have been many beautiful and wonderful days both in America and overseas. Allah has blessed me in so many ways. One of my greatest delights has been to see several other Arabian horse enthusiasts follow their own paths to Islam with Allah's guidance. In some cases, I learned of their conversions after the fact, but in some instances I was able to participate in their conversion, and was able to be at the *Masjid* (mosque) with them when they publicly said *Shahadah* (the testimonial of faith that there is only one God, and that Muhammad is His prophet and messenger). Among these, were our Brother Tim and Sister Stephanie, who followed their own beautiful path to Islam. To this day, this is one of the most beloved and extraordinary blessings that Allah has provided, *Al-Hamdulillah*.

After all my struggling with the Christian doctrines, being half in and half out, it still astounds me that Allah has given me the blessing to be a whole and complete Muslim, right down to my little toes. It is my objective, aspiration, goal, struggle, dream, and vision not only to talk the talk, but to walk the walk of Islam.

Today, everyday is a new challenge, and a new opportunity to serve Allah. Every prayer is a chance to do the prayer to the best of my ability and understanding, in the hope that Allah will accept my prayers. However, like all humans, I get busy, and occasionally have to remind myself not to approach my prayers as though they were interruptions to my daily schedule. Each and every day, I try to remind myself that I have been given an opportunity to worship Allah. It is still an attitude adjustment to remember to approach my prayers properly. However, the five daily prayers always provide a welcome reminder of the path that I am attempting to follow.

Give Me That Old Time Religion: Searching for God

KHADIJAH R. BERUNI

As I reflect back on my past, I can recall one particular event that stayed with me for the rest of my life. I was sitting in my little rocking chair, and singing to my little doll in my grandparents' home in Williamston, North Carolina. It was the home of my mother's parents. I was either four or five years old at that time. It was a beautiful, warm, sunny day, and I could see my grandfather working on the farm and feeding the horses, cows, and chickens. He would always have a pleasant smile on his face, and his demeanor was always peaceful. I can vividly remember my grandmother sitting on the porch in her rocking chair, and singing this hymn: "Give me that old time religion; give me that old time religion; give me that old time religion; it's good enough for me." I could hear her voice echoing throughout the house. She sang in a soprano voice that was so penetrating to the soul that I would often times feel chills up and down my spine.

Sometimes, I would peep outside the door and wait until my grandmother had finished her hymn. At that instant, I would politely ask her why she chose to sing that particular song over and over again. Her reply to me was: "My little, happy child, your grandmother knows that there is a God somewhere Who hears our prayers, and sometimes I just wonder." I would then enthusiastically ask my grandmother: "What is it that you wonder, Grandmother? Please tell me! Oh Grandmother, please tell me!" At that particular moment, she would stare into my eyes, and then look away. Somehow, I could tell from the gaze that she had in her eyes that she would never reveal these, her innermost thoughts. As time passed by, my grandmother continued to sing that same chorus.

GREAT GRAND MOTHER: Sara Jane Johnson at the age of 98. She started her life as a slave.

Until today, I have never known what my grandmother meant by her statement when she said, "Sometimes I just wonder!" I can only speculate about what she meant. Could she possibly have meant that she was searching for God? Was Christianity really the religion of my people and of my ancestors? These types of questions remained in my mind throughout my childhood years. The memories of my grandmother's song were so penetrating in my heart, mind, and soul that searching for God was a task that I eventually pursued. In the meantime, questions concerning religion were something that we as kids were forbidden to ask. So out of respect for my grandmother, I just kept my thoughts to myself; realizing that as time progressed, I would find the answers.

As a youngster, I was taught that children should not be a

nuisance, and should not pry into grown folks' business. In other words, if grown folks don't give you a direct answer to your question, then it is not necessary for children to ask over and over again. As a matter of fact, religion was a topic that was not discussed. We would simply listen to our preachers, parents, and grandparents preach and interpret the *Bible*. Therefore, I accepted things the way they were, and went on about my business, abiding by the rules of my household.

As a child, I spent my school year with my parents in Philadelphia, and my summers with my grandparents on a farm in North Carolina. I enjoyed my childhood life of playing with my relatives in the South during the summers, and of being with my friends in the North the rest of the year. I loved my parents and grandparents so dearly, and cherished every moment of my days with them. Summer life in the country was carefree, and there was no need to worry. My mother used to say, "Let the grown folks worry, and just enjoy your life as a child". Life in the northern city was also carefree, and there was no need for a child of my age to worry. But somehow, deep down inside of my heart, I could not forget the song that my grandmother used to sing, and that song lingered in my mind for years to come.

It was always a blessed occasion spending time with our extended family in the South. My brother and I spent most of our summer days as a vacation in Williamston, North Carolina, where my parents had been born and raised. Every morning before dawn, you could hear the sounds of birds chirping and of roosters crowing. It was always a pleasant trip traveling down south, as well as being a joyous event whenever I saw my extended family. My brother and I eagerly looked forward to the day when my parents would gather the suitcases out of the closet, and would hand us our bags to pack with much enthusiasm. We were excited as we threw our clothes in our bag, and then headed towards the car.

As I ponder those days, I believe that my parents were also just as thrilled to spend some quality time alone without us, as we kids were to be able to spend our summers in the South with our grandparents. Yes indeed! I do declare that those were the good old days of spending time with our grandparents and relatives. My parents would leave us with our grandparents for the duration of the summer, and would come back to get us before the school year began. I had the best of both worlds. I had caring parents and grandparents who loved me dearly. My world was filled with no worries and no stress. All the worrying was in the hands of my parents. Their favorite phrase was: "You are too young to be stressed, and you should just enjoy the childhood days with which God has blessed you".

Each summer in the South was a period of segregation for my family, who were African-Americans. I was born in Philadelphia, Pennsylvania, in the late 1940s. My parents had been born in Williamston, North Carolina. They had lived in a time and place that had been dominated by racial segregation. The Whites had lived in one part of town, and African-Americans had lived in another part. At the time I was a child, African-Americans in the South were isolated from other races of people. During my childhood summers in the South, there were no Italians, Spanish, or any other race or ethnicity of people in our community. In my mother's home community, everyone was all related to each other, and their last name was Bell. In my father's home community, everyone was all related to each other, and their last name was Lee.

As a young child, I didn't give it too much thought as to why we lived in that type of environment where everybody was related. But today, I can see the need for families to live together in the spirit of oneness, peace, love, and harmony. I see can why the institution of family life is so important in today's society. I see that it is crucial to put God first, family second, and then the community. All three of these principles should be incorporated into making the family a strong unit in society, and family was always an important part of my life, ranking right up there with love of and reverence to God.

Everyone of my relatives in the South owned his or her own property and land. My grandparents had acres of land that were used for raising animals and for harvesting crops. It was indeed a blessing to wake up in the morning to the smell of fresh farm eggs and breakfast simmering on the stove. It was also a tradition back then for families to gather and savor each other's cooking. This tradition was started by my grandparents as a way of bringing the family together through family reunions. It brought all of the extended family together in peace and harmony. We stayed among ourselves, and enjoyed the privilege of being in each other's company. Although most of my relatives worked on the White man's farm for meager wages, we kept to ourselves and made the best of our situation. I have, however, heard horror stories from my relatives of how African-Americans in other parts of the South were treated very badly. I used to hear terrible stories of how African-American people were beaten and killed unjustly. There were laws that were made to insure freedom, justice, and equality for one race of people, and unfortunately those laws did not include the African-American race. African-Americans were still being treated like slaves. They had no rights, no freedom, and no justice. This was the South in the era of the 1960s, and I witnessed it as a child.

My family members who lived in the South minded their own business, and kept themselves entertained. The White race of people also minded their own business, and kept to themselves. My grandparents were always busy raising animals, and tending to their crops. It was very seldom that they had to go to the store to buy any produce. Their motto was to believe in yourself, take pride and accomplishment in what you can do, motivate yourself, and strive for improvement in all areas of learning. Although it was hard for the elders to achieve this goal, the concept was preached and passed on to the children. It took a long time for my family members who lived in the South to move forward in progress, and to move past racial tensions.

Community's Name
changed to Bell Town

Since all the Bells lived in one community, my family petitioned to have the name of their community changed to BellTown. It was a long hard struggle to get that accomplished. It took years and lots of patience and work. Finally, the petition was approved, and the name of the road was changed to Bell Town. Today, it symbolizes respect for a community of people who have worked and lived together in peace and harmony.

I think the majority of those people still live in that same community, which is still primarily populated by the Bell family. The name change was approved by the city council in the late 1980s. This was an honor for my family to have a road named after them in this respected and decent community of hardworking people, who cared for their homes and family. What a wonderful blessing from God to have a caring and generous family.

Also, during this era, we were called "Colored people" or "Colored folks". As Colored folks during the 1960s, we were not permitted to sit in the restaurants with White folks. Whenever we wanted a snack or lunch, we had to sit or stand outside of the restaurants to eat our meals. As such, I can understand why we always ate at home with our families. There were also signs in front of water fountains and bathrooms that separated the White folks from the Colored folks. Segregation was prevalent in the schools, churches, and movie theaters. In the movies, we had to sit in the balcony away from White people. I didn't mind sitting in the balcony, as long as I was able to enjoy the movie. If it hadn't been for the cohesiveness, warmth, and love that I received from my family, I would have been deeply affected by the racist attitudes of my childhood society. Nonetheless, I always sympathized with my race of people. In fact, I was a person who admired and respected people of all races, cultures, and nationalities. But when it came to the suffering and inhumane treatment of African-Americans, my love for self and kind was quite naturally projected toward all members of my race.

With segregation being so prevalent during those days, it seemed as if Christianity was all that our people had to hold onto for salvation. There were no other religions known or taught in my family except Christianity. However, there had been an earlier time when racial issues even impeded the religious education of African-Americans. For example, my grandmother used to tell me that she remembered when her mother was not allowed to read the *Bible* or even talk about religion.

I can also recall my grandmother telling me certain other things about her past. She admitted that our ancestors had come over to America by way of slavery. Her mother's name was Sara Bell, and she had been born into slavery. My grandmother explained how our ancestors had been brought here as slaves to raise tobacco, rice, sugar, and cotton. They were a people who had been uprooted from their own homes, families, and culture, and had been brought to an unknown land with a foreign language, an unknown culture, and a set of bewildering and strange customs. That was all the information that I was told by my grandmother. From that day forward, I never inquired or checked out my family's historical background and heritage. All I can recollect is that my family practiced Christianity, and that we were raised as Baptists. I also remember hearing a phrase from someone who had said that, "Children learn what is practiced in their homes".

Our religious life was all we had to which we could look forward.

It was a way of keeping our sanity and lives in one piece, in the face of the cruel and unjust treatments that were placed upon us by society. At that time, African-Americans were known for, and stereotyped by, their singing, dancing, and praising the Lord. However, that was their way of escaping from the crushing hardships that were being placed upon them on a daily basis. Our people would work from sunup to sundown with no rest in between. We were, and had been, an oppressed and exploited people.

In spite of the racial tensions, my childhood summers in the South were definitely "the good old days". It was a time of peace, love, and spending quality time in the presence of family. I even remember the days of playing church roles. We kids would pretend to be in the church, and would pray for God's grace to spare us as children and to bring peace and happiness into our lives. Playing church roles was one of my favorite childhood pastimes in the South, and it kept my mind occupied with good and pure thoughts. This play activity was done among family and relatives.

In Philadelphia, the games we played were different. There was no segregation in the North, at least as compared to the prevalent segregation in the South. Back in the North, we used to play hopscotch, jump rope, hide-and-go-seek, and other fun games with the children in the neighborhood. The neighborhood was integrated with Jews, Italians, and other people of diverse background who congregated in the spirit of peace, warmth, and love. I was able to play and go to school with children of different races and nationalities. Besides playing outside with the neighborhood kids, we would often take trips to the zoo, park, and library. There was no obvious discrimination among families in the North. We could go inside the restaurants, sit at a table, and eat without people staring or wondering why we were there. Looking back on it, I had the best of both worlds in my life – the summers of country living in the South, and the winters of urban integration in the North. Back then, the South and the North were just different, with that difference being based on lifestyles, habits, and people.

There have been times in my life that I used to wonder why there were racial conflicts happening in the South during my childhood years. I used to wonder if things would ever change and improve for African-Americans. Although my southern relatives appeared to be at peace when I was around them, I would often wonder if they were really happy with their situation. Most of my extended family never finished high school. Some of them never completed the sixth grade. I had an uncle who couldn't read or write, because he had to work on the farm as a boy to help his parents survive. He was my uncle on my father's side of the family. Against this background, it was very interesting to discover that my father, who was raised in a family of ten (including his parents), was forced to finish high school and go to college. I remember my father telling me that, when he was a child, his family had really emphasized to him the importance of finishing school. He was the youngest son in the family, and it was imperative that he stay in school.

My father was a humble and blessed man, who was a veteran of the Navy. In spite of the racial prejudice he had experienced during his life, including while being in the military, he had served his country, even though his country had not always served him. My father was the neighborhood chairperson, and we used to have block parties on our street. He enjoyed his position, and was often looked upon as an astute and wise leader. He was a very talented man, as well as being a gifted musician who played the guitar. Besides being an aircraft mechanic who worked on airplanes for a living, my father was also a carpenter by trade, and would frequently be called upon to build cabinets for various neighbors. My father provided for the family and made sure that the bills were paid.

My mother was a kind and generous person. She was a housewife who stayed home and took care of household chores while keeping us busy and out of trouble. She would always have the meals prepared, and the family would gather to pray and to enjoy her home cooked meals. Mealtime was a time of peace and harmony, laughter, and spending quality time with family. Occasionally, our father would take us out to dinner. This was a way of giving my mother a break from cooking. At least, when we went out to eat in the North, we didn't have to sit on the outside of the restaurant to enjoy our meals. We were able to sit among civilized people of all races.

My parents owned their own home in Philadelphia. My grandparents used to say, "God bless the child, who's got his own". We were raised in a home with love, respect, and honor for God and parents. There was less talking and more spankings. However, this was definitely needed in our household. During those days, there was no such thing as child abuse. Parents, teachers, friends, and neighbors all agreed that children should grow up in an environment that encouraged respect for self and others, and spanking was definitely enforced in my home as a way of achieving those goals. Those spankings represented discipline and love, and were something that I truthfully appreciate today. Through it all, we learned respect and love for God, family, relatives, neighbors, and ourselves.

Philadelphia was a neighborhood that consisted of people who were friendly, kind, and respectful of each other's feelings, and who also valued other people's privacy. Occasionally, we had neighbors who liked to gossip and start rumors. But overall, the street on which I lived consisted of neighbors who worked together for the common good of the neighborhood. If someone needed a helping hand or was just seeking advice, we could depend on each other for assistance. This was the City of Philadelphia, the so-called "City of Brotherly Love", in which I was born and raised. My parents were proud to be owners of their first home, and were proud to have bought it in Philadelphia, Pennsylvania.

My brother and I were occasionally forced to go to Sunday school and *Bible* classes. My brother would sometimes walk with me halfway to church, and then go somewhere else until Sunday school was over. As a rule, we were not allowed to come home without each other. Therefore, my brother would make sure that he was always there to meet me. However, there were days that I too wanted to stay home, or take an alternate route away from church. Most of the time, it looked as if being at church was more of a social gathering than anything else. Anyway, I dared not tell on my brother, because when he received a spanking, I was usually somehow destined to get spanked also.

Besides a few dramas in our lives, which were nothing compared to the dramas of today, we lived a happy and peaceful life. My life involved a circle of friends and relatives whom I loved and cherished so dearly. As time progressed, I was still bothered by the racial problems in parts of the South, and my mind was never at ease with the Christian religion. When it came to asking questions about Christianity, we children were not allowed to question our parents about religion in any negative sense. We just accepted things as they were.

I was always a happy-go-lucky child, who could have been nick-named "happy child". I was indeed loved by my parents, as well as by my grandparents. However, at the age of seventeen, my life began to change. I used to wonder if God was testing my faith when I began to lose my family. In 1965, my mother, who had been very sick for several years, became so ill that she had to be hospitalized. She died the next day. In 1966, my grandfather on my mother's side of the family died as a result of a stroke. In 1967, my father was killed in a car accident that made headlines in the newspapers and on television.

(He had been driving, and there had been two passengers. At the time of his death, it was reported that none of the three of them were wearing a seat belt. In the same year, Philadelphia finally enacted the seat belt law.) I was traumatized by the news of his death, and I began to wonder if the world was coming to an end. In 1968, my grandmother on my mother's side of the family died and returned to God. Then in that same year, I also lost my grandfather on my father's side of the family. It was probably one or two years later that my paternal grandmother also died. My paternal grandparents had been much older than my mother's parents, and had been in their 80s when they died.

Given the love and admiration that I had for my dad, the way he died was very shocking. It took awhile for me to get over his death. My life felt empty as I struggled to find meaning and answers as to why God would take my parents and grandparents away from me. I can remember sitting in the church during the funeral services and hearing the crying and screaming of others, as I stared ahead at the casket and wept silently to myself. I also wanted to scream and yell, but somehow my emotions were contained. I just sat in silence, and wept to myself. Years later, I found the comfort for which I was looking in two verses of the *Qur'an*, which I used to say over and over to myself for many years after I became a Muslim.

> Nay, seek (Allah's) help with patient perseverance and prayer: it is indeed hard, except to those who bring a lowly spirit – who bear in mind the certainty that they are to meet their Lord, and that they are to return to Him. (*Qur'an* 2: 45-46)

Somehow, deep down inside of me, I knew that there was a God Who listens to our prayers, and I knew that He was a God Who would judge us by the intentions in our hearts. Throughout the years, I have always kept myself morally decent, and maintained my virtue as a God-conscious person. In spite of all the tragedies that have happened in my life, I was a person who was strong-minded, outgoing, and determined to survive. I somehow knew that perseverance and prayer are the keys to survival, and that somewhere there is a God Who listens to and hears our cry for ease and comfort.

I was always an open-minded person who was seeking out the truth and listening to other people communicate their opinions about God and religion. I used to wonder how I would go about searching for God. I used to ask myself over and over again whether God took my parents and grandparents away for a reason. Sometimes, I would think that God was testing my faith, and that one day He would bring me into the religion that I so ardently desired. I also believed that God does not give you what you want, but He gives you what you need. Therefore, as time passed by, I continued to live my life as a decent and respectable person. I wanted my parents and grandparents to be proud of me, as I was proud of them.

When my father died, he had left us with a large sum of money that was immediately put away into a trust fund. He had stipulated in his will that his children were to get all his money in equitable amounts, and that the money was not to be touched until we had reached 21 years of age. He had paid off the mortgage on our home, so we had a place to stay without being plagued by the financial burden of mortgage or rent payments. My sister was only seven years old at that time, my brother was 15, and I was 19. Given our ages, my relatives didn't feel that we should be alone in the house, and suggested that my father's brother move in to give us support. He was a very caring, kind, and thoughtful person. He was there to support us mentally and spiritually.

During that time shortly after my father's death, a lady approached my brother and me, and told us that she was supposed to have married my father after he returned from his trip. My father had been traveling to Williamston, North Carolina, to take care of some business, and he had taken his nephew back home, along with a friend of the family. My father was then supposed to have picked up a wedding gift from this woman's grandmother. Unfortunately, my father never made that last trip to her grandmother, as all three of them in the car were killed on impact in January of 1967. The lady who was going to marry my father was Mary Williams. She had asked my brother and me if she could be our stepmother and live with us. At that time, it was hard to make a decision, but we nodded our approval. However, since my uncle had already moved in with us, she decided to stay in her home and to come by and visit us regularly. Nonetheless, she is still today my honored stepmother.

After my father's death, life went on as normally and as usual as possible in our household. It wasn't an easy adjustment to make. It was difficult living in our home without my parents. Being the oldest child, I often had to shoulder the responsibility to make decisions for my brother and younger sister.

(Presently, my brother lives in California, and my younger sister died in 1983, at the age of 25. She was killed in a car accident on January 1, 1983. She and her husband were coming home from a party, and my brother-in-law was the driver of the car that killed my sister and four other passengers. He was the only survivor of the crash. Unfortunately, there was another car that was also involved in the accident. An elderly man was driving his car when both cars collided into each other, killing all parties except for my brother-in-law. I was living in Denver, Colorado, when I received a phone call concerning my sister's death. It was shocking news, and I immediately called my brother, and told him the story.)

It was during the early 1970s, that I was first introduced to the Nation of Islam, and I was attracted to the spirit and love of brotherhood and sisterhood that I witnessed among its members. As I would discover later, the Nation of Islam was a totally different religion than the Islam revealed to Prophet Muhammad, peace be upon him, although the two religions have some commonalities. Likewise, the Nation of Islam was not the universal religion of Islam that was taught and practiced for centuries by millions of devout Muslims. In truth, the Nation of Islam was nationalistic and racially oriented. It simply was not the universal Islamic religion for all of humanity. It was not the Islam that is practiced all over the world without regard for racial or ethnic descent, and in which Muslims believe that there is no God but Allah, and that Prophet Muhammad is the last prophet of Allah.

With regard to its history, the Nation of Islam was started in Detroit, Michigan, in 1930. The author and founder of the Nation of Islam was a man by the name of Wali Fard Muhammad, who was also called W.D. Fard. It has been reported that Wali Fard Muhammad came by himself from the East to America in the year 1930. His message was strictly based on the liberation of the African-American people. He preached and taught a strange doctrine in and around Detroit for about three and a half years. Before he left, he taught a man named Elijah Poole, who later changed his name to Elijah Muhammad, and who was appointed by W. D. Fard as the latter's spokesman. The Honorable Elijah Muhammad was then left with the responsibility of building and establishing the Nation of Islam in North America. The Nation of Islam grew, and attracted hundreds of thousands of African-American people, with two of its most outstanding attractions being Malcolm X and Muhammad Ali, both of whom later left the Nation of Islam for the true religion of Islam. The teachings of the Nation of Islam were a dominant message among African-Americans, and many African-Americans viewed the teachings of the Nation of Islam as the pure religion.

In the late 1960s and early 1970s, I would see the young men of the Nation of Islam standing on the street corners of Philadelphia, and selling the *Muhammad Speaks* newspaper, as it was called during those days. These young men all had a certain, distinguishable look, and were easily recognized by their style of dress. Their apparel consisted of a suit, white shirt, and bow tie. Their grooming was typically impeccable, and was characterized by a close cut hairstyle and clean face (no facial hair). However, they would sometimes wear blue and red FOI (Fruit of Islam) uniforms. The brothers, as they were called, had an appearance of cleanliness and intelligent behavior. As they stood on the street corners in various locations, they would be heard shouting enthusiastically, "Get your *Muhammad Speaks* newspaper, and read the truth about America". Sometimes their phraseology would be different, but the message was similar. This was the Nation of Islam inviting all African-Americans to come to the mosque and listen to the minister talk about the rise of the Black man and the fall of the White man.

The women or sisters, as they were called, were also easily recognizable. Their dress resembled the typical dress of Muslim women. The women wore heads scarves that covered their hair completely. No hair was allowed to be shown outside the home. Their outer garments were two-piece outfits that were worn loosely fitted and that covered the body in a way to preserve modesty. These "Muslim" women, as these Nation of Islam women were usually and erroneously identified during that time, were to be found in their homes cooking and doing household chores. The women were taught that they should cover their hair, wear long dresses, and never expose their body in public in any immodest manner.

At 21 years of age, my attraction to the Nation of Islam was simply to find a good husband. I had begun to visit the temple, as it was called in those days, and would socialize with the sisters. An additional benefit were the Muslim Girls Training (MGT) classes where we were taught how to be women, and how to take care of our bodily needs, such as cleanliness of the body and hair. We were also taught how to keep our homes neat and clean, cook and sew, and take care of our children. The men were taught how to be respectful towards their wives, and how to be responsible providers for the household.

What I liked most about the Nation of Islam was the unity and cohesiveness among the sisters and brothers. I also witnessed love, respect, and a willingness to create businesses within the African-American community. This last issue was important, as the development of African-American businesses directly contributed to the economic advancement and uplifting of the entire African-American community. Whenever we would travel, we would see the same spirit in other states. African-American businesses were being developed around different parts of the town, and the "Muslims", as they were called, were ardently selling the *Muhammad Speaks* newspaper. Everyone that joined the Lost Found Nation of Islam, were given an "X" as a last name. It meant that we as African-American people were lost from our land, our people, and our religion, and now we had been found. The "X" represented that unknown quality of our racial heritage and history. Therefore, we were called by our first name, but had an unknown or "X" quality as our last name. However, the Honorable Elijah Muhammad did say that one day we would be given Muslim names.

I came into the Nation of Islam under the teachings of the late Honorable Elijah Muhammad in 1970. It was also during that time that I had met my husband, and we were married into the Nation of Islam. He used to be the minister at one of the temples in Philadelphia.

The Nation of Islam was a slight improvement over what I had seen in the churches, but somehow it wasn't the religion for which

I had been looking. It fact, it was no different from the Christian religion in its racist attitude towards African-Americans. The Nation of Islam was more of a Black Nationalist movement to free African-Americans from the residual shackles of slavery. Elijah Muhammad had been taught a type of reverse psychology and racial ideology, and his teachings were taught to his followers.

Here, it might be helpful to give a brief description of some of the concepts that we were taught in the Nation of Islam. Firstly, as "Muslims" in the Nation of Islam, we accepted the idea that Master Fard Muhammad was God, and that he came to us from the holy city of Makkah in Arabia in 1930. Secondly, the Nation of Islam taught that God is a man, and that He always was a man (*Message to the Blackman*). Thirdly, it was taught that God lives, dies, and passes on his knowledge and god-ship from one God/man to another. Fourthly, for over forty years, the Nation of Islam taught and preached that Elijah Muhammad was the last messenger of God (*Message to the Blackman and Muhammad Speaks* newspaper). Fifthly, not only did the Nation of Islam teach that God was a man, it also told us that Satan (i.e., the devil) was a man (i.e., the Caucasian, White man). The Nation of Islam taught that the White man was the devil, and that the White man was evil by nature. Sixthly, we were taught to pray differently from the Muslims of the universal religion of Islam, and fasting was always done in the month of December, as opposed to fasting during the lunar month of *Ramadan* as specified in Islam.

As time went on, my former husband was among the first to recognize that Elijah Muhammad's son, Warith Deen Mohammed, was teaching a religion that was completely different from that being taught by the Nation of Islam. When Elijah Muhammad's son, Imam W. D. Mohammed came on the scene, he recognized the truth, and began to reject the way that had been taught by his father.

A second force for change within the Nation of Islam was a man by the name of Malcolm X, who had become the spokesman for Elijah Muhammad. As noted in various books and articles, Malcolm X had gone to New York City where he became the minister of Temple #7, which is now known as Masjid Shabazz. He was described at the time as a fireball preacher and as an effective purveyor of Islam. Because of his verbal eloquence and preaching style, and because of the timely message of some of Elijah Muhammad's teachings about the need to advance the cause of African-Americans, Malcolm X became very popular, especially in certain civil rights circles and among young African-Americans. As a result, he began receiving many requests to speak on college campuses. Eventually, as Malcolm's popularity grew, widespread rumors about him began to be circulated. African-Americans generally believed that the FBI and CIA had instigated these rumors with the goal of undermining the growing popularity of Malcolm X. Whatever the actual source of those rumors, it was undeniably Malcolm's exposure of the mistreatment of African-American people at the hands of the White man that made Malcolm X a man to be scrutinized most closely by the establishment and by the government.

Negative political forces were used against Malcolm X, and it began to destroy his relationship with Elijah Muhammad. Malcolm went from being seen as one of the foremost proponents of the Nation of Islam to being seen as a substantial threat to the Nation of Islam. Malcolm was choosing to take a different route, a route that would lead him to the universal religion of Islam. He first went to Egypt, and then he made the *Hajj* or Islamicly prescribed pilgrimage to Makkah. It was in Makkah that he recognized that the White man was not a devil, as he had previously been taught to believe by the Nation of Islam. Instead, Malcolm realized that the White man could be a fellow Muslim, a brother who genuinely submits to do the will of

Allah. While he was in Makkah, Malcolm came to a new religious understanding, and began to abandon the teachings of the Nation of Islam while embracing the universal religion of Islam. Malcolm talked in his autobiography about the racist situation in America, and about his pilgrimage to Makkah. He reported that while in Makkah he shared truth and true brotherly love with many white-complexioned Muslims who never gave a single thought to the race or the complexion of another Muslim. "My pilgrimage broadened my scope".

Malcolm X said that he was blessed with new insights. In two weeks in the Holy Land of Makkah, he saw what he had never seen in 39 years in America: "I saw races, all colors, blue-eyed, blond to black skinned Africans, in true brotherhood, in unity, living as one, worshipping as one". There were no segregationists, and no liberals. Malcolm added that his fellow Muslims at the *Hajj* would not have known how to interpret the meaning of those words. Malcolm admitted in his book that in the past he would have made sweeping indictments of all White people. He said: "I will never be guilty of that again. As I know now, that some White people are truly sincere, that some truly are capable of being brotherly towards the Black man". Malcolm reported that the true and universal Islam that was revealed to Prophet Muhammad "has shown me that a blanket indictment of all White people is as wrong as when Whites make a blanket indictment against Blacks".

In his Farewell Address, which was given during the year in which he died, Prophet Muhammad said: "An Arab has no power over a non-Arab, a non-Arab over an Arab, a Black over a White, or a White over a Black. The best of you is the one that is most God-conscious." Therefore, it is not skin color that determines one's greatness, as was taught in the Nation of Islam. It's not about Black or White. When Malcolm X made the pilgrimage to Makkah, he broadened his scope.

He then changed his name from Malcolm X to El Hajj Malik Shabazz, established the Muslim Mosque Incorporated, and set up a *Masjid* (mosque) in New York City.

As formerly noted, Imam W. D. Mohammed, the son of Elijah Muhammad, had previously recognized the true message and religion of Islam, and had already seen the difference between the Nation of Islam and the universal religion of Islam as revealed to Prophet Muhammad. In fact, according to Malcolm's autobiography, it was Imam W. D. Mohammad who said that the only real hope for the community was for us to accept orthodox Islam. Malcolm and Imam Mohammad had shared a close relationship, and Imam Mohammad was one of the ones that really influenced Malcolm. Malcolm X died as El Hajj Malik Shabazz. He died the death of a Muslim. Surely Allah (God) knows best. He was also given an Islamic burial.

Elijah Muhammad had been sick for quite sometime, and died in 1975. His son, Imam W. D. Mohammed, assumed the leadership of the Nation of Islam. My former husband had recognized the true leadership in Imam W. D. Mohammed years before the death of Elijah Muhammad. Both my former husband and I were discontented with the Nation of Islam, and were hoping for a better way, life, and religion. I had sensed in my heart that the Nation of Islam was not the religion about which my grandmother used to sing and ponder. I had wondered how we could isolate other people of different races and nationalities when there is supposed to be one God for all humanity. We are talking about a God who created the heavens and the earth. We are talking about a God who created humankind for the purpose of serving only Him. As true Muslims, we are to follow the *Sunnah* or customary religious practice and example of Prophet Muhammad, and to live in peace among each other.

In the beginning, the message of the Nation of Islam had been powerful, and it had once had meaning for disenfranchised African-

Americans. However, at least in Philadelphia, the Nation of Islam began to attract the wrong people, i.e., people who were looking at the Nation of Islam as a haven for gangsters. Too many people wanted to cloak their nefarious schemes and ill-gotten gains under the mantle of the religion of the Nation of Islam. In Philadelphia, even some high-ranking officials within the Nation of Islam were crooked. When Imam W.D. Mohammed came on the scene, we knew it was a blessing, as much-needed change was soon evident.

With the leadership of Imam W. D. Mohammed, the African-American community overcame the limits of the Nation of Islam's nationalistic philosophies, racist ideology, and flawed religious teachings. However, some people stayed with the Nation of Islam under Minister Louis Farrakhan's teachings, while most congregants followed Imam W. D. Mohammed into the universal religion of Islam, which is practiced by more than one billion people worldwide. After the death of Elijah Muhammad in 1975, Imam W. D. Mohammed set the community on a course that furthered the growth of true Islam among African-Americans. His leadership was based on the universal teachings of Islam's holy book, the *Qur'an*, and on the practices of Prophet Muhammad, to whom the *Qur'an* was revealed. For the past 20 years, Imam W. D. Mohammed's leadership has fostered progress in the Muslim African-American community, as well as expansion of Islam among all races throughout the United States. The heights of such progress have also cast their influence on the international community of Islam.

Imam W.D. Mohammed was spiritually equipped with knowledge of the past and a vision for the future. He put into motion a plan to bring African-American Muslims into the true teachings of Islam. In that effort, Imam W.D. Mohammed was faced with major obstacles to overcome in his first year of leadership, and that included purging the myth of Master Fard Muhammad as God, clarifying concepts of the devil, and redefining the role of Elijah Muhammad. Imam W.D. Mohammed was on a mission to remake the world. Through articles in the community's newspaper, in speeches, and by example, he introduced and explained Islam's five pillars of faith. Particularly noteworthy were his series of articles on God is One, prayer, fasting in the month of *Ramadan*, charity, and *Hajj* or the pilgrimage to Makkah. He formally transformed the Nation of Islam's concept of Caucasians as "a grafted race", and reworked it to focus on any human being's corrupted behavior and mentality as a "grafted mentality".

It was the teachings of Imam W. D. Mohammed that made me look at religion in a different way. I began to know God as Allah, the "One God for all humanity". My consciousness was awakened to the truth of the unadulterated religion called Islam. It gave me a new way of thinking. It was, as described, "a way of life". Actually, it was in 1975 in Philadelphia, Pennsylvania, that I decided to take my *Shahadah* (a Muslim's declaration of faith). From that moment on, I began to live my life as a true Muslim.

Islam is based on five pillars of practice. The first pillar is the *Shahadah* or testimonial of faith, in which one acknowledges that there is no God but Allah, and that Prophet Muhammad was the last messenger of God. In making this attestation, a Muslim also acknowledges that Allah is One in His Unity, that Allah is the sole and universal God for all mankind, and that Prophet Muhammad's life was, and continues to be, the best example of how to live the Islamic life and of how to be a true Muslim. In first saying the *Shahadah* with understanding, a person enters the fold of Islam.

The second pillar is *Salat* or obligatory prayer. Upon becoming a Muslim, I was taught how to pray five times a day to Allah, with each prayer being said within a prescribed timeframe. Prayer is the most special act of worship, and all Muslims who have reached 10 years of age are required to worship Allah in this manner. Prayer is described as the foundation of faith.

The third pillar consists of fasting during the lunar month of *Ramadan*. During the month of *Ramadan*, Muslims throughout the world fast from dawn to dusk. I now learned how to fast correctly during *Ramadan*, and I also learned about the special joys and religious significance of this month. As multiply recorded in both *Al-Bukhari* and *Muslim*, it is stated that *Ramadan* is also a blessed month for another reason besides fasting, i.e., *Ramadan* was the month during which Allah began revealing His message to the blessed Prophet Muhammad. Allah said:

> Ramadan is the (month) in which was sent down the *Qur'an*, as a guide to mankind, also clear (signs) for guidance and judgment (between right and wrong). So every one of you who is present (at his home) during that month should spend it in fasting. But, if any one is ill, or on a journey, the prescribed period (should be made up) by days later. Allah intends every facility for you; He does not want to put you to difficulties. (He wants you) to complete the prescribed period, and to glorify Him in that He has guided you; and perchance ye shall be grateful (*Qur'an* 2: 185)

The fourth pillar is *Zakat* or obligatory charity from all those Muslims who have an economic surplus. There are pronounced spiritual benefits to be obtained by giving in charity, as illustrated by the following statement of Prophet Muhammad, when he once reminded us of something Allah promised to us.

> Narrated Abu Huraira (may Allah accept him): "Allah's Apostle (the peace and blessings of Allah be upon him) said, 'Allah said, 'O the son of Adam! spend (on what I have given to you on the poor), and I shall spend on you'.'" (*Al-Bukhari Hadith* # 7: 264)

The fifth pillar is *Hajj* or the pilgrimage to Makkah. It is the journey that all sane, adult Muslims must undertake at least once in their lives, provided that they have the financial and physical means to do so. If Allah's wills, I intend to make *Hajj* once in my lifetime. Once a year, Muslims of every ethnic group, color, social status, and culture gather together in Makkah and stand before the Ka'bah, praising Allah in one voice, one harmony.

There is so much to learn in the religion of Islam. Everyday is a learning experience. Prophet Muhammad is reported to have said that Muslims are to seek knowledge from the cradle to the grave, even if one has to go as far as China. Allah has blessed me to come into the religion of Islam. Surely Allah hears the prayers of those who call upon Him. Not only have I been blessed by Allah with this religion, but my children have also been blessed to be Muslims. All praises are due to Allah for His mercy, guidance, and blessings upon me and my children. All praises are due to Allah for Imam W.D. Mohammed. I thank Allah for all the good that Imam W.D. Mohammed has done for the African-American Muslims in America. Imam W.D. Mohammed is a wise and patient man, who has devoted all his energy and time to guiding the Muslims in America to the *Qur'an*.

Khadijah Beruni

I had come home to the pure religion of Islam that is followed by Muslims all over the world. It is a universal religion, and Prophet Muhammad is the last prophet of Allah and the seal of all the prophets. There was no need for me to look any further for a religion. I bear witness that Allah is God, and I bear witness that Prophet Muhammad is the last messenger of God. I accepted this religion of Islam to bring my spirit, mind, and soul closer to Allah, the creator of the heavens and the earth. I had found peace within myself. I had become a Muslim, and it was time to put into action and deeds my religious faith and beliefs. I was happy to be a Muslim, and to be in the company of other Muslims who were also practicing the religion of Islam. I like to think that I had found and embraced "that old time religion", about which my grandmother used to sing.

As a Muslim, I saw and interacted with Muslims from a great variety of cultures, nationalities, and ethnic and racial affiliations. It was always a beautiful sight to see people of diverse origins and backgrounds who were warm and friendly, and who treated me the way they wanted to be treated. I was always invited to attend their homes for dinner. I never witnessed any adverse racial attitudes or any indifference to people of other races in their behavior. They were Muslims who loved Allah and His Prophet Muhammad, and who thus loved all of their brothers and sisters in Allah. As Muslim women, we would stand and pray together side by side. We would embrace and hug each other in the spirit of sisterhood. This is what inspired me the most. It was seeing my Muslims sisters react in a warm, kind, and friendly way. I didn't feel unwanted or nervous. I felt like I was in the company of my own family.

In 1978, my husband and I moved our young family to Denver, Colorado. It was there that I became involved with the Muslim community. At that time, it was a small community, but it was a community with growth potentials. You could say that we were a family. There were always activities for the children, and we were able to stay busy and occupied. One of the things that propelled me forward was the love and warmth of the Muslim women, of my sisters in Allah. There was something special in the way they respected each other. Our community was like an extended family. It was a blessing from Allah to have His mercy, guidance, and protection to keep us from going astray from our faith. I was at peace knowing that I had Muslim sisters to call upon during times of distress, and that I could just pick up the telephone and give the greetings of peace, i.e., *Al-Salam 'Alaykum,* to my fellow sisters.

The two *'Eids* or Islamic holidays were my favorite times of the year. All praises are due to Allah for giving us the month of *Ramadan* to fast. It was a time to be thankful and grateful to Allah for His blessings. As I mentioned earlier, this is the month of fasting, but only from dawn to dusk, and fasting during *Ramadan* is the third pillar of Islam. It is strongly recommended that during this month you eat a small meal before dawn, i.e., before the first light of the sun has risen over the darkened sky. This small meal is called *Sahoor* in Arabic. When *Sahoor* has been completed, Muslims make their intentions to fast for the whole day. Then it is obligatory to pray the *Fajr* prayer before sunrise. During the daylight hours, it is also strongly recommended to read and study the *Qur'an* to obtain spiritual guidance from Allah. Thus, I would regularly occupy myself with reading and studying the *Qur'an*. It is also preferred that Muslims read about 1/30th of the *Qur'an* each day during this blessed month. By the end of this month they have read through the entire *Qur'an*, as *Ramadan* is 29 or 30 days long depending on the sighting of the new moon.

The first time that I fasted, it was in the summer. It must have been at least 90 plus degrees in the shade. My biggest mistake was being outside too long. I will never forget the burning heat (which is what *Ramadan* means), which seemed to scorch my throat. I couldn't wait until it was time for the sun to set. I was more thirsty than hungry. The smell of food didn't even excite my appetite. All I wanted was plenty of water to drink. This fast lasted for thirty days. As is the case for all menstruating Muslim women, I was excused from fasting throughout the days of my menses, and had to make up those excused days later on in the year.

When I was simultaneously fasting and working outside the home, I would be conscious of my actions, and would center my thoughts on Allah during the daylight hours. When Muslims fast, they are abstaining from all foods, liquids, sexual activity, and any medicine. If a fasting person must take medication during the daylight hours of fasting, then that person is not allowed to fast. It was always an exciting time for my children to participate in the fasting month of *Ramadan.* The lessons that we learned from fasting were many. We learned what it meant to be hungry, and we felt more compassion for the poor. Our spirits were more humble, and we learned how to control our anger, to practice forgiveness, and to perform good behavior. The importance and joys of fasting during *Ramadan* are illustrated in the following saying of Prophet Muhammad.

> Narrated Abu Huraira (may Allah accept him): "Allah's Apostle (the peace and blessings of Allah be upon him) said, 'Allah said, 'All the deeds of Adam's son (people) are for them, except fasting, which is for Me, and I will give the reward for it.' Fasting is a shield or protection from the fire, and from committing sin. If one of you is fasting, he should avoid sexual relations with his wife and quarrelling, and if somebody should fight or quarrel with him, he should say, 'I am fasting'. By Him in Whose Hands my soul is! the smell coming from the mouth of a fasting person is better in the sight of Allah than the smell of musk: there are two pleasures for the fasting person, one at the time of breaking his fast, and the other at the time when he will meet his Lord: then he will be pleased because of his fasting." (*Al-Bukhari, Hadith* # 3: 128)

All praises are due to Allah (God), for His Mercy and His Favors. The month of *Ramadan* was indeed a blessing not only for me, but it was also a blessing for my family. In particular, my children were especially excited, because they anticipated the rewards that came with fasting. When my children were younger, and throughout their childhood years, we would faithfully gather at the *Masjid* with other Muslim families, in order to pray and break our fast. As soon as the sun would set, it was time to pray and eat. Sometimes, we would stay at the *Masjid* and pray a special pray called *Tarawih.* The *Tarawih* prayer is performed after the *'Isha* prayer (which is the last obligatory prayer for the evening).

If you were to ask my children what they enjoyed most about

the religion of Islam, they would be in agreement, and say that it was fasting during the month of *Ramadan* and the celebration of the *Hajj*. Besides the love for Allah and His Prophet Muhammad, they would excitedly recall the day *Ramadan* began, the day it ended, and the celebration of both '*Eids*. This was the time that everyone in the family would receive presents for completing the fast for Allah. The purpose of fasting was for the pleasure of Allah, and is a religious obligation on all Muslims who are sane and physically able to fast. All praises are due to Allah! Sometimes, my daughters or I had to break our fasts early. Valid reasons for breaking the fast include sickness, travel, taking medication, and menses. Fasting in the month of *Ramadan* for the pleasure of Allah has uplifted my spirits, given me self-discipline, self-control, self-obedience, and love and submission to the Creator of the heavens and the earth. With fasting, I have been able to improve my health, personality, and behavior – all for the pleasure and love of Allah.

For the first few years after my father died, I had no longer felt the desire to visit my parents' hometown in Williamston, North Carolina. Therefore, I lost contact with my extended family. My brother was an exception as we stayed in close contact. We would often speak to each other, and would visit each other occasionally. Over time, I had become very isolated from the rest of my extended family. I guess I needed time to collect my thoughts and to focus on what direction I wanted to pursue. I wanted a family life, and I also wanted to finish my education.

The institution of family is a very important part of my life. As a matter of fact, this is how I was raised. Likewise, my parents had been raised in communities in which they were surrounded by a network of close-knit families, and my grandparents had instituted a system of family reunions that were responsible for holding the extended family together. Today, my extended family still carries on that tradition of family reunions. I have been back to visit, but that was ten or fifteen years later on in my life.

As for my former husband's family, there was never any close relationship established between me and them, except with his parents. As far as I can remember, his parents never objected to his reversion to Islam. They would always ask questions, and had agreed that there was One God for all humanity. But deep inside of their hearts, and because of the Christian environment in which they lived, they still claimed that Jesus was the Son of God. Without disrespecting his parents, he would read the *Qur'an* where Allah said:

> And (Jesus) shall be a sign (for the coming of) the hour (of judgment): therefore have no doubt about the (hour), but follow ye Me: this is a Straight Way. (Qur'an 43:61)

My former husband's relationship with his extended family was completely different than the closeness that my family had shared in my youth. His parents did not socialize with their different family members. He was raised in a large family, and he never really knew his grandparents or played with his relatives. His family was also from the South. He grew up in a small town in Virginia. He was the youngest among his brothers and sisters, and they were all much older than he was. His parents lived until they were in their seventies or eighties. My former husband was in his forties when his parents died. Because of the distant relationship my in-laws had with their families, there were never any family reunions. However, my former husband had a close relationship with his parents, and he loved his mother very much.

My children didn't spend time getting to know their relatives because of the geographical distance that separated us. But as my children grew older, I felt the need for them to become acquainted with their extended family. Sometimes, I wish that things had been different. I used to wonder if my relationship with my former husband had been closer, perhaps our children would have spent time getting to know their extended family when they were younger. As time progressed, my husband and I grew apart in our relationship. Our lives were going in different directions. We were not communicating our feelings to each other, and it was beginning to affect our children.

In spite of the hardships from losing my parents, grandparents, and sister, deep down within my heart, I truly feel that I was blessed by Allah to be a Muslim and to have my health and strength. I also feel blessed by Allah to have a beautiful family with four children. Their names are Zaneta, Abdul, Ayesha, and Muhammad. Today, I thank Allah for blessing my children by allowing them to survive in America and still be Muslims. As a family, we prayed and worshipped together. The traditional practices and behavior that were done in my childhood days are still prevalent within my family today. I have tried to raise my children the way that I was raised, but in an Islamic household. *Al-Hamdulillah*, Allah instilled in my children's hearts and minds the love for Allah and His Messenger Muhammad. I have shown them love and warmth, and have spent quality time with my children. Whenever I would meet other people who were Muslims, I made certain that they also had children that were equal in age with my children.

Living in Denver, Colorado, was quite an experience. This is where I lived with my family for 23 years of my life. Our lifestyles, habits, and pattern of dress made life easy when and where it mattered. It was all consistent with the religion of Islam. There was nothing strange in the way we did things. It was all for the love and pleasure of Allah. Because it is much easier to live an Islamic life when one is frequently around other Muslims and their families, we stayed in contact with the Muslim community, and became involved in daily activities that kept us focused on Islam.

At the time that we moved, I had only three children. My fourth child, Muhammad, was born in Englewood, which was a suburb of Denver. As a family, we used to have lots of fun and numerous projects to keep us busy. My sons were involved in sports, and my daughters were involved in gymnastics and other recreational activities. We would visit the parks, zoo, and have picnics. I would even take them to the mall, and I would find a place to sit while they would have fun shopping together.

Most of the sisters with whom I socialized had other children who played with my children. As a result of our interactions, there were always positive things to do in the society. In Denver, we would have various committees to support our sisterhood. We had a committee to help sisters who were ill, and who were not able to visit the *Masjid*. In fact, visiting the sick is one of the Islamic social customs that was established and encouraged by the Prophet Muhammad, who made it a duty upon every Muslim man and woman to visit the sick, and made such visitation a right that one Muslim may expect from another. "The rights of a Muslim over his brother are five: he should return his peace, visit the sick, attend funerals, accept invitations, and 'bless' a person when he sneezes." We also had a committee that was established to help a sister with her daily chores and to provide needed food and transportation.

We would often gather at the *Masjid* for Arabic classes, or meet at each other homes for lunch or classes. Most of the time, my children were included in my activities. It was a family gathering for Muslims. We would take our children to the park or zoo. Sometimes, we would just hang out at the park while the children played until they were tired. Being a Muslim in America doesn't mean that you have to stay indoors and away from public areas. There are lots of fun and good things that Muslim women can have and do by themselves or with their children. We used to have swimming for the Muslim women and their children. We would make arrangements to have the pool available on certain days for Muslim women only. I have also heard of Muslim women exercising at a facility where only women were allowed to attend.

Even after we were married for 23 years, I would sometimes think that everything was going to be all right. I used to wake up in the morning thinking that it was all a bad dream! I guess I stayed in an unhealthy relationship too long. I wanted my marriage to work, and I didn't want my children to be affected by my unhappiness. But as it turned out, my children were affected after all. It became more unbearable throughout the years. Some days would be good, and then we would argue. I can't say that he was fully responsible for our failing marriage, because I also had my faults. I know for sure that I needed a change in my life, and that change was Allah. My husband and I had gotten away from our religious beliefs, and it was definitely affecting our lives. We had allowed other people to influence our way of thinking, instead of relying on Allah to make the final decision through prayers, perseverance, and patience. As noted previously, Allah said:

> Nay, seek (Allah's) help with patient perseverance and prayer: it is indeed hard: except to those who bring a lowly spirit – who bear in mind the certainty that they are to meet their Lord, and that they are to return to Him. (Qur'an 2:45-46)

I also adamantly feel that if we had prayed together more as a family, then that would have possibly strengthened our family ties. There is an old adage that says, "A family that prays together, stays together". I believed that this was part of the problem in my marriage. Besides a lack of communication, we lost the trust that we had for each other. I feel that Allah was not in our lives or in our hearts. Instead of being friends, we became enemies. Another wise adage is that "hindsight is 20/20". I was not looking to go back to a relationship that I knew would never work. Allah said that He will never change the condition of a person until they change what is in their hearts (*Qur'an* 8: 53). I can only learn from my experience and move on to a better life; if it is the will of Allah.

During that period, my husband owned a bookstore, and most of his time was spent away from home. I was working fulltime, and attending college part-time. I guess we were so caught up in our every-day activities that we didn't spend any quality time with each other. Anyway, it was to the point where we would argue and disagree about everything. We would insult each other with offensive name calling, and bicker for unknown reasons. Allah said:

> O ye who believe! let not some men among you laugh at others: it may be that the (latter) are better than the (former): nor let some women laugh at others: it may be that the (latter) are better than the (former): nor defame nor be sarcastic to each other, nor call each other by (offensive) nick-names: ill-seeming is a name connoting wickedness, (to be used of one) after he has believed: and those who do not desist are (indeed) doing wrong. (*Qur'an* 49: 11).

After a while, my children no longer saw any respect and love in our household. As a result, they began to feel uncomfortable being around us. With everyone feeling uncomfortable and unhappy, I knew that I eventually had to start all over again. But this time, it would be just me starting over. I needed a rebirth. I needed Allah back in my life more completely than before. I knew that Allah was testing my faith, and that it was time for me to learn how to submit myself more fully to do His will. There is a proverb, attributed by the *Bible* to Prophet Solomon, peace be upon him, that states: "Pride goes before destruction, and a haughty spirit before a fall" (*Proverbs* 16: 18). I was to the point that I was too proud to admit my wrong-doings and inappropriate actions. I told my children that "hindsight is 20/20", and that one should learn what went wrong from the past, and then move ahead in a positive direction. I had made mistakes in the past, and I have asked Allah to forgive me for my past mistakes. I can pray that my children learn from my mistakes, and try to be the best they can for the pleasure and love of Allah. In this society, the challenges in life can be difficult, especially when all the odds of doing what is right are against you.

I had tried unsuccessfully to make my marriage work by doing what pleased my husband. Nevertheless, it was a hard lesson to learn that you cannot change the ways of your spouse. Only Allah can make that change, if the person is willing to change his or her ways for the pleasure of Allah. It took a long time to learn that lesson and to apply it in my everyday life. I am thankful to Allah for having given me patience when I searched for guidance, and for having given me a way to get out of a relationship that was not benefiting me or my children. When I look back, I have no regrets, although I wish I had been a better Muslim for the sake of myself and my family. But, I have truly learned to trust in Allah, and to worry about pleasing no one except Him. Surely Allah hears the prayers of those who call upon Him. We as Muslim are being tested in this life. As a Muslim, I ask Allah to grant me good in this life and good in the next life, and to save me from the chastisement of the fire.

As a Muslim mother, I had tried to give my children an Islamic upbringing. I would make sure that we were always occupied with activities. Besides being busy in academics, my sons were involved in football practice and other sports. My daughters were involved in musical lessons and exercise classes. Islam places responsibility on the shoulders of every individual; not one person is left out. Parents, especially mothers, are responsible for providing their children with solid nurturing and a sound Islamic education. I was close to my children, and would read to them before they went to sleep at night. Our children are a blessing from Allah, and I truly thank Allah for blessing me with four children. Allah said:

> Whoever works righteousness, man or woman, and has faith, verily, to
> him will We give a new life, and life that is good and pure, and We will
> bestow on such their reward according to the best of their actions.
> (*Qur'an* 16: 97)

There is one particular night of *Ramadan* that has extra special significance. It is the night when the first Qur'anic passage was initially revealed to Prophet Muhammad. It is called *Laylat Al-Qadr* or the Night of Power. According to the sayings of the blessed Prophet, it falls on one of the odd-numbered nights in the last ten days of *Ramadan*. During this time, many Muslims stay up all night seeking their Lord's forgiveness and guidance, for Allah has said:

> We have indeed revealed this (message) in the Night of Power: and what
> will explain to thee what the Night of Power is? The Night of Power is
> better than a thousand months. Therein come down the angels and the
> Spirit by Allah's permission, on every errand: peace!...this until the rise of
> morn! (*Qur'an* 97: 1-5)

Being in school and fasting during *Ramadan* were no problem for my children. Usually, I made an appointment to speak with my children's teachers, and explained the reasons why they were fasting. I requested that their teachers allow them to be present at the library during their lunch period. I didn't have any problems with the teachers honoring my request, and I would always invite my children's teachers to come to the *Masjid*. In fact, when the '*Eid* was in the spring or summer months, we would have outdoor activities during the '*Eid* celebration. These were open to the public, regardless of their religious background or affiliation. We would always send invitations to the school, inviting the principals and teachers to come out and participate in our social events. It was a time of learning and educating one another about religion.

When the children came home at the end of a *Ramadan* school day, we would go the *Masjid* and have our meal. It was a blessing being in the company of other Muslims when breaking the fast. My children were then able to be around their peers who were also fasting. This made the entire month very exciting, and it was indeed a blessed month for all Muslims who participated.

I was always especially grateful to Allah when *Ramadan* came in the month of December. I would exert extra time and effort to make that month a joyous occasion for my children. Although we were fasting during the daylight hours, I would sometimes decorate the house with balloons or have a special treat for them when it was time to break our fast. Every morning for breakfast, the children would have their choice of favorites. I have always tried to make this a special month for celebrating. When it was time for the 'Eid celebration, we would always go out shopping and have more fun. But, of course they always realized that the most important blessings that came from fasting were through Allah. We kept in mind that we were not fasting for ourselves, but that we were fasting for the pleasure of Allah, and praying that Allah would forgive our sins.

Between fasting during the month of *Ramadan* and being in the company of Muslims, I was propelled to increase my worship and study. If it wasn't Allah's mercy upon my family, I would not be as strong in my faith as I am today. By practicing the religion of Islam on a daily basis, it has made me stronger and more appreciative of Allah's blessings, of my family, and of the Muslim community. Surely, Allah is most merciful and most gracious to the Muslims. I found peace within myself, and appreciated having Muslims surround me, who also loved Allah and Prophet Muhammad. All praises are due to Allah for the members of the Muslim community who are striving for the pleasure of Allah.

It was important to spend time with our children, guiding them and giving them the proper education. That is why it is so important for Muslims to have their own schools, colleges, banks, and stores. Schools and colleges are crucial for giving our children a strong Islamic education. I don't know how I would have been successful in raising my children, if it weren't for Allah's mercy, guidance, and blessings. I have truly been blessed. I can only hope that my children feel the same way today, and appreciate what they have learned as kids growing up in America. I did the best that I know how in raising them. They say that children learn from their parents' habits and lifestyles. I know that they appreciate their mother. They have shown it in their actions. I am always told how much they love me. I have told my children how much I love them also, and I tell them that I pray that Allah gives them good in this life and good in the next life, and that Allah saves them from the chastisement of the fire.

As Muslims living in America, we are faced with different types of religious celebrations. Christmas seems to be the most celebrated holiday in American society. When I became a Muslim, it was sometimes difficult for me to adjust to the holiday season. It was a challenge for me to be at work among my co-workers and to observe their gleeful interaction with their peers. Sometimes, I would feel isolated when they would have Christmas parties and when the office would be decorated with Christmas themes. They knew that I was a Muslim who didn't celebrate Christmas. However, I was always approached by my co-workers, and was asked if I would be offended by their decorations. In a respectful way, I would respond that I didn't mind, because as Muslims, we have two important holidays that are celebrated all over the world. I would briefly explain that the two holidays were called 'Eid Al-Fitr (the feast of fast-breaking) and 'Eid Al-Adha (the feast of sacrifice). I knew that Allah was testing my faith, and I was thankful for the opportunity to talk about the religion of Islam to people who were receptive to hearing about it.

With regard to other holidays, such as Easter, it was not as hard to overcome the Christian's way of worship. We had taught our children the truth about the falsehood that kept the masses of the people ignorant and divided among themselves. However, it was at times a struggle to keep my children's minds focused and occupied on Islam. Then again, it was also a blessing for us to have a Muslim community that had classes and activities in which families could participate and learn the Islamic way of life. My children had learned how to be creative, and therefore keep their focus on Islam. I have often given thanks to Allah for blessing us with a Muslim community that was active in its faith and deeds. It has helped my children and me to grow stronger in our faith. We stayed involved with the Muslim community, and it helped us overcome our anxiety about and sometimes frustration over the Christians' celebration of New Years Day, Valentine's Day, Halloween, St. Patrick's Day, and whatever else I didn't include.

After being married for 23 years, I finally realized that the only person I could change was me. I wanted to be a fully committed Muslim, and to practice my life according to the teachings of the *Qur'an*. When a family does not pray or worship together, it takes away the relationship of Islam. My children were grown and my daughters had already moved out of our home. In January of 1998, I was finally divorced. It was as if a heavy burden were lifted from my shoulders. All praises are due to Allah for His mercy and guidance. I feel very grateful to Allah for blessing me to be a Muslim. Surely, Allah said:

> Because Allah will never change the grace which he hath bestowed on a people until they change what is in their (own) souls: and verily Allah is He Who heareth and knoweth (all things). (*Qur'an* 8:53)

My children are now young adults. My older daughter lives

outside of Baltimore, Maryland. She keeps a busy schedule with work, and loves to cook. She also attends the *Masjid* and different Islamic events. My younger daughter lives in Washington, D.C. She also works, and attends the *Masjid* and different Islamic events. She is learning to speak and write Arabic in her spare time, and spends quality time with other Muslim sisters. Her plans are to attend an international school abroad and to further her learning skills in Arabic.

My older son is married to a Muslim woman, and has two small sons. They spend quality time together learning Islam and raising their family. My younger son is going to a private college, and is working. He is very fluent in Arabic, and spends time with his Muslim friends. I have asked Allah to bless all my children, and to help my unmarried children to find a suitable mate who is also a Muslim, and who loves Allah and His Prophet Muhammad. I wish the best for my family. I want my children to be selective in choosing a marriage partner, and have asked them to pray the prayer of guidance. Surely, Allah hears the prayers of those who call upon Him.

Every society has a way of organizing its social and family structures. Where families are strong, societies are more prosperous and united. Where families are weak and disunited, there is crime and chaos. Islam is a way of life bequeathed by the Creator to us. It involves our personal life, our social life, and our family life. The family is the first unit in society, and it should be the same way with the entire Muslim community. We could say that the Muslim community is our extended family. In the Islamic family structure, both the father and the mother are considered equal partners. The husband is not a god for the wife to worship, nor is the wife a servant or slave. Allah said:

> And among His signs is this, that He created for you mates from among
> yourselves, that ye may dwell in tranquility with them, and He has put love

and mercy between your (hearts): verily in that are signs for those who reflect. (*Qur'an* 30:21)

And those who pray, "Our Lord! grant unto us wives and offspring who will be the comfort of our eyes, and give us (the grace) to lead the righteous". (*Qur'an* 25:74)

In today's society, we are witnessing a breakdown in the moral fiber of families. Mothers are raising their children without the presence and influence of the father. The fathers are raising their children without the presence and influence of the mother. This suggests that something is wrong with society. When I was growing up as a child, I could see the love between my parents and grandparents. They were my role models. I saw the love of God in their hearts, minds, and souls. Their love and respect for self made it easier for me to also love and respect myself. The family values with which I was raised and my life as a child had important affinities with the Islamic concept of family. The ideal Muslim family is what is known as an extended family. That is a home where the parents, grandparents, and children live together, or at least in the same neighborhood. This is synonymous with the way I was raised. The importance of family is clearly reported in the following statement of Prophet Muhammad.

'Aisha and 'Abdullah ibn 'Abbas (may Allah accept them) narrated that Allah's Messenger (the peace and blessings of Allah be upon him) said: "The best of you is he who is best to his family, and I am the best among you to my family. When one of you dies, speak no ill of him." (*Al-Tirmidhi, Hadith* # 3252)

Learning to live in Islam is truly a test and a blessing from Allah. Islam is not just a religion, but a complete way of life that is patterned after the natural trend in the universe. Its goal is to help people live in harmony with the natural order of nature and existence. However, those challenges are not continuous difficulties without relief, for Allah said:

So, verily with every difficulty, there is relief: verily, with every difficulty there is relief. Therefore, when thou are free (from thine immediate task), still labour hard, and to thy Lord turn (all) thy attention. (*Qur'an* 94: 5-8)

Surely, Allah speaks the truth. I would recite the above verse in times of difficulty or hardship. I would also recite the verse in times of ease – whenever I was relaxing or reading a magazine. When I was in a state of happiness, I would think about that verse, and as a result tears would flow down my cheeks. They were tears of joy and appreciation for Allah's mercy and guidance. I would also draw strength from the fact that Allah said:

On no soul doth Allah place a burden greater than it can bear. It gets every good that it earns, and it suffers every ill that it earns. (*Qur'an* 2: 286a)

Surely, Allah speaks the truth. Being a Muslim in America is a trial from Allah. We are tested with our wealth and our children. Thus, it is stated by Allah:

And know ye that your possessions and your progeny are but a trial; and that it is Allah with whom lies your highest reward. (*Qur'an* 8: 28)

There have also been some difficulties in being a Muslim woman in America. For example, when I began working outside of the home, I mistakenly thought it would be easy wearing my *Hijab* or scarf. I didn't think that I would have any problems in the workplace. I have since come to realize that there is a certain amount of discrimination against Muslims, and especially against Muslim women, in the workplace. A lot of job sites generally expect women to wear clothing that is appealing to the eye of the opposite sex. A woman is too often looked upon in America as a sex symbol and as nothing more. Therefore, being a Muslim woman in America can be challenging. The fears and insults that most Muslim women in America have to confront on a daily basis, particularly from non-Muslim women, can prove to be a test from Allah and a challenge to one's commitment to Islam. Specifically, I am referring to the challenge of wearing the *Hijab*, which Muslim women wear as part of their everyday dress.

At first, it was uncomfortable for me to wear my head covered in a public place, and it was especially uncomfortable in the workplace. I would sense that people were staring, and that made me even more uncomfortable. Sometimes, I would have non-Muslim women ask me why I was wearing my head covered. Their curiosity made them bold enough to say such things as: "Do you have any hair? How can you wear your hair covered in hot weather? Do you have to wear your hair covered inside your home?" Of course, not all non-Muslim women would be so bold, for fear of embarrassment to you and themselves. However, sometimes their remarks would be aggressive and insulting. "You look very unattractive with your body covered!"

I would like to address all non-Muslim women with regard to covering one's hair. The *Hijab* represents modesty, purity, and chastity. When a Muslim woman covers herself, she is rejecting the role of a woman who half-nakedly portrays herself for the voyeuristic pleasures of society, and especially for male society. She is rejecting the role of the mere sex object who is disrespected and stared at in an inappropriate manner. As I stated earlier, at first I felt uncomfortable wearing my hair covered, but now I realize that I am not alone in the way I dress. I have the love of Allah, and that is most important to me. I also have the love and respect of other Muslim women who dress the way that I do, and wear their *Hijab* for the love of Allah. Still further, I have the respect of my Muslim brothers, who treat me with the respect and honor that I deserve. I refuse to take off my garment for the world to gawk and stare. I am not looking for the libidinous approval from any ungodly man who might wish to whistle at me, or who might want to put me to shame or embarrassment. I am not interested in having my manner of dress fit the half-naked, pin-up "ideal" of a hedonistic society. Yesterday, I felt ashamed, because I wanted to "fit in" with the American way. I wanted to be accepted in the workplace, and to be liked for being someone other than myself.

As a Muslim woman, I am dressing for the pleasure and love of Allah. I have heard people say that women should "Dress for Success". As Muslim women, we can dress for Allah, and still be successful in our professional and personal lives. More importantly, we dress for success in our spiritual and religious lives. In the *Adhan*, which is the Muslim call to prayer and worship, it says, "Come to success, come to success." Allah is therefore calling Muslim women and Muslim men to come to success in their prayers. Oh, yes indeed, I am dressing for success. I am dressing for Allah to grant me good in this life and good in the next life, and, *Insha'Allah,* to be spared from the hell fire.

The Muslim women's *Hijab* is also a protection for her in today's society. This modest dress elicits respect and honor from one's fellow Muslims, even from many non-Muslims. However, a Muslim woman does not have to cover her hair inside the privacy of her home. In fact, it is in the privacy of her home where she can look attractive for her husband and where there are no restrictions on the way she chooses to wear her garment. She can dress anyway that she chooses in her home. Regardless of her status, single or married, she is not required to cover except to be modest in front of men who are not her immediate family members. The right attitude and right spirit is to dress to please Allah. A Muslim woman has dignity, and carries herself in a dignified way that represents her character, attitude, and belief in the One God Allah. Islam is a way of life, and Allah does not place any hardship on anyone greater than he or she can bear. Sometimes, I believe that we put hardship on ourselves A Muslim woman is conscious of her actions and deeds, and her goal is to please Allah by being modest in her dress and behavior. There are two consecutive verses of the *Qur'an* that speak directly to this issue of modesty and dress, the first of which is directed to Muslim men, and the second of which is directed to Muslim women.

> Say to the believing men that they should lower their gaze and guard their modesty: that will make for greater purity for them: and Allah is well acquainted with all that they do. And say to the believing women that they should lower their gaze and guard their modesty; that they should not display their beauty and ornaments except what (must ordinarily) appear thereof; that they should draw their veils over their bosoms and not display their beauty except to their husbands, their fathers, their husbands' fathers, their sons, their husbands' sons, their brothers or their brothers' sons, or their sisters' sons, or their women, or the slaves whom their right hands possess, or male servants free of physical needs, or small children who have no sense of the shame of sex; and that they should not strike their feet in order to draw attention to their hidden ornaments. And O ye believers! turn ye all together towards Allah, that ye may attain bliss. (*Qur'an* 24: 30-31)

When I was a youngster growing up in America, it was considered modesty to wear your skirt or dress below your knees. In fact, it was common seeing a woman with her skirt or dress to her ankles. I remembered the days when my mother and grandmother would wear their clothes to their ankles. They also wore hats and gloves when they went to church. The women of that era were modest and decent. However, in today's society, personal dress has become much more immodest. Nowadays, it seems that the clothes women wear are much shorter, much more revealing, and more vulgar looking. My mother used to yell at me for attempting to leave the house if my clothes were tightly fitted. My father used to give me a look that would make me think twice about the way I dressed. I knew better, and would not hesitate to dress in a way that represents modesty and decorum. I thank Allah for blessing me to be a Muslim, and I thank Allah for protecting me from the evils in this society.

The Muslim woman who understands the teaching of Islam adheres to the principle of modesty in all things. I was keen to look good, but without any extravagance or excessive waste. Muslim women do not blindly follow those who throw aside new clothes after wearing them only once, and do not exhaust themselves trying to keep up with the latest fashion, which is forever changing. Thus, she is careful not to fall victim to the enslavement of fashion and those behind it, who are people who often have no fear of Allah, and who do not have the best interests of women at heart. In my personal life, I try to abide by the limits of moderation set out in the *Qur'an*, which describes moderation as one of the qualities of the believing slaves of Allah.

> Those who, when they spend, are not extravagant and not niggardly, but
> hold a just (balance) between those (extremes). (*Qur'an* 25: 67)

The sisterhood in Islam is an important aspect of our community. A Muslim woman loves for her sister what she loves for herself. The love that I have for my sisters-in-Islam is for the pleasure of Allah. The sisterhood of faith is the strongest of bonds between hearts and minds. Muslim sisters should enjoy being in each other's company. They should be thankful to Allah for having the camaraderie that is based on God-consciousness and respect for one another. It is a love that is untainted by any worldly interest or hidden motive. By having this strong bond with my sisters, I feel connected to the Islamic way of life. Being a Muslim is a blessed experience. I have Muslims sisters whom I love and trust. We are bonded in our relationships.

The sincere Muslim woman is one whose heart is filled with the kindness of faith and who desires for her Muslim sisters what she wants for herself. We should never forget to pray for our sister in her absence. We should pray a short prayer that is filled with the warmth of sincere love and sisterhood. We should also schedule lunches or meetings and have them in our homes. In our meetings, we should learn how to become better Muslims in society and at home. To gain this knowledge, we should study the lives of Prophet Muhammad's wives, and learn how they conducted themselves in society.

There is always something to learn about Islam, which keeps Muslim women busy and occupied. When the weather is warm and sunny, we may meet at the park where it is convenient for our sisters who have children. It is a blessing being around our sisters. Learning to live in Islam is all about pleasing Allah, asking Allah for forgiveness and mercy in this life, and petitioning Allah to be granted paradise in the next life. We also ask Allah to save us from the chastisement of the fire. Islam is a growing religion, which makes it easy to practice among other Muslims. There is always strength in numbers, and when the *Ummah* comes together, it is a beautiful sight to see everyone in peace and harmony. We pray together at the *Masjid*, and I particularly enjoy being in the company of Muslims from other cultures.

Living within Islam continues to bring me closer to my Muslims sisters. The Muslim woman who is sincere in her Islam, whose faith is strong and whose mind is open to the guidance of Islam, is always active in the cause of goodness, enjoining what is good and forbidding what evil. She offers sincere advice to her sisters, and strives for improvement in her own daily life. She is not selfish or niggardly. She believes in sharing with her sisters. The Muslim woman is of good and noble character, friendly, humble, gentle of speech, and tactful. She likes others, and is considerate of others' feelings.

It is important to try to exemplify the *Sunnah* or customary example of Prophet Muhammad, who was an excellent example for all Muslims to follow. We are taught to be truthful with all people. A Muslim woman should have absorbed the teachings of Islam that encourage truthfulness, and she should regard truthfulness as the chief of virtues. We are also taught that lying is forbidden, and is regarded as the source of all evils and bad deeds. The Muslim woman therefore believes that truthfulness naturally leads to a goodness that will admit the one who practices it to paradise. In contrast, falsehood leads to a wickedness that will send the one who practices it to hell.

The Muslim woman not only strives to free herself of negative characteristics, she also seeks to offer sincere advice to every woman with whom she comes in contact who has deviated from the guidance of Allah. We are all in need of spiritual advice from our sisters, and it helps us to know that we have Islamic sisters upon whom we can depend to help us grow in Islam. There are a lot of benefits from being a Muslim, and this is especially true for the Muslims who live in America. It is a blessing from Allah when one has the sincere love and support of the *Ummah*.

As I look back on the past and my present situation, I must admit that I would not have made it this far without the mercy and guidance of Allah. Living in Denver proved to be a challenging experience. I have lived long enough to have learned how to be a God-conscious Muslim. I am a Muslim who loves Allah and His Prophet Muhammad. I have learned how to put all my faith and trust in Allah. When I look back, I also see a person who has developed and grown in the way of Allah. I have learned to appreciate the favors that Allah has bestowed upon me and my children. A day does not go by without a teardrop of joy and gratitude in my eyes.

When I was asked to write about my reversion of Islam, I was more than excited to participate. As I began to unfold my life story, it made me seriously think about life in general. Some of the events that have been told in my story made me ponder on how blessed I have been by the mercy and guidance of Allah. Some of the events even made me get up from the computer and pray to Allah for strength and courage to write more. Oh Allah! Oh Allah! How thankful I am for the blessings that You have given me. Oh Allah! Oh Allah! Please forgive the errors of my ways and please continue to guide me on the straight path of righteousness.

I have truly found peace in my life. In the beginning, I thought I had peace of mind, but it was only an illusion. I was too deeply involved in the material world, and had left the spiritual world behind me. It was indeed a test of my faith. I strongly believe that I have passed the test, and I am prepared for Allah to test me further. I pray that Allah accepts my prayers and forgives me my wrongdoings. I pray that Allah gives me the strength and courage to do what is expected of me as a Muslim. Oh Allah, please guide me on the straight way, and not on the path of those who have gone astray.

After my divorce from my former husband, it took me two years to recuperate and to restore my self-confidence. I had prayed the prayer of guidance to Allah for a more peaceful life. With my first marriage, I had asked Allah to give me a good husband. In my second marriage, I was more specific. I asked Allah to bless me with a Muslim man who loves Allah, and who follows the *Sunnah* of Prophet Muhammad. I asked Allah for a Muslim man who is kind, considerate, and passionate, and who can communicate his feelings in a respectful way. Surely, Allah hears the prayers of those who call upon Him. As I contemplate what I have just written, I have come to realize the need for self-evaluation. I needed to look at myself, and to understand how I have made improvements over the years for the pleasure of Allah. A lot of times, we have the tendency to blame others for our faults and misguidance, instead of honestly evaluating ourselves.

In Islam, marriage is a blessed contract between a man and a woman, in which each becomes acceptable to the other, and in which they begin the long journey of life in a spirit of love, cooperation, harmony, and tolerance. It is a relationship where each feels at ease with the other, and each finds tranquility, contentment, and comfort in the company of the other. As previously noted, Allah said:

> And among His signs is this, that He created for you mates from among yourselves, that you may dwell in tranquility with them, and He has put love and mercy between your hearts: verily in that are signs for those who reflect. (*Qur'an* 30: 21)

In my search for a blessed marriage from Allah, it was through a Muslim network that I met a Muslim man who lives in Wichita, Kansas. In our conversations, we expressed our love for Allah and Prophet Muhammad. We also had a lot in common, and were compatible in our social lifestyles. He came to Denver to meet me, and we decided to get married.

It has been almost three years since I married my current husband and joined him at his residence. I truly believe that Allah has blessed me with a sincere, trustworthy, and God-conscious Muslim man, who dearly loves Allah and His Prophet Muhammad. Since I have remarried, I have attended school fulltime at Wichita State University, and have graduated with a degree in business.My husband has been very supportive of my education, and has always given me encouragement whenever I began feeling discouraged and overwhelmed by studies. He is my blessing from Allah.

Moving from one state to another has made me think about life in general, and I have become more appreciative of what I have accomplished in the time that I have been living in Wichita. My husband often asks me if I am happy and at peace. I have always responded to him in a pleasant way by saying, "All praises are due to Allah for His mercy, guidance, and blessings." I am at peace within myself, and I have found happiness in my life.

I have also been blessed by Allah to have three beautiful sisters who are my dearest friends. They have been good to me spiritually and morally. Whenever I need spiritual advice or just someone to hang out with, I can count on my sisters to be there for me. All praises are due to Allah for my beloved sisters. I treasure them all exceedingly. The true Muslim woman is cheerful of countenance, and always greeting her sisters with warmth and smiles, as the Prophet Muhammad said:

> Abu Dharr reported: "Allah's Apostle (may peace be upon him) said to me: 'Don't consider anything insignificant out of good things, even if it is that you meet your brother with a cheerful countenance'." (*Muslim, Hadith* # 6359)

One of the virtues of a Muslim woman is that she is completely sincere towards Allah, His prophet, and the leaders and the masses of the Muslims.

> It is narrated on the authority of Tamim Al-Dari: "The Apostle of Allah (may peace and blessings be upon him) observed: '*Al-Din* (the religion) is a name of sincerity and well-wishing'. Upon this we said: 'For whom?' He replied: 'For Allah (by obeying Him, attributing to Him what He deserves, and performing *Jihad* for His sake), His book (by reading it, understanding it, and applying it to one's daily life), His messenger (by respecting him greatly, by fighting on his behalf both in his lifetime and after his death, and by following his *Sunnah*), and for the leaders (by helping them in their task of leading Muslims to the right path, and by alerting them if they are heedless) and the general Muslims (by being merciful towards them)'." (*Muslim, Hadith* # 98)

The attitude that I have for my Muslim sisters and brothers is based on sincerity. Without sincerity in my heart, soul, and mind, I feel that my faith would be invalid and my Islam worthless. I truly wish for my sisters what I wish for myself.

> Narrated Anas: "The Prophet said, 'None of you will have faith till he wishes for his (Muslim) brother what he likes for himself." (*Al-Bukhari, Hadith* # 1: 12)

I feel love for my sisters-in-Islam in the depths of my soul. It is one of the conditions of true faith and religion. The love that I have for my sisters in Wichita, Kansas, is the same love that I have for my sisters in Denver. I have grown to love my Muslim sisters, and I feel that they have grown to love me for the pleasure of Allah.

My children are very supportive of my relationship with my husband. When I graduated from Wichita State University, they came to cheer me on, and were elated to meet my friends. They also enjoyed their visit with me and my husband. Everyday, I ask Allah to bless me with the knowledge to give back to the Muslim society at least some of what Allah has given to me. When I was asked to write this chapter, I felt honored and obligated for the pleasure of Allah. I feel that this is the first step in making a God-conscious effort to please Allah, and to be thankful for His blessings. I would like to continue to do more positive things for the pleasure of Allah. At this moment, I am thinking of doing something that will not only benefit the Muslim community, but society in general. My precious husband has been trying to get me to become an entrepreneur. It would be a wonderful blessing from Allah to be able to have a business that includes my Muslim sisters. Allah knows best. In my prayers to Allah, I will ask for His mercy and guidance in making the right decision.

Dear Grandmother,

I would like you to know: In searching for God, I have found Islam. I have also found peace within myself and my life is full of joy and happiness. I will never know for sure what was in your thoughts when you stated, "Sometimes, I just wonder!" In my heart, mind, and soul, the words of "Give me that old time religion" is a phrase that relates to my ancestors. I believe that they were robbed of their Islamic religion and brought to America for use as chattel. Recent studies estimate that as many as 05 to 10% of all of the African slaves who were brought to America were Muslims, and that there may have been as many as 400,000 Muslim slaves laboring in North America at some time or another before emancipation.

Further, many of these Muslim slaves were highly educated and could read and write Arabic, and some of them even had university degrees or training. Nonetheless, our women were tortured, raped, and killed, and our men were also tortured and killed. What type of human would treat another human in such a cruel and sadistic way? My grandmother said that my great-grandmother had been a slave. Could she not have been one of those 05 to 10% that had been a Muslim?

All I know from this day forward is that I am thankful to Allah for giving me this religion called Islam. Allah said:

> This day have those who reject faith given up all hope of your religion: yet fear them not but fear Me. This day have I perfected your religion for you, completed my favour upon you, and have chosen for you Islam as your religion. (Qur'an 5: 3b)

Surely, Allah speaks the truth. Allah is most merciful and most gracious when it comes to His servants. I am a servant of Allah. May Allah grant my sisters in Islam peace of mind, and May Allah grant us all good in this life and good in the next life. Oh, Allah, please spare us from the chastisement of the fire. Surely Allah hears the prayers of those who call upon him. I briefly want to mention that I am thankful to Allah for Sister Debra. I would not have been able to write this chapter if it weren't for her kind gesture in asking me to participate in this blessed and wonderful experience. In writing this story, it has broadened my horizon and made me more appreciative of my religion. I am thankful and grateful to Allah for blessing me to sit at my computer and to type my life story.

May Allah bless and guide the sisters who have written their chapters. May He grant us success in this life and the next life, and give us the inspiration to write more stories. Only Allah knows what the future holds for each and everyone of us. All we can do from this point forward is to submit to His will, which is the meaning of Islam. All praises are due to Allah for His mercy, guidance, and blessings.

Waiting for The Prophet Yet To Come

JENNIFER MANZOOR

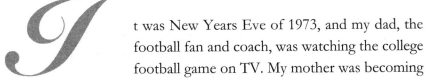t was New Years Eve of 1973, and my dad, the football fan and coach, was watching the college football game on TV. My mother was becoming more and more uncomfortable as she started into labor. However, she was content to wait until the game was over before heading into the hospital. Along the way, Dad decided to stop for gas, which Mom considered to be pushing things a bit. After getting the gas, they went directly to the hospital, and I began trying to put in an appearance. However, the nurse, after preparing everything, felt that we should wait while they located the doctor. Finally Mom told Dad to get the nurse as the baby was coming NOW! The nurse came hurrying back to Mom, and saw that I was indeed coming. Fortunately, the doctor finally showed up, just in the nick of time. Unfortunately, he was slightly inebriated. Mom, who could not wait any longer, just prayed that the intoxicated doctor wouldn't drop me. Thus, on January 1st at 12:45 A.M., I became the first 1974 baby born in the small town

of Chanute, Kansas. While the Doctor was trying to make amends for delaying my appearance into the world, he offered to backdate the birth certificate to before midnight to allow my parents to claim me as a tax deduction for 1973. While my dad thought this was a great idea, my mom was not going to lose the honor of having had the first baby of the new year! The gifts and certificates from the local businesses would just have to make up for Dad's loss of the tax write off.

When I was one year old, Mom and Dad parted ways and divorced. My older brother, Wade, and I remained with Mom after the divorce. One year later, Mom married my stepfather when I was two years old and Wade was five. This resulted in our moving to Kansas City where we lived for the next three years. I guess we did not see much of Dad during this period of my life, as I remember one time when I did not recognize him when he did come to see us. In spite of this separation from my father, I had a very safe and stable childhood.

When I was five years old, we moved to Wichita, where we lived for about a year. When I was six years old, our family moved again and we ended up landing in Andover, Kansas, a small town of about four thousand people, which is located a few miles east of

Wichita. It was small town America, but well within commuting distance of the "big city" of Wichita. One major advantage to being in the Wichita and Andover area was that Wade and I were reunited with our dad who had moved to Andover some time before the rest of us, having previously remarried. Andover was to remain my home throughout most of my youth.

JANURAY 1977: Jenny with her brother Wade

While in Andover, my brother and I attended a private school, which we could afford to do, because we received a tuition discount, since

Dad was the history teacher and football coach at he school. It was a private, non-denominational, Christian school. The core curriculum included Christian studies on a daily basis, and church service on Wednesday mornings. Ironically, my brother and I rarely attended church outside of school. If we did attend church, it was usually for Christmas service. My dad and stepmother occasionally took my brother and me to church when we were little, but that ended when I was about six years old. In contrast, my mom was a firm believer that one did not need to attend church to worship God. I remember that she taught us that God was everywhere, and that He would judge us by our hearts and actions, not on whether we were at church every Sunday morning. I also remember that my mother loved listening to Gospel music. I can't remember who the singer was, but he had a beautiful voice.

I was close to both my dad and my stepfather, and I was a real tomboy due to the influence of Wade. As many families moved in and out of our neighborhood in Andover, the only consistent playmate I had was my brother. His idea of teaching me to play football was to give me the ball and say, "Run, or I will have to hurt you." In fact, many games were played under this threat, but I must have been fairly compliant, because I do not recall him actually "hurting" me with any frequency. In reality, we were always the best of friends.

I remember being a shy child, although my mom claims that I was bossy with other family members. Consistent with my shyness, I was a bookworm, and I loved any subject in school that had us reading stories, whether it was in English class or in reading class. I stayed in the background most of the time during elementary school, despite my love for reading. When I did get any recognition at school, it was always a surprise to me. I recall one time when we were having an awards assembly. All the parents were there, and the teachers were handing out special awards. One teacher said, "She reminds me of

The Little Engine That Could in her determination", and I was shocked when she then announced my name.

When I was in the fourth grade, I was extremely fortunate to have had an exceptionally talented teacher. Mrs. Jones was incredibly good at motivating the whole class and had the knack of making our studies interesting. She was very advantageous for me at that time in my life, as she helped to change how I saw myself. I was struggling with some of the classroom subjects, and she not only noticed but presented a viable solution for this. She told me that she thought I could be a straight "A" student, and offered me a candy bar as an incentive to accomplish that goal. In those days, at least for me, a candy bar was a really big treat, so I studied very hard and tried my best. I ended up surprising myself by actually realizing that straight "A" standing in my classes. She really helped me to believe in myself and in my abilities, and boosted my self-esteem.

There were other special people in my life, including my paternal grandparents who lived on a farm outside Arlington, Kansas. When Dad would take us to visit, Grandma would pack up a picnic lunch for Wade and me, and we would start off on a whole day devoted to exploring and tramping through pastures and woods. Wade and I were like Lewis and Clark, exploring and investigating the uncharted expanses. However, there was one thing that topped a day of exploring the farm, and that was the riding lawn mower. My grandparents would let us drive it! As a result, their grass was the most thoroughly mowed and shortest around. The sighting of any slightly taller blade of grass was cause, or excuse, enough to celebrate, and to drive over and mow it, regardless of how far away it might be!

Grandma died while we were still fairly young. After that, we did not go to the farm very often. However, I have always wondered if the end of visiting my grandparents' farm was not, in fact, a result of a baseball-fetching incident. As I now recall that event, Wade and I were out in the yard and were playing ball. At one point, Wade threw the baseball up, and it lodged on the roof of the chicken coop. This building was old and rickety. However, as I refused to go onto the roof by myself to retrieve the errant baseball, Wade led the way, and I followed a few feet behind. I must have stepped on the wrong spot on the roof, as all of a sudden, I was sailing downward at an alarming rate of speed. I landed headfirst on a railroad tie (a 10 inch by 10 inch post), which was lying on the ground. My two front teeth went right through my bottom lip, and there was blood everywhere. I was frightened by all the blood and certain that my brain was bleeding! My horrified and terrified screams brought Dad at a run. He brushed me off, cleaned me up, and told us to stay off the roofs. However, when he returned us home, Mom gave him quite the earful. I don't recall going to Grandpa's farm after that.

Mrs. Jones and my paternal grandparents were positive and influential forces in my childhood life, but Mom was always the person with whom I was closest. She stayed at home throughout most of my childhood, and always had time for me and my questions. It marked a big change in my life when she resumed her teaching career when I was in junior high school. At school, she was busy teaching children with learning disabilities in the special education program, and when at home she was occupied grading papers. I really missed her having lots of time for me and my questions. This was the first of many changes in our family structure that had a long lasting influence on me.

While in elementary school, I tried Brownies and Bluebirds, but I was not really into any clubs or extracurricular activities until junior high when I started to participate in sports, especially in tennis, track, and basketball. Mrs. Hammersmith was the junior high school gym teacher. Everyone in gym class had to run a mile against the clock. Most only tried to beat what they called the "standard time," so they could move on to other things. Others were the real milers, and they had to work at breaking the "excellent time." Mrs. Hammersmith had noticed that I was a determined person, and decided to make use of that fact. She took me aside, and told me that she thought I had a lot of determination, enough to reach the "excellent time," if I really tried. She said, "If you make up your mind to do anything, you can do it!" Thus, I practiced and ran untold miles until I finally could break that "excellent time" standard.

All through grade school, I was always searching for a way to feel closer to God. My belief in God's existence never wavered, but I continuously questioned the purpose behind our creation. The *Bible* seemed like a collection of stories rather than a guide about how we should lead our lives as Christians. Other than the Ten Commandments, I felt as if there were no boundaries or restrictions being placed upon us. However, the ultimate challenge to my beliefs came in my eighth grade at school. It took place during one of the morning church services at school. The speaker was lecturing on the passage in *John* 14: 15-30 that referred to the promise of the Holy Spirit.

> "If you love me, you will keep my commandments. And I will ask the Father, and he will give you another Advocate, to be with you forever. This is the Spirit of truth, whom the world cannot receive, because it neither sees him nor knows him. You know him, because he abides with you, and he will be in you. I will not leave you orphaned; I am coming to you. In a little while the world will no longer see me, but you will see me; because I live, you also will live. On that day you will know that I am in my Father, and you in me, and I in you. They who have my commandments and keep them are those who love me; and those who love me will be loved by my Father, and I will love them and reveal myself to them." Judas (not Iscariot) said to him, "Lord, how is it that you will reveal yourself

to us, and not to the world?" Jesus answered him, "Those who love me will keep my word, and my Father will love them, and we will come to them and make our home with them. Whoever does not love me does not keep my words; and the word that you hear is not mine, but is from the Father who sent me. I have said these things to you while I am still with you. But the Advocate, the Holy Spirit, whom the Father will send in my name, will teach you everything, and remind you of all that I have said to you. Peace I leave with you; my peace I give to you. I do not give to you as the world gives. Do not let your hearts be troubled, and do not let them be afraid. You heard me say to you, 'I am going away, and I am coming to you.' If you loved me, you would rejoice that I am going to the Father, because the Father is greater than I. And now I have told you this before it occurs, so that when it does occur, you may believe. I will no longer talk much with you, for the ruler of this world is coming. He has no power over me; but I do as the Father has commanded me, so that the world may know that I love the Father. Rise, let us be on our way." (*John* 14: 15-31)

The speaker brought up that there were those who believed this passage was translated incorrectly, and that the passage actually referred to the promise of another prophet who was to come after Jesus. I stopped paying attention after he said that. I was astounded! I remember thinking: "God's message is incomplete. There is another prophet coming." Then, I was gripped by fear. If there was another prophet and more revelation to come after Jesus, then how did I know that I was following the right paths, and that I would go to Heaven. This doubt would later plague me for years, and caused me to turn away from the *Bible*, because it did not hold the answers for which I was looking.

Oh, I would still go to the occasional youth revival or youth group meeting, but I was never able to find satisfactory answers. I knew in my heart that there was more to God's message than what I had been taught, and I had a fervent prayer in my heart that God would not let me die before I learned about the prophet who was to come after Jesus. I must admit that, while I was terrified of dying before I found out about this prophet yet to come, I did not go out actively seeking additional religious knowledge. I was under the impression that the prophet had not yet come. I knew that Judaism came before Christianity, and, as far as I knew then, no one else worshipped the same deity, as did the Jews and Christians. I never even considered Islam as a religious option at that time; because I erroneously thought that Muslims worshipped a different god or idol, and that they viewed women as being inferior.

That very next year, the school dropped its Christian education courses, in order to attract a larger student body. In other words, the message to me was that money was more important than religion. I remember thinking, "If you do not think it is important, why should we (the students) think it is important." While this may have been a convenient excuse for a young girl to shed religion when entering high school late in the 1980's, it was not just a passing thought, but was part of my awakening to the way of the secular and Christian world.

When I was starting my sophomore year in high school, Wade was going away to college. This was the second of the changes to our family structure that left a lasting impact on my life, and left me feeling that I had been set adrift on some uncharted sea. With Wade passing from my immediate and always present circle, life was changing, and I felt abandoned and forsaken.

Despite my feelings of abandonment, there were classes to which I had to direct my energies. My favorite class in high school was German. I loved it! I loved the language, and was learning rapidly. However, I must admit, it did not hurt that I was the only girl in a class of boys. Obviously, my teacher gave me special attention, as she used to call me her "rose among thorns." Otherwise, high school was a really stressful time period from which I do not have a lot of pleasant memories. I was focused on my studies and sports for the first year or so. However, I dropped all sports at the end of my sophomore year.

At sixteen, I was allowed to get a job, so I worked at the Andover Dairy Queen, which I enjoyed. One thing that made it special for me was the assistant manager, Cindy. She was a college student, and Cindy and I really clicked. She even took me walking with her a couple of times at the Heskett Center at Wichita State University (WSU). She convinced the owners of the Dairy Queen to give me a 10-cent raise each month I worked there. This was quite extreme for a teenager. I worked there until the tornado that changed so much of my life.

It was about five or six o'clock in the afternoon on a day in April of 1991. I had been pestering Mom about being allowed to go into Wichita for the day, but Mom had refused, because of some rather ominous weather reports. Mom and I were inside our tri-level home, in the living room, and I was upset about not being allowed to leave for Wichita. My stepfather was still at work. Suddenly, Mom developed a funny feeling that something was amiss weather-wise. She ushered me down into the basement where we turned on the TV to listen for any possible weather alert.

Sitting down there in front of the TV, we were confronted by nothing but the regularly scheduled programming or reports of storms that were quite some distance away. There were no reports of tornados or even severe weather alerts for our area. No weather alert sirens were going off outside. Nonetheless, Mom's feeling persisted, and she turned on the radio to search for any additional news on the weather. No sooner did we get the radio dialed in to the proper frequency than we heard an emergency weather bulletin that a tornado was down on the ground only a block away from our home. Hurriedly, Mom pushed me under a basement bed and crawled beside me.

Cramped under that bed with Mom, all I could hear was Mom loudly praying for our safety and deliverance. Mom would later say that the tornado sounded like a freight train running full speed through water, but all I could hear was Mom's desperate prayer for our safety.

I don't know how much time went by before Mom's praying came to an end. However, she eventually told me to remain under the bed while she ventured up the basement stairs to survey the situation. She reached the landing at the top of the stairs, and I heard her exclaim, "Oh, my God!" I hastily crawled out from under the bed and ran to Mom. We stood there on the landing looking through the passage that once held a door to the main floor. Windows and doors were blown off all over the house, and the house had been noticeably shifted on its foundation. Apparently, the tornado had lifted the house up just enough to turn it slightly, before setting it back down askew on its foundation. Everything in front of our home had been completely flattened by the tornado. Our home, while sitting markedly awry on its foundation, was setting on the edge of an area of several blocks where the tornado had consumed everything. Behind us there was a gap of almost one block and then the tornado touched down again destroying everything in its path.

It took some hours before my stepfather could reach us, as the police had cordoned off the area struck by the tornado. Once he was home, we packed up a few clothes and headed to Wichita where we checked into a hotel. We never moved back to Andover and remained in Wichita. That initial hotel was followed by another hotel. After a few days, we rented an apartment before we finally bought a condominium in Wichita.

While we were physically uninjured by the tornado, we had lost our home and way of life back in Andover. The stress on the entire family was enormous, and our lives were never the same. Mom was placed on antidepressants, and my stepfather responded to the stress by becoming a workaholic. In the midst of this chaotic environment, I managed to convince them that I should attend Wichita Heights High School, which my best friend was already attending, for my senior year of high school. It was a decision I regret until this day.

This tornado marked the single biggest change in my youth. It was immediately thereafter that I became a full-fledged, acting-out teenager. I became rebellious and irresponsible. I lied and was manipulative. I even became disrespectful and disobedient to my parents and family. I was going on a downhill slide, and all sorts of things were going wrong in my life. Even the friends that I kept were the wrong ones. They were the kinds of friends that all parents hope their children will never have, and they were into doing things that all parents hope their children will never do. I was truly forlorn. I felt lost and confused, and gradually I started down a dark path from which I would not emerge for several years.

I no longer saw any answers, restrictions, or boundaries. I disrespected my parents by not obeying them, and by lying to them about my whereabouts. I would scream and curse at them about what terrible people they were, and yelled that they should just let me do whatever I wanted to do. It was the beginning of six years of my life that I would like to erase from existence. Those six years caused me

so much pain and grief…I will never forgive myself for not only what I did to my family, but also what I did to myself.

Despite my anchorless lifestyle and acting-out, I graduated from Wichita Heights High School in 1992, and started my college career

High School Graduation, May 1992:
Jennifer with her father and Grandpa Bainum

that fall by attending the University of Kansas (KU) in Lawrence,

Kansas. For me, KU meant complete freedom, no rules, no anything. I was living in the KU Towers, but all my friends were "off campus". Many of them were a year or more older than I, and they were mostly not attending their classes. Despite their influence, I was an okay student for my freshman year, managing to obtain all A's and B's, with the exception of C's obtained in two courses that I did not like or attend.

I can remember going to see my assigned academic counselor (who was to advise me on a major and how to proceed through college, etc.) early in my freshman year. I told her that I wanted to major in German, and asked about careers with this field of study. The only thing she told me was that there was no career for a person with a degree in German, unless one wanted to teach. That was the beginning and end of her help. I was so very lost. I needed boundaries and focus, but was literally set adrift to sink or swim. I sank. During the first semester of my sophomore year, I had to drop out, because I was otherwise going to fail all my courses, as I was neither doing the work nor attending classes.

My college career over, I moved to a small town in Kansas in the hopes of trying to find myself. I met my future husband during this time. We married in December of 1994. He had been previously married and had a son by that prior marriage. Thinking back on it, I realize that the signs that he was not ideal husband material were there before we married, but he asked, and I accepted without a backward glance. Why not? I had nothing better to do, and I really had no aspirations for this marriage, no dreams. It was not until after I found myself married that I started thinking at all, and then it was a little late.

My marriage was a disaster, and I was sinking fast. Nonetheless, my mom was always there for me, even in this difficult time. As rudderless as I felt, she had never abandoned me. My parents even initiated help for me one time, but I was not ready to be helped, and

I ended up going back to my husband. Even then, Mom seemed to understand that I needed to work through this myself, but always let me know that she would stand by me. I still had a ways to go before I could accept the needed changes. In the meantime, Mom listened to my tearful telephone calls.

I was working, supporting my husband and family, and was taking a couple of classes at the local college. I completed one class just before my first daughter was born. The second class was to have the final on the 27th of June. However, Courteney arrived on the 26th. Before her birth, I had arranged with the professor of that second class that if I gave birth before the course ended, I could belatedly take the final examination, and still get credit for the class. However, after Courteney's arrival, I was so busy with her that I never got around to taking that belated final examination. Imagine my surprise and gratitude when I discovered that the professor had not only passed me, but had given me an A.

During this time, right after Courteney's birth, there was one unexpected bright spot to lighten the hopeless and forlorn road on which I found myself. I started a new job as a temporary worker for a small company just outside of town. The people there were wonderful to me! The boss was Gary Campbell, and his wife Dorothy also worked at the company part time. They were both very supportive and helpful, making me feel wanted and accepted. Even the other people who worked there were nice, kind, and caring. Just shortly after they gave me a full time and permanent position, I discovered that I was again pregnant. I felt that I was letting them down tremendously to quit right then. I spent time in Gary's office crying my eyes out. I just did not know what to do.

I had changed into a person that I could not recognize, and it wasn't until after the birth of my first daughter that I started to recognize what a dark and twisted path my life was taking. My first daughter helped me begin to see what was wrong with my life and with how I was living it. However, I was stubborn and thick headed. Fortunately, God knew all that about me. With time, I am sure that I would have changed my habits, but it would have probably been after I had done irreparable harm to my daughter and myself. God knew this, and He saved me from myself through the gift of my second daughter.

My first daughter was only nine months old when I found out I was pregnant. The news of a pregnancy should be grounds for elation; however, the pregnancy hit me hard. I was actually distraught, because I had finally gained enough sense to leave my husband and had filed for divorce. My husband was also surprised about the pregnancy and became convinced that the baby was not his. I had not been unfaithful, but his accusations made me feel ashamed, and I knew he would never accept the child. He offered to give me money to have an abortion, and I seriously considered this possibility for a while. However, after talking to some people at an abortion clinic in Wichita, I just suddenly knew that I had to keep the baby, and that I needed to turn back to God for help. I remember calling my mom, scared of what she was going to say, certain that she would tell me to have the abortion. I told her that I was pregnant, that I had looked into getting an abortion but that I had decided to keep the baby and that I wanted to move back to Wichita to be near family and friends. My mother never ceased to amaze me. Despite the abuse that I had heaped on her for the past six years, and in spite of all the stress and worry she had suffered because of the stupid choices that I had made, she was very forgiving and supportive. She was glad that I had chosen not to have an abortion, and that I wanted to move back home. She helped me turn my life around.

My divorce was finalized in February of 1997, and I was terrified of facing life as a single parent. In March of 1997, my mom came, packed me up, and moved Courteney and me back to Wichita. Before leaving work, Gary and Dorothy gave me a wonderful party. Dorothy gave me a pack of starbursts as a joke, saying that I should have one fruit a day. The whole staff had put money into a piggybank for me. What a great gift this was for a single mother who was starting out on a new life! It meant the world to me.

From the time when my grade school had stopped having religion courses at the end of my eighth grade year, I had not had any real religious training or affiliation. Plus, from the time of the tornado until I hung up the telephone after talking to the abortion clinic, I had not thought about God. I think I had managed to almost forget that He even existed. Now, it was time to turn back to Him, although I was not exactly sure how to do that.

For six long years, I had been too proud and too embarrassed to go back to my parents. However, they not only came and moved me back to Wichita, they rented an apartment for me, provided financial and moral support, and helped me get my footing. I went to work for my stepfather, as it would have been very difficult to find a job while being pregnant. They babysat Courteney for me, and Mom was the one in attendance at the birth of my second daughter. Faith was born on September 30, 1997. Just over a month before Faith was born, I started back to school at Wichita State University.

I did not expect to ever marry again. I was a working girl (still for my stepfather). I did not date, did not want to see a man. I was just going to get on with life with my two daughters. Even with the support of my family, this was a very trying time. My ex-husband called every six months or so, and would only ask about the older of our daughters, never having really accepted the second daughter as having been his. As he never saw her as a baby, he could not have known that at that time she had some of his features. He never came to see the girls, even though he would make it a point to go see his son by his former marriage. After a long delay, he finally did start to pay some child support.

These were still challenging times for me, but God began working so many miracles in my life through my mother and my children. However, I was still unsure how to show my gratitude and devotion to Him. I thought about attending church, but it just did not seem like the right path. Then, God answered the prayer I had been fervently making for years. He led me to His final prophet.

June of 1998 found me busy with my girls, work, school, and family. I took an evening off to go out with an old girlfriend who happened to be in town. At one point that evening, as I was momentarily sitting at our table alone, Nasir, a lifelong Muslim and my current husband, walked by on his way to leave the establishment. He suddenly felt drawn to speak to me, even though it was his policy to have nothing to do with women who were out alone. When he finally paused and spoke to me, my first instinct was to stay away from him. One look at him, and I was certain that he was a wife beater, and that he came from a country where women were oppressed, and where they had their children taken away from them for not obeying their husbands. Of course, I had no accurate idea of what country he was from, but just knew that he was not native to the United States!

I mentioned something about my perceptions of him, and he asked me where I thought he was from. I told him he looked like he was from the Middle East, but was informed that he was from Pakistan. In a complete reversal of his usual behavior, he asked me out. Still caught up in my mistaken illusions, I told him that I had two young daughters, and that I was not a submissive woman. He gave me a strange look and asked me what I was talking about. As I spewed forth my ignorance and all my mistaken and erroneous stereotypes, I became aware that the more we talked the more comfortable I was beginning to feel.

Personal comfort and his rational explanations aside, my mind was busy thinking he was probably a wife beater who would want me to wait on him hand and foot. In truth, I knew less than nothing about Islam, and I just assumed that he was an idol worshiper, as that is what I thought Islam was all about. While all this was running around in my brain, he was gently smiling at me, then he asked if we could meet somewhere and just talk for a while if I didn't want to go out with him. He was so nice and polite that I could not totally refuse him, so I settled for giving him my phone number, without setting a time and place for another meeting. I thank Allah that He sent me such a patient and understanding man. My husband later admitted that after our second "date" (we never went anywhere, we would just sit at my apartment with the girls and talk), he thought about never calling me again, because I already had two kids, and because my family would probably be as ignorant about Islam and Pakistani culture as I was. However, Allah opened his heart, and we were married within six months.

During our first meeting he had dispelled many of the myths I had about Muslims, but I still did not believe much of what he told me. I started looking on the Internet for websites and for books that I could order to learn more about Islam. I also went to Borders, a large bookstore in Wichita, and browsed through their limited, but surprisingly unbiased, books on Islam. I had found my answers! I could not put the books down, reading two or three at a time! Each time that I talked to Nasir, I bombarded him with more questions about Islam and demanded clarifications regarding certain information that I had recently read. I was ecstatic! Of course, I didn't embrace everything wholeheartedly and all at once. I still had issues with why Muslim women had to cover and Muslim men didn't. I kept wanting to hear more reassurance and clarification about the role of women within the religion of Islam, as I had yet to develop enough patience, and still haven't, to be a stay at home mom twenty-four hours a day, seven days a week. I also wanted to understand why so many people were so afraid of Islam that they felt the need to distort its beliefs and teachings.

Despite all my questions and doubts, I began to know that I would eventually become a Muslim. Allah had brought me to this point and had opened my heart to His word. I could not turn my back after He had brought me to the path that would lead me to Heaven. However, I was afraid of how my family might respond to having a Muslim in their midst. Furthermore, at that point in time, even though I knew I would become a Muslim, Nasir and I had not discussed marriage. As such, I thought that my journey into Islam would be a path I would have to follow on my own and by myself. As one example of my concern about how my family might respond to my becoming a Muslim, I remember a discussion that I had with my dad when he first met Nasir. He told me not to marry or get involved with a Muslim, because Muslims were fanatical and treated their women badly. I knew that by making my own journey into Islam, I was risking the possibility of losing my family. However, by this time, I also knew that Islam was the path for which I had been searching for so many years.

I discovered that Islam was what I had been looking for by the time I was half ways through my first book on Islam, a book that was authored by reverts to Islam. I was surprised to discover that some of the same prophets and stories were as central to Islam as they were in Christianity. However, my understanding of Christianity was still flawed at that time. For instance, I thought that Lot/Lut (peace be upon him) was not a prophet, but just someone whose biographical story appeared in the *Bible*. I had to relearn about Christianity, as I learned about Islam. The only prophets who I was certain that Christianity recognized, were Noah/Nuh, Abraham/Ibrahim, and Moses/Musa, (peace be upon them all). Then, of course, there was the issue of the prophethood of Jesus/Isa (peace be upon him). While I was aware of stories about other people in the *Bible*, I had never realized that they were actually prophets.

I was not the only one who did not have a perfect understanding and practice of my childhood religion. Nasir always went to the *Jumaah* (Friday noon) prayer, but doing five prayers every day was not easy for him, although he always accomplished at least two or three of them. However, as soon as he met someone who came along and challenged his ideas and religious practice, like I did, he became a lot more conscientious about his religious practice and tried to do better.

Between the books and the conversations with Nasir, I knew that Islam was for me. In many ways, it was all over except for the formal announcement of my reversion to Islam. However, after all the help and comfort they had been to me, I did not want my family to think that I was turning my back on them. I put off doing *Shahadah*, the Islamic testimony of faith whereby a non-Muslim becomes a Muslim, to give me time to introduce them slowly both to Nasir and to Islam.

As I now reflect back on it all, I realize that over the years there were many things that bothered me about Christianity, many areas where I had unanswered questions. For many of these questions, I am now able to find answers within Islam. For example, I was always curious why it was that after Jesus came his followers supposedly did not need to obey all the divine rules and laws that had been given before him. What exactly was the reason that the Mosaic laws of the *Old Testament* were not "in effect" on the Christians? Shouldn't Christians refrain from eating pork? Christians eat pork all the time and think it is okay. Yet, that is not what the *Bible* says!

The pig, for even though it has divided hoofs and is cleft-footed, it does not chew the cud; it is unclean for you. Of their flesh you shall not eat, and their carcasses you shall not touch; they are unclean for you (*Leviticus* 11: 7-8).

And the pig, because it divides the hoof but does not chew the cud, is unclean for you. You shall not eat their meat, and you shall not touch their carcasses (*Deuteronomy* 14: 8).

"Do not think that I have come to abolish the law or the prophets; I have come not to abolish but to fulfill" (*Matthew* 5: 17).

Jennifer Manzoor

When I was a Christian, it never made sense to me that we ignored so much of what the *Bible* actually said, and that realization had been a source of discomfort in my life for many years. Now, as a Muslim who is encased in Allah's religion of Islam, I can begin to see how a rebellious or ignorant mankind had either misinterpreted or changed the actual words of Allah in the book of the *Injil* (Gospel) that Prophet Jesus originally gave to his people.

I also think the women's libbers ought to figure out that Islam is their best religious alternative. First of all, there is this thing in Christianity that Eve was the evil tool of the Devil, and tempted poor Adam into trying the forbidden fruit of the tree of knowledge. As a result, Adam and Eve became aware of their nakedness, covered their loins with fig leaves, and were thrown out of the Garden of Eden. Not only that, but all the descendants of Adam and Eve right down to this very day are stuck with the inheritance of their original sin. Traditional Christianity says that all this came about because of just one little act on the part of Eve. Now, that is a lot to blame on one sex.

In Islam, Prophet Adam and his mate are both guilty of eating the fruit. It was a shared choice and a shared punishment. However, there is no concept of original sin in Islam. According to the teachings of Islam, we are all, male and female, born pure Muslims, and stay that way until we reach the age of rational choice. Then, we must each exercise our freedom to choose. Whether we recognize it or not, even refusing to choose is a choice. Secondly, Islam not only freed me from my questions, but it liberated me from my understanding of my role in the world. I found Islam's teaching that the men were to care for the women reassuring after having had a bad marriage where I had been both the breadwinner and the child bearer. Also, in Islam, I was free to work or go to school, but if I worked, the money that I earned was my own. As a Muslim, I was not expected to put my earnings into the family budget, as had been the case for me before I became a Muslim.

Plus, I had finally found the prophet that was yet to come after Jesus. To me this was like a postscript that changed the entire meaning of everything I had known before.

In November of 1998, Nasir and I were initially married before a justice of the peace. We then went to the *Masjid* (mosque) where I said the *Shahadah*. Immediately after my formal statement of the *Shahadah*, we were married in an Islamic ceremony and under an Islamic marriage contract by Sheykh Siddiqi. I had known that I was Muslim for some time before this, and my marriage was just a convenient time to say *Shahadah*, although I sometimes wish I had done it officially earlier, as many people incorrectly assume that I became a Muslim because my husband was a Muslim. I make a point of clarifying that I did not become a Muslim because of my husband. My husband will even point out to people that he had very little to do with my becoming a Muslim. Nasir never pushed me to be Muslim, but he helped me to understand what Islam was, and what it meant to be Muslim, although his understanding and practice were not always perfect at that time. For example, one thing that enhances my memories of our wedding day is that he did not know about doing *Mahr* (the "dowry" given to the bride by the groom), so when the Sheykh asked for the *Mahr* at our wedding, Nasir had to borrow money from one of his friends in order to pay it to me. By the way, it needs to be emphasized that the *Mahr* was not paid to my parents for me, but was rather paid to me to do with as I pleased.

At times, I have been accused of not having had a strong faith in God, and that is why I converted to Islam "so easily." The people who make those judgments do not know my heart and mind. I had been searching for a way to feel closer to God for so long and had finally simply found Him. Also, in Prophet Muhammad, I had found that elusive prophet that was yet to come.

I tend to tell others who ask about Islam to wait to convert until they are sure of every detail. However, that is not what I did. I made sure Islam was the religion for me, and then made my private *Shahadah*, even though I waited to do my public one until my wedding day.

One sad thing was impacting my happy life while I was getting to know Nasir and coming to understand Islam. My stepfather and mother divorced in 1998. It was really quite traumatic for me as my relationship with my stepfather was and is so close. He is still a part of my family, both for me and for my children. I continued working for him until this year when I started nursing school at Wichita State University and changed my place of employment to work at a hospital to reinforce my training at nursing school.

I did have some questions about why Muslim women dress the way they do. I was not at all certain I would like giving up the freedom that I thought came from my American style of clothing. I thought of my clothing as a type of self-expression. I looked at the scarves and loose, "modest" clothing of Muslim women and was very unconvinced that I would feel like myself in it, let alone find it not only comfortable, but comforting. Once I decided, and it most definitely was my decision, to try the clothing, I was amazed at the feeling of total freedom that comes from being inside these clothes. They are not binding, and I no longer have to be concerned about anything showing. It moves with me, and flows around me, without being in my way, allowing me to concentrate on everything else. It was a freedom that I had never experienced before. However, one frustration that remains is trying to explain this to anyone else. It just does not translate into words as easily as it does into practice.

A little more than a year after Nasir and I married, my third daughter, Hadiya, was born on January 25th, 2000, adding extra joy and bliss to our lives. Our family was blessed and expanded simultaneously.

Finally in 2001, my ex-husband came to see my two older daughters during Courteney's fifth birthday. At that time, he agreed to give both of his daughters up for adoption. With Nasir's adopting them, we changed their first names as part of the adoption procedure, so that we now have Anesa (Courteney) and Iman (Faith – the Arabic word *Iman* may be translated as *faith*) as well as baby Hadiya. However, we did not change the girls' last name, as Islam requires that their identification with their biological father not be severed.

SPRING 2001:
Daughters (L to R)
Iman, Anesa and Hadiya

I was recently asked what is the best thing about my marriage to Nasir, and I immediately said, "Everything!" Nasir is a wonderful father and is very patient with both me and the children. He takes good care of us. He even cooks! Plus, in a final behavioral refutation of my one-time misconceptions, he does not expect me to wait on him hand and foot! He is what every red-blooded American woman want: a faithful, caring husband

and provider who allows me the freedom and time to explore my own agenda and who supports me as I tackle that agenda.

One of the concepts that has come to my attention since joining Islam is that not all the misconceptions about religion are what the Christians do not know about Islam. It is just as easy for a Muslim to misunderstand Christianity. Misunderstanding and erroneous conceptions are just not a one-way street. How confusing is Christianity if seen only through the following exposure to it? By the way, I should note that the following is a true story. A new Muslim to our country met a single woman who was a self-professed "devout Christian". She even wore a ring on her finger like a wedding ring, in order to signify her marriage to Jesus. However, she did not let this stop her from having casual sex. She would just take off the ring before having casual or recreational sex, and would then put it back on afterwards. If this type of behavior were accepted as normal Christian practice, it would give a pretty distorted view of Christianity.

Not all the issues with my family about Islam are fully resolved, even though they did not take my conversion as hard as some other sisters' families have done. Some of the members of my very extended family have felt that I am now an anti-Israel fanatic and extremist, because I once participated in a peace walk for Palestinians. This was a local, peaceful demonstration in support of the Palestinians. It was not anti anything, and its participants included Christians as well as Muslims.

Unfortunately, I have not yet been able to explain Islam well enough to Wade so that he can agree with my embracing Islam. However, I ask Allah to give me the right words and ask Allah to guide Wade. It is not nice to have to face disagreements within your own family. One thing that I simply cannot understand is my family's positions on what is acceptable and what is not. To me, it is totally illogical to accept Wade's lifestyle and not mine. I have tried to break it down logically and cannot find any. Wade does not accept Christianity, and he openly claims that the *Bible* no longer applies to us and is outdated. He says he will never marry and that he has no desire to marry, although he stays sexually active. How can this lifestyle possibly be more acceptable to a family of devout Christians than mine as a follower of Allah, the same God that is talked about in the *Old Testament?* Surely, my current lifestyle is closer to the life example of Jesus, along with the lifestyle of a whole host of other prophets, than is Wade's. However, despite our differences, Wade and I do remain close. When we see each other, especially if we are the only two present, it is right back to how it always has been, and I treasure that tremendously.

I feel that I can discuss Islam with my mom, and that is a blessing from Allah. She has been willing to read up on Islam, and to try to understand why I love it so. She always told me, "You can talk to God regardless of where you are, and He will always listen." This belief fits perfectly with Islam.

Meanwhile, I continue to benefit from Islam. I like the structure and the form of Islam. I like knowing the rules and having those rules be specific. For example, a Muslim must fast during the Islamic month of *Ramadan,* unless one of the following criteria is met: one is traveling; one is unable to fast because of impaired health; one is menstruating; or one is bleeding from childbirth (within 40 days of the birth of one's last child). If any of these apply, a Muslim must make up the days not fasted later in the year, unless one's health does not allow fasting at all (like in the case of a

December 2001:
Jenny's mom

diabetic or a cancer patient on chemotherapy). In that case, the Muslim must feed an indigent person for one day for every day not spent in the prescribed fasting, if one is financially able to do so. These rules are easy to follow as they are so concise and clear.

Another benefit that I derive from Islam is that I never feel inferior for being a woman. I have my own set of rights, and these rights were divinely ordained for me in the *Qur'an*. I can have my own money and property, and hold them independently from my husband and family. As a Muslim woman, cooking, laundry, and housekeeping chores are not my labor in life. These rules are also clear and easily comprehensible. I find it freeing to know where I stand and to be able to work within that structure, rather than guessing and hoping that everything will work out somehow.

In spite of the perfection of Islam, the Muslim *Ummah* (community) still has some problems. Muslims are human, and thus not perfect. Only Allah is Perfect. As I look at our *Ummah*, I want to pull all the factions and parts together and erase any and all divisions of nationalities, ethnicity, and cultures. These differences are for sharing our uniqueness, not for creating divisions. The night I took my *Shahadah*, there were a couple of Arab sisters at the *Masjid*. They were very helpful and friendly to me, and I looked forward to meeting them again. The very next night I went to the *Masjid*, as it was during *Ramadan*. As we gathered for the evening meal to break our fasts, I found the same two sisters and was so very delighted to find them. However, they took me over to another American sister who was married to a Pakistani, introduced me to her, and promptly left. I was amazed and somewhat hurt, as it was obvious they did not want to work with me. Fortunately the sister to whom I was introduced was very kind, and I am quite fond of her. Nonetheless, it did show me right away that there are some cracks in our *Ummah*. The members of the various cultures within the *Ummah* need to be more accepting of those who are outside their experience, and need to include everyone whenever possible. There are plenty of sisters and brothers that can translate, and they need to take the time and effort to do so whenever they have a person within their midst who is not fluent in the language being spoken at the moment.

Currently, one of my greatest joys is when people approach me in public, and ask questions about Islam. I love to explain what a great joy it is, and why I am a Muslim. I always have loved the comparative religion aspect of my journey into Islam. Perhaps the reason why I like to explain it so much is that it is such a special gift from Allah. I have often wished that I could have been born a Muslim, rather than having to have found my way through the Christian and secular world to my final religious home in Islam. However, I do not believe that I could have appreciated Islam the way I do now, if it had not been for my own personal passage into Islam, whereby I found the light of Allah shining on me.

Back To Square 1

STEPHANIE PARLOVE

Before you begin my journey: some events in my life have been quite harsh; I blame no one. I thank Allah for cozying me into an entire family of completely imperfect people. That's where I learned the best stuff: to forgive, to respect, to work hard and do my best every single day – regardless of the outcome – to love, be loyal, to move forward and through and to give thanks. My parents did great! They love me and I love them back. Allah be praised!

If life is a Stephen King novel, mine has been IT. Yes, there were big, ugly, scary spiders, but none of them were aliens and that is not the point I am trying to make. One of Stephen King's observations on how children handle a horrific experience goes something like this: they are able to encounter demons in the morning and return the same afternoon to enjoy a nice picnic and a good game of make believe. Children, with their expanded consciousness, as yet unsullied by the demands of society, are able to roll the abominable and the splendid into their reality and accept them without judgement.

Mr. King was able to say in a sentence or two what I couldn't articulate: kids don't hold their experiences up to the goodness scale, they just experience. It's later in life that we come back and weigh where we've been and determine the goodness quotient or evil factor in the events that have befallen us. It is in this light I remember my childhood, my early childhood especially, with a warmth and sweet fondness that surpasses my reality.

I was born in Long Island, New York. My first five years were blissfully spent in the old family home purchased by my Grandpa and Grandma Wujick in 1926 or thereabouts. It was as extraordinary a place to live as a child could imagine. It smelled great in every season, at all times. Fresh. Mom left the windows open as often as the weather allowed and to this day sheer curtains tossing lightly in a breeze take my breath away and overwhelm me with emotion. Sheers, as well as dark forest green and deep red anything will stop me immediately and send me swirling into childhood joys. My world was vibrant then.

Our home territory covered three lushly landscaped acres. We have the gardening gene in our family, giving weeds little chance of survival and fairly well ensuring a treasure trove of greenery; but the Long Island home stands alone when it comes to types and numbers of foliage, trees and adornments to soothe the soul. It was a landscaping lollapalooza. The property was bordered and cross-sectioned into four somewhat equal squares (see illustration: pg. 247) by six foot tall, thick, bushy hedges sporting waxy green leaves and some sort of inedible berry in the spring. The hedges were a garden-ing extravaganza providing an air of complete privacy and yet were not foreboding enough to ward off the creation of secret passages and escape routes masterminded by us wee folk. The house itself – a giant in its' time – was in actuality, a modest, wood frame, two-story, attic, basement number with an enormous wooden front porch. For all the

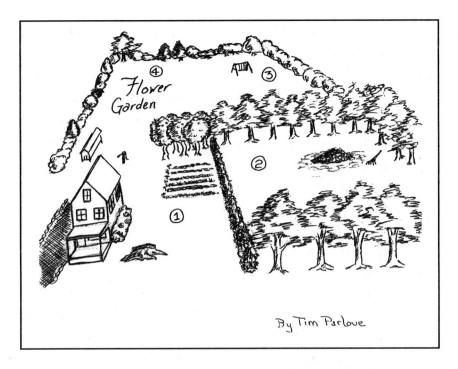

By Tim Parlove

acreage, the house and the driveway bumped right up to the property line on what I'll call the left side (as I do not know the direction and there is no one left who does) and faced the street. The square (heretofore referred to as Square I) including our house was host to Grandpa's vegetable garden, no doubt, the best place to take a salt shaker on a summer's day. We were unobtrusively under the watchful eye of the master gardener as we enjoyed the plump, red, juicy tomatoes – paying due respect not to crush or damage any of the precious plants. In retrospect, Square I was clearly my favorite. In addition to the veggie garden, the apple trees grew in Square I and my grandpa would climb the trees and throw down the ripe apples for me to catch. Mostly I ran after them as they bounced on the ground, but Pop Pop always commended my apple catching abilities and I had no reason to doubt him. He would then wash and cut the apples for us and we would enjoy them mightily. My source of income grew in Square I –

hydrangeas of colors I can't even describe with words. These mammoth beasts of beauty I would pick, with all the care four-year-old fingers can muster, and sell to the neighbors for a penny. Due to the inherent stealthy nature of four, I thought I was running this business on the sly, but in actuality the neighbors were calling my mother, telling her where I was and asking her permission to purchase the beautiful flowers I offered. Most of my daily activities took place within the joyful confines of Square I, that's where the old water pump was, that's where the cellar was, that's where my Pop Pop spent his time gardening with me gleefully in tow. Square II, which shouldered Square I and also faced the street, was a great expanse of lawn. Three sides were laced with dogwood trees and other leafy Behemoths that obliging dropped their foliage at the onset of winter. From my point of view Square II was good for two things: 1. Running away from home – which I did twice, both times neglecting to take any food and packing my little suitcase with dolls for their extraordinarily good company. And 2. The raking of leaves in the fall, when Pop Pop would drag both leaves and me around on a tarp. All over that green expanse we would travel, swishing and circling – until I could take no more laughter and joy – rolling off the tarp to lie exhausted on the carpet of lawn.

In a child's eye, Square III really didn't have much going for it. The swing set was there, but there was much too much to do in Square I to play there often.

Square IV held treasures. The old chicken coop – used for paratrooper exercises when the cousins came to play and no adults were watching, and a flower garden extraordinaire. The Lily of the Valley lived here. Magic grew in Square IV and it was five feet high or taller. Walking in this Square was like living in *The Secret Garden*, a world all its own, perfect, fragrant, delicate tiny flowers winking and waving; immaculately groomed, kid safe and never off limits.

I have few memories of either my mother or my father during this time of my life, but my father's hand was in each bloom and delicious scent that delighted us on the light breezes of sweet spring days. He was in every peaceful moment I shared with my Pop Pop. He was the back-breaking work behind all that grew at our home then, and Pop Pop was still the Master Gardener. That's where my father was then. He was in the respect and pride he allowed my Grandfather, he was in the quiet sustenance he provided for Pop Pop by slipping him money, in addition to paying the mortgage and caring for all his needs. He was

POP AND DAD
... picking strawberries from the Garden of Square I

in the dignity my grandpa had until the day he died. It was a raucously good five plus years.

We were inside taking a break, my sweet Pop Pop and I, when the soft ka-thump of my world crashing emanated from the bathroom. He was down. No worry. A seizure. At that time there weren't the epilepsy miracle drugs we have available today. My little feet went running to get Mom, my young faith as yet undistorted by the quirky turns of life. Pop Pop died. No more walks, no more apples, never again does anyone ride me around in the leaves, no more long adventures with an ice cream or candy treat in the middle, no more best friend. Gone forever. I did not understand death then and I do not understand it now.

I am, however, a testament to the concept of our early childhood years being the most significant and am convinced that the intense love and devotion of my sweet Grandpa did indeed, provide the strength that has carried me through thus far.

Back at the ranch...two of the eight (there are nine counting my father) brothers and sisters wanted "their inheritance." One of the eight, my sweet Aunt Jackie stood on two premises: (1) with the exception of my father, none of them ever paid for anything, not the house and certainly not the care of my Pop Pop; (2) their inheritance is their US citizenship – the greatest treasure they could have, next to God. But there's greed at work here and my father says "never argue about money, let it go." And he walked. The property was sold to a contractor who built a house in each of the squares. They each pocketed a few thousand bucks and with the exception of my sweet Aunt, my father, although loving them all and never speaking of the sale of

THE 10-YEAR OLD STEPHANIE
....already a shovel in hand
and working with rocks!

the house again, had very little contact with them from then on. We're going to California.

My life-long love of road trips began when my parents packed us all up in a flashy, turquoise, 1959 Buick Special. The colors on this tugboat were so bright, you were blinded just looking at it for more than 4.2 seconds at a time. I was six then. My sister Mary was two and my sister Ellen, eight. We were the back seat contingent. There were no seatbelt laws and we were three, free-flying, young girls bouncing those fully padded seats from New York to California. I was in charge of watching the gas tank – it was to become a lifelong obsession – apparently, I took that job seriously. We saw every sight along that New York-California Route, but we never stopped at more than five of them, not counting motels. Dad made the trip in three days – the back seat noise compelled him to make it to California in record time no doubt. One of my great loves began with the Painted Desert in Arizona – the mochas and muted pinks, faded and washed greens, warm breezes accompanied by the quiet, quiet tones of desert life. Being there was the first peace I had experienced since the death of Pop Pop. Give me a desert any day, any time – it's where I can hear my spirit whisper and feel the hand of Allah brush against my life; my heart is free there in the shifting, sandy places.

We moved to our new home and I was happy. There were massive dirt piles beyond our house as we lived in a new development and almost every weekend when the wonders of the California fall rolls around, my father drove us to the desert in the turquoise monster to pick up the beautiful rocks with which he landscaped. Today as I write, there is a dirt pile in my back acre that is approximately fifteen feet high and runs 60'-75' long, maybe forty feet wide. My husband, Tim, would like to use this material to fill over the leech field, a sensible thing to do; but I would like to just keep it as is, a spiritual thing to do.

I have just finished collecting rocks from the side of the road to finish a landscaping project (Allah sent in my dreams, but that is a whole 'nother ballgame) that my children call "the crop circle." So this rock/dirt connection was my father, and it is me. My sister, Mary, has a modified version, in that she will climb any rock, anytime, anyplace. She's like a petite, well-groomed, mountain goat. So two of the three of us have some form of the rock and dirt gene passed down from at least two generations before us.

New houses, rocks, and childhood mountains gave way to the fall and a new school year where I spent a large portion of the initial semester of first grade outside the classroom door crying. Everyday I started crying for apparently no reason. Voluminous, constant, yet quiet tears would trail down my six-year-old face. Of course, I was finally grieving for my Pop Pop. The teacher couldn't tolerate this behavior. Apparently she couldn't take the time to call my mother, either, as my mother claims to this day she had no idea I spent a significant portion of my first grade experience cleaning the hallway with tears. One day I stopped crying. I was just finished. Until I sat to write this "sharing," I had not cried again for my Pop Pop.

Life was smooth in kidland until I was ten and my maternal grandfather molested me while we were on a trip to New York. The Stephen King observation applies to this portion of my life, thereby, leaving this to be dealt with at a later date.

My Paternal Grandmother was Russian Orthodox, and, although she attended an Orthodox Church in New York on occasion, the family was 100%, bona fide, New York children of immigrants, first generation, US citizen, Catholic. This was a tough group. They lived and breathed the Catholic Church; many of them still do. Don't forget, my Dad had nine kids in his family, all but one had children (he did have an awesome trained parakeet who lived in birdy splendor); and my mother had five in her family – all but one had children (no parakeet). That's twenty-seven aunts and uncles, one parakeet, and around thirty cousins. The stereotype of working hard Monday through Friday, partying on Saturday and asking for forgiveness on Sunday was no doubt, created from watching two generations of my extended family.

We moved to California to build a new life, new connections, still the Catholic Church. My mom and dad hooked up with a brand new congregation and helped build a church from the ground up. We belonged to something again. Weekends became a time of gathering, hard work, and potlucks. My mother, who to this day is the most social person I know, made (and still does) friends everywhere, at church, in the neighborhood, walking down the street, standing in line at the grocery store. Our world started to grow. Upon the completion of the church and school buildings, Catechism (religious instruction) began on Saturday for the young ones and one weeknight, per week for the teens. We being the young ones attended on Saturday. Our schedule was school Monday through Friday, Catechism on Saturday, church on Sunday with perky hats, or the

Mexican mantillas we all came to love: crisp, pastel, flowered dresses, white ruffled socks, patent leather shoes in white or black; and pancake breakfast after church – these were the days of fasting before communion and that pancake breakfast was nothing short of divine inspiration.

Church was not next-door. We were on the road almost as much then as I am now and now I live twenty-seven miles from the nearest good-sized town. I thank Allah for Catechism. If it wasn't for my Catholic "learning experience," it might have been too easy to leave my search for God incomplete, to accept the norm and to live happily ever after. But the holes and unanswered questions, or my favorite response "have faith," which sounded remarkably to my young ears like "go away little girl," told me there was a mystery to be solved.

I was a quiet child up until ten years old, but quiet didn't eliminate curious and I was on the God trail.

There wasn't enough faith in the cosmos to cover the crucifixion theory, AND since Mother Theresa (I loved that woman – and I am not referring to the one in Calcutta; I am referring to the one in Southern California) had assured me a mustard seed's worth (of faith) was all we needed. I even had the mustard seed necklace; I knew how very little faith that was. The entire concept of God's only begotten son dying by crucifixion prompted me to suspect "something is rotten in Denmark" as my daddy was known to quip.

Even so very young, I realized one person could not have all the answers and that not all people knew everything. So year after year I continued to ask the same questions:

1. Why if You had all the power in the universe would you allow your only son to be crucified?

2. Why, if You were God, would You need a son at all?

3. Why would we need saints?

4. Why do we need to confess to a priest? Why can't God listen on

His own – He doesn't have time, not enough ears, what?

5. What's the deal with purgatory? And what if you don't have some-one to pray you out of there faster – which lacks certain fairness?

6. Babies and limbo – no baby baptism, and it's limbo for the baby. It's a baby for goodness sake!

At some point after my first holy communion (as though we really accepted that body and blood of Jesus Christ (pbuh) concept), I started counting my sins at night, mortal and venial. I couldn't fall asleep, wondering if I was "good enough" to make it into Heaven, or if I was too sinful. My only hope was to die after communion and before I had a chance to sin again. I stopped counting around the time I turned twelve. I don't even want to get into the nun and priest issue. Catholicism was not working for me.

My parents were both open and honest about being Catholic. There were serious lapses in other areas, but when it came to this religion, when they knew the answer, they told, and when they didn't, they said that too. For them, it had been no question as so many issues of their generation; there had been too much hard work and too little time to devote to change, especially as they saw the options as so limited.

Despite my religious frustration, I enjoyed the social aspect of the church and fully expected that someday I would, indeed, "get it." But at sixteen, I had an epiphany, the truth was not coming from the Catholic Church and I was not staying. So, I told my daddy I was not going to church or catechism ever again: God did not live in that church. Dad was quite angry, furious to be precise. I knew this by the smoke shootin' out his ears and the flames racing out his nostrils. But this was not the first subject my father and I were to disagree on, nor would it be the last. It was to remain forever the biggest.

I was getting ready to explode. Three years earlier my maternal grandfather had died. My mother was weeping and I was trying to comfort her. It was then she said, "My sister was so rotten to him (her father). I don't know how she could say those awful things."

I was opening the door to the refrigerator to get a cool beverage for her and I asked, "What awful things?"

She said, " My sister always said Grandpa (her father) had molested her. I never believed her. She just wanted attention. She hated him."

The nausea and realization of what happened during my tenth summer froze me in time. I could not breathe; my mind was suspended in the knowledge, pain, and betrayal of molestation. It seemed fitting and just that this pedophile predator had been run over by a Volkswagen while Grandpa attempted to cross the New Jersey Turnpike during the wee hours, sloshed to the gills of course. The driver of the car, an unsuspecting sweet person, attended Grandpa's funeral, where the family took him under their wing and assuaged any feelings of guilt he may have carried.

For me from the moment at the refrigerator on, I never missed that man one single moment of my life. It was clear, Mom wouldn't believe her own sister, she wouldn't believe me either, and the truth was tucked back into the safe spot where we keep our secret hurts.

Within a short period of time, my elder sister had gone nuts. Since it is often difficult to differentiate between the teen years and mental illness, it took us a bit too long to understand it was a combination of the two that had driven her into the abyss. Uncontrollable violence. Explosive anger. Verbal abuse. Obsession with her appearance. My younger sister was often the focus of the rage, as she was the easiest target. My mother had taken a job to "get out of the house" which left Mary and me in the untenable position of having to depend upon my oldest sister to pick us up from school daily. It was the Russian roulette of transportation. We never knew if big Sis would show up even close to on time, and if we so much as mentioned her extreme tardiness, there would be a violent outburst, often ending with her threatening us or attempting to drive us off the road. We told my parents over and over, but Mother couldn't hear us anymore and Father was too deeply in the bottle by then to care. We were on our own. One day, as my eldest sister verbally tortured Mary, chasing her around the house and threatening her life, I had reached my limit.

I chased my eldest sister down, catching up with her on the second story, I grabbed her by the neck, pinned her to the wall, lifting her six inches above the floor. As her feet dangled and she began to sputter, I looked into her very crazy eyes and said, "If you ever touch that little girl again, I will kill you." Both of us knew it was true and to my knowledge she never laid a hand on that child again. It was not my finest moment. It should never have had to be, but it was. Whatever speck of innocence I may have held onto, vanished at that moment. And from that day forward, I was acutely aware of all my capabilities, both beautiful and evil. I was keenly aware of my situation. My father was drunk, my sister was dangerously mentally ill, and my mother was absent. No one was coming to rescue us – not then, not ever. I was hellaciously angry. For the next decade and a half I was going to burn with that intensity. Cleansing fire.

The summer of '71 I graduated from high school. Mary was able to fend for herself, so I was off to live on a commune in Oregon. In theory the concept of loving all our brothers and sisters is a sweetness we should all be able to savor. In reality, I can respect most people, tolerate even fewer than that, and there's always going to be that amazing someone who is just so dangerous it's best to get as far away as possible. I was under the illusion that people actually said what they believed, so as an example, when people on the commune talked about loving each other, I thought they did or at least were striving toward that goal. When there was talk of equality and respect that was good, I thought that was truly where we were headed. When there was talk of changing society and living differently I believed that to be possible and was certain we would form a different type of society. Less greed, less structure, more caring, more gentle ways, this was not true. I learned that even though some people may break away from the masses to form a new unit, they will most likely structure that new unit as a microcosm of the larger whole. I learned that greed and envy travel in every circle, so watch for it and dispel it as quickly as it shows its ugly little head. I learned that there is no free love, true love comes with a price – commitment. Peace was not in the back-woods of Oregon. I went home.

Two weeks later I met and fell deeply in love with a young man just two months back from Viet Nam. He had been a helicopter gunner shot down twice behind enemy lines while trying to extract our troops. He had the GI Bill, a bad attitude (and a great sense of humor), and post traumatic stress disorder before it was labeled as such. Between my anger and his fear, there was no place for happiness to grow. It broke my heart. Thus began THE BLACK ERA, otherwise known as Stephanie's Maniacal and Godless Quest for Power and Control through the Dark Arts. The tarot was my friend; astral projection was not a strange form of transportation to me. I had no heart. I had no conscience. And compassion never even crossed my mind. Psychics, mediums and metaphysical dabblers recognized me immediately as a kindred soul. Inch by inch I became "the darkest person" most of my contacts would ever come across. I was no longer afraid. During one card reading, done for me by a "Christian" woman, who just read the cards as a "tool," the reader turned white as she placed the cards on the table.

"What do you see?" I queried.

"I don't want to talk about it." The reader was clearly shaken.

"You've already dealt the cards; it's out of your hands. What do you see?" I answered.

"I don't like to talk about the negative." She responded.

"The cards are just what they are, now tell me."

"These are the darkest cards I have ever read. There is darkness over your head. There is darkness all around you. I see death – yours." She could barely control her fear and anguish.

"I'll watch out for the darkness, sweet lady, don't worry. And I assure you I am not dying anytime soon. Be calm. It's alright." I paid her, kissed her forehead, and left. I never saw her again – nothing she said had done more than prompt me to watch who was coming in around me; but, we were finished, because I had outgrown her and needed the associations of the more powerful to guide me. I found them. A woman who called herself Hertha opened new avenues to me. With her assistance, I numeralogically changed my name to attract more power and began past life regressions guided by my new "mentor." Hertha didn't want to "ment". She was more interested in trying to glean any strands of power that might fall from her students and stuff it in her own power bag. She was electric with evil. Even I wanted a distance at least the size of the Grand Canyon between us. Self-preservation runs strong in the world of hocus-pocus.

It was around this time that a friend of mine from San Diego came to visit. Mary and I were now roommates, which means at that time I had been running the metaphysical gamut for about eight years straight. Now my visiting friend had started down the granddaddy of slippery slopes, satanic worship. Wow! Jump Back! My friend related her story to Mary and me as this:

For some time she had been quite attracted to a fairly well to do, self-employed, businessman, drug dealer in San Diego. She felt she was making, slow, if any, progress in engaging him in an exclusive relationship with her (in retrospect I say "smart man" except for the drug thing, of course). While discussing her romantic frustration with a new acquaintance, she was offered an avenue that would guarantee her success. For lack of better phrasing, we'll call it the "love spell." No obligation – just guaranteed to work!

Just a note to anyone reading this who may be tempted to take this route, when it comes to Satan, THERE IS ALWAYS AN OBLIGATION! Well, of course, girlfriend started seeing results. Why wouldn't they both be affected? they were both walking in the shadow side of life; Satan pretty much had them anyway! This thought apparently never crossed her mind.

Mary and I listened as girlfriend relayed how the spell had achieved results and this had prompted her to spend more time with her friendly coven member. Satanic worship wasn't bad, just a different perspective. She was experiencing dramatic, positive results in her life based on the spells and incantations she had begun using. The warning chill ran through both Mary and me as girlfriend continued to relay how blurred the lines had become for her. She thought she was describing a much improved life condition. For Mary and me, the warning lights were flashing, and the foghorn of danger was blowing full on. At the conclusion of her tale, I told her, "Wrong answer, friend. Start to finish, there is no part of that that's gonna' fly with me. What you are doing will cost you what you cannot afford to lose. You will pay the highest price; make no mistake." We told her, "You may not bring drugs here and you may certainly not bring Satan into this house." Mary and I spoke to her for what seemed like ever, and finally it appeared she understood and determined to not return to the coven and Satan's friends.

That night, as Mary (Sis) and I sat in our living room, we heard the unmistakable sound of cloven hoof beats click across our enclosed walkway. My friend's activities had literally brought the devil to my door. Had we not been there together, Mary and I may have later doubted what we heard. We were graced with having the impact of the experience, without the doubt.

You might well be wondering, exactly as I am in retrospect, what was I thinking? At that point in my life I was only two shakes of a cloven hoof away from coven central myself. But in metaphysics it remains an accepted distinction that the Satanic guys are the dark ones, everyone else is simply striving to improve their talents and e x p a n d themselves. I was headed for Hell.

Two years later I had one foot in the fire and it was getting hot. I was surrounded by bad, bad people; mercy, I was one of them. And that was my miracle – mercy. I was sitting around my apartment (no longer roommates, with sweet Mary) when it occurred to me, if I had no problem accepting that evil spirits could exist, then I should have no problem accepting that good spirits even dare I consider it God could exist. I got up and went into my bathroom where there hung an enormous mirror and I said, "God, if you exist, then show me what is really going on in my life." I watched my reflection as it distorted into a twisted demonic apparition. That's not good, I thought. Right there I shut the door on that life.

I went to church. Not Catholic Church, but born again Christian church. Now, that was going to church. I loved it! Dancing and singing with my arms up to God, born again church was fabulous! My father was openly miffed at my new religion. One day I had had enough of his snide comments and I said to him "Daddy, for years you prayed to God that I get religion, and now you complain that it's the wrong one!" He laughed from his eyes to the ground and back up, never to complain again.

Christianity not only fulfilled my need to celebrate the Lord; it resolved many of my religious issues. The saints were gone. Confession was between the Lord and me, and Purgatory was no problem. My new found expression of faith, however, continued to dangle the issue of Jesus (pbuh) as the Son of God. The crucifixion and now the third element in the Trinity, i.e., the Holy Spirit, came strongly into play. But I was happy in this place. I was joyful sitting closer to God than I ever had before. Years of living research had brought me to this place, and it was good.

At this point we plug in an almost six-year marriage to a man that eventually had an affair, quit his job, took the only decent vehicle we had, and left our 4-$^1/_2$ year old daughter and me with no money, a broken down truck and all the bills. He scooted off to Arizona to live with the then object of his affection and we did not hear from him for months – four to be precise. I divorced him.

Abandonment would appear to have been a bad thing, but in this case, it was not. Little Leslie and I were free. We were finally rid of the abuse, the neglect and the roller coaster that had been our life, and we openly cherished each other, healing as we lived. So I took a look at my life and here, in tiny Kiowa, the woman child, Leslie, and we women lived in harmony. I thanked God all day every day for giving me the strength and the ability to do what needed to be done, for the extraordinary kindness one or the other of his children might show us, and for the peace He provided.

We worked like ants. Sis and I went back to school, we worked, and we took care of our tiny charge. A baby tree shot up in our field, a place that has grown little but the dreaded yucca plants which are in such abundance our very existence may be in danger! This tender seedling became our symbol of hope.

Even before we were abandoned, my parents had planned to move to Colorado. Leslie has always been a sparkle in the night sky and her grandparents wanted to be with her as she grew. The divorce was a perfect opening for their arrival. Instead of moving to a separate home, they slipped in here perfectly. Sis was able to move to town to finish her teaching degree and there were plenty of eyes to stay focused on our busy little girl. There was a mondo glitch wedged right between reality and our perfect family picture—my Dad's love of his liquor. Having grown up in the household of an alcoholic, there was no room for pretence as to what that meant and there was no part of me that would allow my Leslie to live in that kind of torment. Prior to my parents' leaving California, I questioned my mother extensively as to whether my father was still hitting the bottle. She assured me Dad was just fine and wasn't drinking at all! I had no reason to think he was drinking; he'd been sober whenever I had spoken to him, and it most certainly wouldn't be the first sweet mercy God had sent my way that year alone.

It didn't take an advanced degree to realize my mother was wrong. My dad was a drunk still drinking. Fortunately for me Lent came around. Dad gave up drinking for Lent. That man, not drunk, was dynamite! But Lent was ending, and I knew from past experience my mother would never address my father's alcoholism – but I would.

One day he said to me, "I can get some scotch in a couple days when Lent ends."

I answered, " Dad, please don't. You're not a good person when you're drinking; you're cruel and unkind. That's not how I see you and I really don't want Leslie to grow up thinking that's who you are."

He said, "OK, honey."

My Dad died eight years later never having tasted another drop of alcohol. In fact, about four years after he quit drinking, he quit smoking the same way. He decided to stop – after having smoked two packs a day for 55 years – and he did. My father was blessed with the strongest of wills and the truest sense of justice I have had the privilege to encounter.

Leslie and the tree continued to grow – Leslie much faster than the tree – and eventually we remarried – Tim.

He loves us – the whole group of us – warts and all. And believe me, when you have that many people living under one roof there are an extraordinary large number of warts! Leslie, precious, brilliant, beautiful, quirky does not scare him, she delights him and he claims her as his own from the first day until forever. Leslie is now eighteen, it is impossible to determine without checking the DNA that she is not Tim's biological child; she is just like her Dad, and her Dad is Tim. In 1991 Stephen was born and now there were two brilliant, lively, quirky kids running around the house. We have three times the adult to child ratio required by law at any daycare center and still we were clearly outnumbered and outwitted.

We've lived in Kiowa, Colorado, since 1987. Kiowa has some real beauty to it and some real ugly to it. It's a rare day I don't marvel at the majestic cottonwoods down by the creek – even this year when someone decided to cut down about a third of them to build a car wash in a drought year. Even then the remaining trees came in full regalia to celebrate the season. Great green leaves and fluffy flyaway cotton puffs pepper the landscape for days at a time. Our little town has an active senior citizen population, well respected and highly cherished. We are an agricultural community which provides an opportunity for children to learn how to take care of animals. And from my home outside the main stream of small town life I can see for miles and miles – a clear view all the way to Pikes Peak some thirty miles away.

The ugly comes in the form of bigotry, prejudice and bullying. The school system is wrought with it. The unchecked ugly filters up into adulthood – allowing for few new ideas, differences or for the correction of old destructive concepts and patterns. I suppose the behavior is an expression of fear, but it's not benign and blocks out so many of life's marvels the environment becomes stagnant.

Still there we were, we in our little home and the Dirks in their little home. Oh, yes, Jerry and Debra Dirks lived diagonally from us on a Southwest tangent. Our fields touch at one small section of fencing where an old wood post and wire gate opens in either direction. The rickety gate was constructed many years ago by the previous owners – they were family. All things important were connected to that gate.

Most mornings come to Kiowa in a clarity that is distinctly Colorado. M & M blue skies and a swish of clean air as it fills your lungs make each day feel like the first ever created. I approach morning with a delicate reverence and a cup of strong coffee.

For years – that were all too soon behind us – I would let our horse, Andy, out into the field in time to greet Debra and Jerry's Davenports (horses). I could feel the Davenports in my feet first, milli-seconds before I could see them. The vibration in the earth began to mount, transforming to a defined sway, a tumultuous shaking and then the THUNDER! The pounding of the earth crescendoed beneath the blast of eighty hooves as they hit the dry Colorado dirt. A spray of particles formed dust clouds around the animals as they took the hill at a full run – a twenty-band rainbow of the rare Davenport, desert-breds, in a graceful exhibition of power and motion. They moved as one, taking pleasure in each extension of their striding bodies. They ran as if all of life was contained in their hoof beats. In one motion, as one being, the herd would stop – right by that old gate – each horse, in turn placing sweet kisses on the lips of our Andy. This was not just an event; it was a daily celebration!

Debra and I have had many conversations about the purity of the Davenport horses, we have held our breath as my then three year old daughter walked beneath a young stallion and staked out her territory, holding onto his legs. That stallion baby did not so much as twitch a muscle while we removed Leslie from her happy place of soft, cuddly equine security. Debra and Jerry had been studying the history of these animals for many years, and it was in 1993, they were able to go to the Middle East to do – what was to become –

groundbreaking (for the Western world) research on these phenomenal horses.

The Dirks had gone and returned, and I had yet to contact Debra about her trip. I thought I'd give her some time to "settle back in," then I'd get in touch and see what wonders her trip had gifted her. Little did I know that none of us were ever going to "settle back in" again.

It was just a quick run to our local grocery store. I loved the old grocery store. It was my vision of what a small-town should be, warm and kind with a dash of peace tossed in. The store was in a turn of the twentieth century building with World War II furnishings. The worn wooden floors spoke at each footstep and the muffled sound of voices and old rickety carts echoed from aisle to aisle. Cans, boxes and plastic bottles were precariously balanced an arm length above my head. The candy racks and newspaper stand were stocked to overflowing at the front registers, which still tallied the purchases manually, bolding taunting the technological age. The store smelled like childhood memories and I slowed down here in part due to the tender nature of the shopkeeper who was a sweet puzzlement in this harsh town. It was here the creaking of those aged, wood floors followed me like a noisy shadow as I tried to snatch a glimpse of the scarved women who seemed to be gleefully floating between the aisles in our tiny grocery. This was not the first time I had seen women covered. Having been raised in Southern California, I had the advantage of having been exposed to people of many cultures and faiths. It was, however, the first time I had ever seen a woman cover in Kiowa and I understood that although these women appeared light and airy, they were also women of great strength. How could I not respect them?

Debra was among these joyful apparitions gracing our rural Colorado town that day. Something bold, perhaps even spectacular had happened in her life – landing her solidly in the company of these covered women of presence and sweet spirit. Apparently Deb's trip to the Middle East netted more than horsey info. A phone call was in order.

And call I did. In fact, after I called I went to her house for a visit. Debra told me then that she had reverted to Islam. I could clearly see this was good for her. This didn't scare me. I was not afraid that Islam would wash off on me like red dye in the whitewash.

Our town, as a whole, was cruel to Debra during this time period. The communal behavior of our local citizenry was nothing short of appalling. I was deeply saddened and disturbed (although not completely surprised given my past experience here) by what people said and did – especially since Debra and I were becoming closer friends every day. I would say to her "My God is not like that." And truly, my God is, indeed, not like that. We were just friends, hangin' out, having some really good snacks (anyone who knows Debra knows she is a phenomenally great cook). We didn't talk much about Islam or Christianity; sometimes we might discuss a similarity or difference when it came about in another conversation. Mostly then we talked about the horses and my Dad's progressing Alzheimer's. The Dirks' home became a haven or refuge for me, providing a forum to learn incredible new information about Arab culture, the desert-bred horses, as well as a gentle break from the duties of caring for my father. Debra and Jerry provided both intellectual stimulation and songs of the heart, which allowed me to grow and be soothed at once.

The Dirks were very active in the "horse community" and were getting ready to host one of their many gatherings. Debra invited us to come: she so wanted to share her beautiful sisters in Islam with me. She said, "You'll like them and they will like you." Well, who would-n't be drawn to people you are sure would like you? However, we are not easily fooled (usually), Tim and I had been around enough Kiowans and US horse people to have become suspicious at best and hermitic at least. There had to be nothing short of a magnetic pull to get us out of our cave. That's when Debra brought out the heavy artillery – her sisters from the Ummah were going to be doing the cooking, OK, color us shallow, but the lure of Arabic cooking will bring us out of our jammies and into party clothes every time!

This was, if memory serves me – and it usually doesn't – an AHHA (Arabian Horse Historians Association) Meeting. Debra and Jerry were not only hosting it, they had arranged to have Mustafa Al Jabri – a renowned Syrian expert on the desert-bred horse – speak at this meeting.

We arrived early, ready to work – we're not horse people, we're neighbors! Many horse people had already gathered and they were busily chatting away as Debra worked hard to ensure their comfort. Always the outstanding hostess, she would not be losing her crown today, I assure you. We went in her house and up the stairs. The house was a bi-level allowing the choice of the upper or lower level. Already the lower level was filled with the whisperings of horse people plotting the course of the Arab horse world. The upper level was the best choice under any circumstance. Tim could only go to the top of the stairs; the sheets were hung separating everything upstairs except those areas the public might need access to. Yup, the sisters were coming and this would provide an area for the women to relax and not need to be covered. Tim is a quiet man and was somewhat uncomfortable with the girl/guy division. We had never been in a situation that might require us to function separately and I think he may have had doubts as to how well he would do (this tells you who the talker is in our family). But I was going through those sheets (that's what Deb used as curtains) Debra needed help and I didn't have time to quibble about the he's, the she's, and the they's. So Tim went off to help Jerry with something in the barn and that was how we made our transition into the concept of united, yet separate. Deb and I got right into step in the kitchen and within moments the cavalry arrived!

It was a twentieth century caravan. A couple of Minivans, a Ford Taurus, and some car I didn't recognize, but was beautifully kept. They parked in a tidy row just short of the front yard, leaving the basketball court open in case the sunlight held long enough for a game. Children began pouring out of the vehicles; I lost count at six. I collected Tim from somewhere and we went to help unload. A man went shooting out of one minivan like a rocket and went to the passenger side rear door, which he opened. A woman began to unfold from the back seat. A streak of a woman enveloped in an expanse of gossamer black fabric that flowed from her in the slight breeze. Her hands were gloved; her face was veiled, all black. Not even her eyes were exposed. I was mesmerized by this vision – the incongruity of this woman standing in the middle of cowboy country – stopped me just short of bad manners. I couldn't tell for sure, but the black draped figure was angled in our direction, so I figured I should say something.

"May we help you with something? I'm Stephanie Parlove and this is my husband, Tim." I extended my hand in a typically American fashion. The veiled figure reached out with one gloved hand and solidly shook my outstretched one. Good handshake, I thought.

"Pleased to meet you. I am Sahar. Yes, please I could use help. There are many dishes and bags in the trunk. Jamal, please open the trunk."

Jamal it turns out, was the rocketman. Everything about Jamal moves quickly, he can translate from Arabic to English so rapidly, it appears he is not translating at all, but holding a normal conversation.

Meanwhile other women had come from the vehicles, but none

were dressed unique to my experience, their accents were different, but I was accustomed to the *Hijabs* and *Jilbabs* – the beautiful scarves and robes – worn by some Muslim women.

We unloaded the vehicles, like little ants making an unbroken trail to the kitchen until all was done. Behind the curtains most of the cover came off and we set to complete the cooking duties. If you ever want to accomplish a task quickly and proficiently, call the sisters. Those women can chop like human veg-o-matics and Mr. Clean has nothing on their ability to restore a kitchen to a "ready to cook" status. They work as one unit with speed, efficiency and good humor. I loved these women from the moment I met them; I cherish their company, and will love them forever. They are intelligent, strong, capable and the sweetest people I have ever encountered. It was a companionable time and hours later when we were to leave, I heard the phrase which was to delight me many times over in the ensuing years, "You can't go yet, you just got here!"

I share the above story in such detail, as this was a loving picture, which was to repaint itself with some regularity over the next few years. I was still Christian and all my most beloved friends were Muslim.

By 1996, we were caring for five horses, four of them Davenports. My sweet daddy was slipping away. However on his journey through Alzheimer's, he stopped at both his days as a soldier in World War II and his teen years. For my sister and I, this was an extra blessing in caring for him. We knew him in every stage of his life as if we had experienced each moment alongside him as he grew. It still stirs my heart to remember.

We were lulled into Islam on the love of our friends and the sweet, precious words in which Jerry Dirks chooses to tell a story as a master storyteller. We enjoyed many an evening living the history of the Arab people, the desert-bred horses and Islamic culture through the magnificent images woven for us by our friend.

In tiny little steps, my heart was changing; I was getting answers about God. But Jesus (pbuh) had been my longtime, constant companion; this is part of the difficulty and at once part of the ease in coming to Islam. Still I wondered – if God has all the power in the universe why would He kill His only son? Why would He need a son? I flat out asked questions, and what questions Debra couldn't answer she asked Jerry, or Sahar, or Jamal. Always I got an answer and always it satisfied my spirit. I certainly had no problems with the concept that women in Islam were a repressed group of people. Please! I'd been hangin' out with covered Islamic woman for a couple years by this time, and they were free, highly respected, intelligent, articulate people who chose to cover for religious reasons. There was not a wimpy little girl in the bunch.

When we had an opportunity to travel to the Middle East in 1996 with a group of people interested in the desert-bred horses, we did everything within our power to get there. Jordan and Syria, Debra, Jerry, Tim and I – yes, there were other people, many of them delightful but when I think back on the experience I most strongly remember we four from our group. I had to get to the Middle East; there beckoned the home of the black tents, the pull of the desert was strong in me. With its rich mix of history and tradition, the Middle East with a foot in the present and a foot in the past. All things worked to get us there. At the last minute one of my knitting machines sold and provided the funds for tickets. My sister agreed to take care of everything on the home front for the three weeks I would be gone; in fact, she did this so well, my children were completely pampered. My sister even warmed their clothes for them in the dryer so they would be cozy in the morning before school! Debra and I were leaving a few days early to take care of some horses she was exporting to Jordan.

From the moment the plane took off in Denver, I was immersed in a seriously spiritual experience. One of the first things to happen to us was at once humorous and perplexing. Debra and I were both covered – Debra as was her custom, and I in respect for the culture we would be moving in. At one point in our journey, an aggressive American woman from a Christian tour group scheduled to spend time in the Holy Land, had left her group and cornered a Palestinian brother. She was on a quest for knowledge and wanted to know the "other side" of the Israeli/Palestinian conflict. This man was trying so hard to be polite and yet be able to remove himself from the situation. Deb and I were seated right behind him and after watching this exchange for a few moments, I whispered to Debra, "I think we need to save this man." Deb took the lead, attracting the woman's attention and initiating a conversation. The very first thing the quester asked was, "Are you a nun?" Now, I was delighted beyond what is reasonable by this comment when our Arab brother soulfully and emphatically answered, "NO! She is Muslim woman." Clearly understanding the treasure that rests within a Muslim woman while paying her due respect. I caught my breath and marveled at the beauty of that exchange – quietly settling into my seat as the brother excused himself and Debra continued her conversation with the quester. I'm not sure our curious guest learned what she wanted or understood what she heard, but I felt reasonably certain that all of us were well aware of the value of a Muslim woman and how she might dress!

As we traveled throughout the Middle East there were some circumstances I was uncomfortable with, for example, armed military personnel at the Amman Airport (this, of course, was years before 9/11); not being able to understand either the process or the language when there was a snag regarding Deb's horses at the Amman Airport, and one comment from an American educated member of a prominent Bedu tribe. It was not having control of a situation that was a problem for me – like having to surrender my passport at the hotel. In retrospect not having control was the predominant theme in my life– my father was moderate to advanced Alzheimer's, I'd been diagnosed bi-polar a couple years before, AND I knew at any time I could be propelled into the throws of a Crohns attack. Did I ever feel I was in danger in the Middle East? Not one moment of the entire time we spent there; everyday life was much more dangerous!

In Jordan, we were pampered by the gracious attention of Dr. Hani, his wife the fabulous Hanadi, his family, and the wonderful people who worked with him. They rented a lovely, air-conditioned bus and took us to many of the wonders Jordan has to offer. We loved the people – those who cared for us and those we met on our journey. Tim and I were in a bit of hot water at one point, when we wandered up to a museum at Jerash and accepted a kind offer of Arabic coffee from the caretaker. I am ashamed to admit we caused our hosts much concern and even caused our guide quite some trouble for having let us linger so long when no one knew where we were. Our guide was trying to be courteous to us by letting us stay as we had wished when actually he should have been herding us down the road to the bus. His sense of duty, would not allow him to do anything other than grant our wish. This was a lesson hard learned for Tim and me. It took half a day to ease the concern the leader of our expedition had experienced. There was a good bit of joking and cajoling that washed over the situation. Tim and I were very sensitive to all of our caretakers from that moment on, especially the dichotomy that existed between duty to us as guests and duty to the leader of the tour as keepers of our safety.

More considerate and with a clear understanding of how this touring thing worked, we were able to enjoy the company of our friends both old and newly acquired. When we got to the Dead Sea, it truly was dead; thick and saucy, not nearly as large as I had thought it would be. Life was beginning to take on the feeling of an illusionist's show. What seemed to be was not. What was, was not what I thought it to be. Although I did see one member of our entourage take a camel ride and that was exactly as it seemed to be – hard, bouncy and requiring a significant amount of coordination which I was glad to see he had.

It was at the Royal Stable of Jordan then under the loving and watchful eye of Princess Alia that we were to visit an old friend. One of the Davenport Arabian stallions had been given as a gift to the Royal Family of Jordan and was now enjoying the life every horse must dream of! We were treated like royalty, but evidently so was he. All the horses were movie quality gorgeous, strong, agile, silky coats and flowing manes and tails. They were horses blessed with enough of everything to make their lives seem charmed.

In sweet Jordan it was ensured we would see as much as possible in the time we had – from the Dead Sea to a working sheep farm which provided much of the *Halal* meat for the region. The people we met took pride in their work – but not personal pride – pride in doing their jobs well for Allah – a communal and spiritual pride.

We could not have left our sweetheart Jordan, had we not been flowing into the arms of Syria.

Syria was an awakening. There were important things to learn. I came eager, with an open heart, an open mind and a smidgen of information. Time frames, considered so very important in American society disappeared as our guides, our friends, and our fellow horse-men, continually made adjustments in scheduling to wrap around the learning curve we were experiencing. In both Syria and Jordan, people were flexible and in only one case, were we shown any indica-tion that we had inconvenienced or irritated anyone at all. We found that often, Arab time moves a bit differently than American time I prefer the rhythmical accommodation of Arab time. It moves to the timing of the spirit.

The ancient places of the Middle East, called to me like an old friend greeting me from a distance. I found it to be the most amazing sensation to come home to places I had never been. Not at all a deja-vu, but a sigh of, "Oh, yes." I could not imagine leaving this new part of me behind when we returned to Colorado. So I tenderly and lovingly folded the song of the Middle East into my heart place to live forever. I plucked from the desert the way the light breezes felt on my face, the sweet, musty smell of the dirt covering the remnants of lives and civilizations that came before and the peace in the spirits of the people I have met. Having walked there, we are now a part of that same history. Some day, *Insha'Allah*, I will walk there again. There it is – the eternal hope of the future.

The AHHA group was in Syria as guests of the Syrian Government. The Syrian government and the dedicated horse breeders of that country have created an incredible National Farm to preserve the purity of bloodlines of the *Asil* horses. The breeders have donated some of the most outstanding horses to have ever stepped foot on this planet to this project. They have come together – with no thought for themselves – to ensure that these "drinkers of the wind" will not be tarnished or polluted by an admixture of blood. These horses, as well as the people who care for them, are part of our Islamic heritage, and, indeed, these horses are mentioned in the *Qur'an*. We must salute our brothers for this outstanding effort.

It was our honor to be guests at the farms of many of these generous people. I regret that I cannot tell each story as they are all excellent examples of how brothers and sisters in Islam behave, not only toward each other, but toward their guests.

Communication was important – especially since we were experiencing another culture. Dr. Absi or Basil Al Jadaan (who watched over us as though we were his own), would help us with the language often, but the Syrian government had sent the most wonderful people on the trip to ensure there were enough interpreters for everyone to be comfortable at all times. We had made a mistake, however, as is apt to happen in a different country. Our Syrian friends would greet us every day with their right hand over their hearts and say "*Salam*" (peace). We, all of us, thought it would be a breach of etiquette to return this gesture, as we were not Muslim. After we had come to know each other quite well, Basil Al Jadaan said, "Every day we greet you with peace and you never return the greeting. Why is that?"

"Oh, we thought it was bad manners to say "*Salam*" if we were not Muslim." Someone from our group quipped.

"No, you can do that!" he said, greatly relieved.

From that day forward we greeted our beloved friends with "*Salam*." *Al'Hamdullilah*, Basil did not keep silent. Communication! We were to be guests of the *Sheykh* of the Naim tribe on our way North. The *Sheykh* was a wonderful host, and had paid careful attention to each and every detail. At the time of our visit, he was having a new barn built (although any one of us would have been more than pleased to have his old barn on our property). He had tents set up for us and, as was the custom, cushions for our comfort. Tim was ill at that point, as the creepy ick had been moving through the group. The *Sheykh* had special herb tea made for Tim, which made him much more comfortable. We were presented with beautiful and thoughtful gifts, which would forever remind us of this special time. The *Sheykh*'s horses were fit, well kept, and when they ran together – it felt as though time had stood still for us.

It was at the Naim, that we first encountered the wonders of making coffee. Oh, no, not like you and I make coffee. When the Bedu make coffee it is both a ceremony and an invitation. There are many things that you and I might consider ordinary that the Bedu approach as extraordinary, and when they do it, it is extraordinary indeed. Let me explain. To make coffee from the green coffee beans the process follows:

The coffee is made over an open fire where the tents have been set. First, the beans are roasted in what we might consider a skillet with slightly upturned sides. When they are roasted to perfection the beans are transferred to a coffee grinder – the most incredible coffee grinder I've ever seen. It is made of wood and is, perhaps, two feet high with a three-foot circumference. The grinder is hollowed in the middle creating a cylindrical opening about one-eighth the size of the circumference. The roasted beans are poured, just a bit at a time, into the grinder. There is a long, solid, wooden, cylindrical tool that is used to grind the beans. The magic begins when that tool is placed in the hands of a Bedu. Slowly this person begins his task. As the beans are ground, the coffee grinder transforms into a drum as the rhythm of the grinding increases so does the volume of the drum until the artist is turning and grinding and drumming the deep song of the desert all at once. And it is a song; it says to all who may be traveling in the desert, we are making coffee here, come and be refreshed; you are welcome. How could we not love the Bedu? Too soon we were to leave the Naim.

Our tour bus caravan had covered many miles of Syria. Now, solidly in the jezeera we pulled into the homeland of the Tai – a Bedouin tribe able to trace their lineage all the way back to Noah. We were befuddled and somewhat delighted, at the sight that met us – thousands of people crowded the area, there were horses – more than we could count – peppered throughout the scene. The gathering was electric with excitement.

Our guide told us "This is for you. These are all members of the Tai tribe, some of them have ridden their horses for days to be here to welcome you."

"Why?" I asked. We all did. This extraordinary behavior was beyond anything we knew.

"Because you are their honored guest, and your coming to the Tai to learn about their horses is a great honor for them."

Please, I thought, a few days ago I was shoveling out the horse stalls; are these people sure they have the right "honored guests"? I was incredulous!

I shared this story in a newsletter in 1996 calling it *The Elder Man:*

In all great adventures there is one defining moment: a clarifier, bringing together all that transpired prior and all that is to come. Mediocre adventures, vacations, mini-tours, of course, do not have this moment, which is as it should be. For me that moment is and will be for always, the horse and the elder man.

Others will tell you of historical fact; I am compelled to tell of historical heart and Spirit—the very components, which propel man to take the actions which create history.

Now the story.

The American contingent of AHHA had been eagerly anticipating visiting the tribes

And this was the day. Our first meeting would be with the Tai, in my most elaborate imaginings, I would not have seen what we were to see.

The Tai are legendary for their generosity and Amir Muhammad Abdul-Razak Al Tai; the *Sheykh* of all *Sheykhs* of the Tai has carried on this tradition. As we approached, thousands of Tai tribe members lined the area, they had come from many miles, some riding their horses two days to be there for there honored gusts. We were treated to horseraces, Bedu style. Few saddles, I don't remember seeing a bridle, per say – sometimes children who appeared as young as eight were riding, they looked like the wind, looked like joy in motion, looked like every horseman's dream.

We photographed our hosts and their inspirational horses. As we viewed each pair, I was humbled by the honor we had received in being allowed to spend time in the presence of such warm and generous people. We feasted with our friends, we shared, and we were cared for lovingly – as good parents for their children. The day ended, some of us slept in the black tents, some not. Morning came. We were graciously invited to stay for breakfast and hesitant to leave, found this a most appealing suggestion.

It was shortly after breakfast when the horse and the elder man came. Someone came to us, I'm sorry to say I don't remember who, and mentioned there was a man who had come to see us. He had not made it in time for the gathering, but would very much appreciate our photographing his horse. We couldn't get up fast enough! In all my life I have never seen anything more beautiful than this. The elder man, although having many years behind him, had a youthful spirit and such pride and respect for his companion we longed to be near him, if just for a moment. For all we did not know, we recognized a noble spirit when we saw it, in both these friends it was clear. Before we could drop our cameras, the elder man turned with his horse and as the horse, still walking, headed back from whence he'd come, the elder man, with the grace and ease of a youngster and the skill of many years, leapt gently onto his companions back and cantered off. As he rode we could hear the whispers of generations past move by us, we could feel the hope and joy of his sons, grandsons, and great-grandsons within us; and as we watched, the horse and the elder man became the horse/elder man, with no distinction between them. This is the spirit; this is the beauty we felt. It was the moment we understood, for the horse/elder man rode with all of history and the entire future surrounding him. At that moment what we were experiencing became a great adventure, a revelationary journey – a journey of the heart.

That was the exact moment I understood the nature of Islam.

Tim and I were flying home a week or so later, I turned to him and said,

"I think we're Muslims now."

"Yup," he replied. We sat quietly and tried to intellectually assimilate this change.

Debra and Jerry returned a few weeks after us. And at some point Debra, Jerry and I were going to the *Masjid* – I had pointed out to Debra that she had never taken me to the *Masjid*, although she had taken other people. I guess I kind of whined about it, if the truth were told. Finally, we three were headed there for afternoon prayer. Deb was explaining *Masjid* protocol regarding prayer – where I would have to stand and what I would have to do as I wasn't going to pray. I said something like "But I can pray, I'm good there."

When Debra realized that I was saying, I am Muslim, the joy on her face was so powerful it literally took my breath away. Jerry, of course, led me in reciting the *Shahadah* immediately. This is our statement of faith. Upon our arrival at the *Masjid*, Jerry found the *Sheykh* who was in charge, and once again, I recited the *Shahadah* with him. After prayer, while we were talking, I mentioned that Tim and I did'nt want to make a big deal of our reversion. Don't forget we have never relinquished our hermit status. Of course, Debra, promised me ... no problem; but we would come to have a small celebration – just them and us – at their house that evening. Huh! Debra had called all our friends – now also our family – it was a raucous celebration Muslim style! But first Jamal, spirited Tim off to the *Masjid* to recite the *Shahadah* – the *Sheykh* had been concerned that one partner in a marriage was reverting and possibly not the other. Jerry had assured him this was not the case and that they would be bringing Tim by later –this detail was quietly handled for me by Deb and Jerry –– knowing me they were doing everything possible to keep that stress level low. I didn't know that the *Sheykh* had any concerns nor did I know Tim would be going to the *Masjid*, until he had been swept away. By the time they returned, it was more than clear reversion to Islam was not going to slide in the back door and sit quietly in the last row of the theatre.

I didn't know how to do this intense community experience – it was too much attention for me. I couldn't see Tim, but I could feel him hitting maximum load as the evening moved forward. Our new family took care of everything for us – prayer rugs, copies of the *Qur'an*, beautiful wall hangings, clothing both prayer and daily, jewelry – I still have each and every one of these items and they remind me of my family's sweet and generous nature. Within a 24 hour time period I had prayed once with each of my three new "sisters", they were all in turn, quite careful to determine what I need-ed and how the other two had instructed me. Sahar, Suha and Debra, were diligently checking to make sure there were no gaps in the infor-mation they were teaching me. Jerry wrote down for me each prayer time and requirement, including prayer during travel, I carried it around then and I still have that sheet. I was now twirling into Islam!

It was a miracle I didn't just lie down and die right there from the mental and emotional overload. Reverting was huge! In fact, it brings to mind years ago when I brought my newborn Leslie girl home from the hospital for the first time. My sister and I were sitting in the living room, just looking at Leslie and I turned to Mary and said, "Well, what do we do with her now?" That was the big question for me when it came to Islam.

I approached Islam with the greatest dedication I could muster, but it was a feeble run toward it, at best. Islam is tremendously com-plicated and beautifully simplistic all at once. Here's the key – it took me years to get my mind around this, but I'm willing to share this with you now and perhaps save you some floundering time –Islam is not just a faith - we are a society, a family, an *Ummah*. Islam encompasses every aspect of life, every day of the week, every hour of the day. In the words of the marvelous Sahar, however, "It is not beyond what a person can do." Clearly she spoke the truth as there are astronomical numbers of us around the world and people are flocking to Islam daily. This tells me Islam is, indeed, within our grasp.

Later Sahar and I were discussing how Tim and I got married at the courthouse with our local judge, my mother, sister and Leslie present. Sahar said to me, "You should have had a celebration. There are far too few things to celebrate, so when something comes up we should take that opportunity to truly rejoice in the occasion." Foreshadowing at its best.

All too soon, there were separations in my Muslim and non-Muslim families. My father died. The time of my father's passing was, quite possibly the most remarkable moment of my life. The nurse on duty had called our home at three am, saddened, as she was certain my father wouldn't remain earthbound much longer. We all came. Oldest to youngest there was not one of us who didn't want to hold him, touch him and speak sweetly to him about how much we loved him, about how extraordinary having him in our life had been, to reassure him and to thank him one last time. My father left this earth surrounded by the love and respect of his family, and when he left, I saw his spirit rise up from his body and gently glide away. I was transfixed by the phenomena and have held dear the vision of our spiritual selves since that day.

My Muslim brothers and sisters were there for me always, but it was a very bad idea to speak to me of Allah's will and mercy. From my perspective there wasn't a whole lot of mercy flying around my house. I had never understood grief until that time and I don't believe I will ever misunderstand the depth of that experience in someone else. I didn't understand death then and I still don't. However, in retrospect I will never know how truly awful the situation may have become had the sweet mercies of Allah not been spread out to cover my life, had my friends not prayed for me.

Considering time as eternity in timeline moments, my father died, ALL of the Muslim family I knew left – some to Jordan – some to Palestine – one was estranged, and then left! The estrangement was a direct result of what I call meltdowns – just like a nuclear accident – life just turns to slush! I didn't have the hang of praying. I would read the *Qur'an* and not make a bit of sense of it. This had happened with the *Bible* also, when I was first "born again" – so I figured SOMETIME understanding would kick in. But mainly I was lonely and seriously depressed, yes clinically. I was absolutely stalled out in Islam and I had just barely started!

One day, Stephen, said, "We have got to learn to pray correctly!" For me that was like the scene in the movie, "Moonstruck," where Cher slaps her brother-in-law to be and yells, "Snap out of it!" We worked hard on prayer, memorizing and practicing from sheets we had. This is where our weird pronunciations come in, I'm afraid. But the effort was honored and pray we did. Just the conscience effort of worship helped us to move forward.

Truth be told, Stephen has the prayer thing goin' on! Aside from the obvious reasons an eleven-year old boy loves to visit his *Amo* (uncle) and *Khaltu* (aunt), Stephen takes great delight in prayer, and especially prayer shared. He chose a special prayer rug many years ago and carries it with him when we go to visit. When it's time for prayer any time, each time, he beams happiness. There is no chore for him in performing *Salat*, and the sparkle in his attitude and purity of his heart light up the room like the noonday sun. My spirit is refreshed.

Most of my non-Muslim family quietly discounted our reversion. Our non-Muslim family consists of Catholics, people who "don't believe in organized religion," and some totally Godless individuals.

It didn't matter which group my family fit into I did not feel support for our choice of Islam at the onset. Having different faiths within our household we try to respect each person's holidays. It took quite some time before ours were given full measure. The process was not without frustration. Now we approach our celebrations with enthusiasm and in turn, our family members are eager participants.

We have never hidden the fact we are Muslim, nor have we taken banners and hung them across the streets of our little town announcing our faith. I'm confident most people in our community know we are Muslim as my sweet son, Stephen would and still does tell everyone, "We're Muslim!" He has an innate sense of the value that lies within that phrase.

We chose to home school Stephen for a number of reasons (Leslie was also home schooled, but graduated this year and will be attending college in the fall). Two of them are to protect him from cruelty and to remove the underlying Christian influence in our local schools and textbooks. In fact, one local school announces in its handbook they celebrate Christmas, although they respect and support religious choice. Another school, last time I checked, still hosts a musical Christmas program each year. It was rather disconcerting when many years ago Stephen came home and told me he knew who was Lord.

When I asked "Who, Stephen?"

He said, "Jesus Christ is Lord."

"How do you know this son?" I asked.

"It says so in the song we learned for the Christmas program."

Oh, I thought learning opportunity, I also thought, great, another trip to the local school!!!!

Having a penchant for being outspoken and to the point (perhaps I'm being a bit gentle with myself here!) I wasn't tremendously popular in this walk-all-the-way-around-it town prior to our reversion and as, Debra will confirm, not being Christian in Kiowa can be a rugged experience. Living outside the town limits and not participating in the local schools has allowed us to circumvent most local activities. Stephen and Leslie have created a circle of close, supportive friends outside our town and since Mr. Abbey sold the old grocery store – I do my shopping elsewhere.

We've been able to weed out phrases from our speech that are rooted in Christianity. Although we don't appreciate every grocery and department store playing Christmas carols in December, we don't have to join in at the chorus anymore. The other day, I drove through town and a sign up at one of the local real estate offices read: Jesus is Lord of Kiowa (first line), buy and sell real estate (second line). I wanted my own sign that said, "Not True (first line), No, Thank You (second line)."

As with other religions, Islam has brothers and sisters from conservative fundamentalist to liberals who interpret their religion quite loosely. I am somewhere in the middle crawling towards conservative. I cover only when going to the *Masjid* or when I am going to be in the company of conservative brothers and sisters who might be caused discomfort by my not covering. I have incorporated many, but not all of the dietary guidelines into our lives. Aside from my unique phrasing, there's no problem in the prayer area and I am quite consistent in meeting the required five times daily schedule.

I am where I am. Everyday I strive to do better, there is never a day I wake up and say, "Gosh, I hope I can go backwards in my faith today." Sometimes I just don't seem to go forward, but I try. Allah honors the effort.

Al'Hamdulillah, our brother Jerry and sister Debra moved back to the US– I know they had other reasons, but I like to think Allah did it for me! It feels as though I'm taking baby steps forward in faith. The other day the *Qur'an* started making sense when I read it. This is very good, I thought. I have recently been introduced to a group of Muslim brothers and sisters who are active in community service and education; these people make my heart sing.

Last year I absolutely had to start a garden for my daughter. I wanted her to be able to see herself through my eyes. With some grass seed I cultivated a little patch of lawn and planted a few morning glories. We were delighted by how well Leslie's garden grew. This year I added to her area by creating a rocky place to represent the contrast that rests within her, moss roses and ice plant (which she chose for herself), two mounding junipers and two birds nest spruce to draw a distinct line between the grassy and rocky terrain. The Leslie garden is lush with morning glories and snapdragons of every color. It is Leslie represented in foliage.

We also began a Stephen garden this year with rocks (his choice). Both pea gravel and cobblestones-scotch moss and elfin thymus grow between the rocks along the border, and an entire petunia convention of lavender, purple and deep red, white, and pink wink and nod at us as we pass.

Both gardens not only remind me of my children, they remind me of my walk in Islam – education, preparation, hard work, perseverance, overwhelming beauty, and tremendous love.

A couple months ago I had a dream to create a circle and walkway of bricks and stone. I was compelled to work on this project. My motto was not unlike the US Post Office, "neither rain, nor snow, nor sleet, nor hail..." As I completed one section, I would have a dream outlining the plans for the next one. To date I have put down 2000 plus bricks and have dreamt portions that will require another 500. After fifteen years of unbeauty, with the children's gardens and the brickwork, our yard has become our oasis in a drought year.

Recently as I stood on my hill with my big old hat flopping in the breeze and I looked across this property, for the first time

I understood what has happened. Leslie is grown, the tree is still in the field, my family has been restored, there is a massive dirt pile in the back acre and I am surrounded by the beauty of my youth.

Allah has brought me home to Square I, wherein lies my childhood joy and sweet peace. That, my friends, is mercy.

The End

Stephanie Parlove

*R*ecently Sister Debra had occasion to visit Denver. Accompanied by the amazing Leslie, we spent a splendid day doing a little "pantry" power shopping (items that are difficult to find in Debra's town). Late in the afternoon, we stopped for a plate of hummus and some Arabic coffee. Naturally, the conversation filtered down to this book. I said to Debra as I chased the elusive hummus around the plate with a nibble of pita bread, "Writing this chapter is the most difficult thing I've ever done. I will never tell this story again." (I was no doubt whining and exasperated at the same time—totally unappealing to witness I assure you!) "I have been crying for days!" Continuing without even a glance at Debra, I was about to move forward with my next expression of frustration when I paused long enough to look at my dear friend. Contrary to my basic nature, I shut up right then. In the minutest fragment of time, I understood what I had been unable to grasp before. Debra had a vision. Not just an idea, but a full blown vision. I had pita bread. She was willing to reach out to grab the hand of a potential sister waiting for her story. I couldn't even get the hummus to cooperate. She was committed to put forth the effort to complete this book in the event that just one woman may be waiting to know that "someone just like her" had come to Islam, and she could too. And for a reason never to be understood, but completely accepted, Debra needed my help. There was an instantaneous conversion of my attitude. When I explained it later to Tim, I said, "At that moment I understood, and no effort would be too great, no requirement too demanding. I determined to do everything within my scope and sphere to ensure that this book would come to fruition, and that Debra's vision, her goal would be attained. I love her. What's important to her is important to me."

Tim said, "That's it! Right there – that's what being Muslim is all about."

Well, of course – you might think – you have known her for fifteen years. It's true, that has been my blessing. I would then submit…how does that account for the other four sisters who have contributed to this book? Most of us have never heard the melodic tones of each author's voice. Most of us have never had the pleasure of an afternoon of *Shai* and sharing. No – longevity has nothing to do with our joyful responsibility to each other. One woman of Islam said to her sisters, people she considered a solid representation of American women in Islam, "I would like to put together this book, and I would like you to write a chapter." And across the great expanse of this wonderful nation, sisters in Islam came together in spirit and support to complete the vision.

As I wrote my contribution to this book, I cried. I picked up tiny pieces of my life and held them gently up to Allah and said, "This one?," and if I received a yes, it went into my chapter – no matter how difficult it was for me to remember, or how my heart was breaking for that little bitty girl who lived so long ago. No doubt, all the sisters cried.

Tears were shed from the depth of sadness and the sweetness of recollection as we told these tales.

As we wrote, crystalline drops of "by-gone" days slid down our cheeks and fell silently to the earth. They did not accumulate in stagnant pools where what has passed would forever keep us trapped and dying. Instead, our sister tears flowed into a gentle stream where each of us, in turn and yet as one, was swept away in the soft current of time and tumbled hither and yon as our rough edges were polished smooth. Our lives were, perhaps, healing in the retelling and for me, the pain was moving out—I truly did not live there anymore. I was no longer the child of abuse or sadness. I had become precious in the eyes of Allah. I had become a Muslim woman.

In 1996, I was in Syria enjoying one of life's perfect days at the farm of Hisham Ghrayeb. My then new friend – now sister, Nura, got right up close to my face and looked deeply into my eyes, she tenderly cupped my face in her hands—a nurturing gesture no one had shown me since childhood—she smiled as she said, "You have the face of Islam." To this day, it remains the greatest compliment I have ever received.

The face of Islam! One has to ponder—what is the face of Islam? Shortcut for you right here. I know, and it is my honor to share it with you.

Islam has only one face; it does not come in disguise, and it does not pretend to be anything else. Islam announces clearly and definitively what is expected of you. Islam is not a shape shifter. Always it is the same, uncorrupted by the times and the whims of humanity. Islam is brutally honest while at once tender and light. It is following the *Qur'an*, which is the Voice of Allah, and guess what – Allah may not think just like you do; Allah thinks like Allah! Although you may find this shocking, it is absolutely sublime! This last revelation adjusted my entire perspective and was presented to me by Brother Jerry.

Finally, my friends, sweet Islam is the whisper of peace embracing the spirit of each Muslim. It is the silent, bubbling joy to which we are privy when we hold the hand of Allah while we climb this mountain of life. It is our safety, our support, and our motivation. The face of Islam is one face, but you will find that face on over 1.2 billion people in the world today. *Insha'Allah*, you will recognize it when you see it; or better yet, someone will see it in you.

Glossary of Terms

Abu   Father, father of.

Adhan   The Muslim call to prayer, pronounced loudly to indicate the time to pray is due. Normally articulated 10-15 minutes before Prayer.

Ahadith/Hadith   Sayings and actions of the prophets, especially pertaining to matters of religion. Normally applied to the Prophet Muhammad. Singular is *Hadith*.

Al-Baqarah   The cow; the second *Sura* of the *Qur'an*.

Al-Hamdulillah   All praise belongs to Allah.

Al-Salam 'Alaykum Peace be upon you. Greeting of peace by Muslims.

Allah   God; i.e., the one and only God.

Amo/Amu   Uncle.

Arkan   Pillars, i.e. the five pillars of Islam.

Asil   Pure from the original.

Baqarah   Cow.

Bismillah	In the name of the One God,
Al-Rahman	Most Gracious,
Al-Rahim	Most Merciful.

Bedu/Bedouin Nomadic people of the Middle East.

Dawa   Witnessing

Deen/Din   Religion, i.e., Islam

'*Eid Al-Adha*   The feast of sacrifice celebrating the end of *Hajj* that lasts for three days.

'*Eid Al-Fitr*   Three day holiday marking the end of *Ramadan.*

Elohim   Hebrew word that is typically translated as God in the *Old Testament.*

Fajr   First of the five obligatory prayers. *Fajr* is performed between the first light of dawn and sunrise.

Five Pillars   1. *Shahadah* (testifying there is one God).
of Islam   2. *Salat* (Prayer).
             3. Fasting during *Ramadan* (*Sawm*).
             4. *Zakat.*
             5. *Hajj.*

Gott   German word meaning God.

Hadith/   Sayings and actions of the prophets, especially
Ahadith   pertaining to matters of religion. Normally applied to the Prophet Muhammad. Plural is *Ahadith.*

Hajj	The fifth pillar of Islam. Islam prescribed pilgrimage to Makkah for those who are physically, mentally, and financially able to do so.
Hajjah	Title for a woman who has performed *Hajj*.
Halal	Something that is permitted or acceptable.
Hijab	A partition or curtain for the sake of modesty, normally refers to a scarf or head covering.
Haram	Something that is not permitted or forbidden.
Imam	In Islam – the leader of the congregational prayers.
Iman	Faith.
Injil	The book of revelation given to the Prophet Jesus.
Insha'Allah	Allah (God) willing.
Iqama	Muslim call to prayer pronounced loudly directly proceeding each of the five daily prayers.
Irhab	Terrorism.
'Isha	The fifth obligatory prayer of the day, performed after the full darkness of night.
Islam	Submission to the will of Allah; the religion of the prophets and messengers of Allah culminating with the revelation of the *Qur'an* to the last Prophet, Muhammad and the followers of the *Qur'an*.

Jamel   Camel.

Jamil   Beautiful or pretty.

Jihad   Effort or striving.

Jilbab   Traditional, loose, outer garment of women.

Ka'bah   The first house of worship made for man. Adam
                    occupied this area first. A square stone building
                    built by Prophet Abraham and Prophet Ishmael in
                    the Great Mosque in Makkah, towards which all
                    Muslims face to pray *Salat.*

Kafir   Disbeliever, one not on the Straight path.

Khaltu   Aunt.

La Ilaha   There is no God but Allah.
Illa Allah

Laylat Al-Qadr   Night of Power.

Ma Salamah   With peace.

Mahr (initial)   The dowry, specified in the marriage contract, and
                    paid by the groom to the bride at the time of the
                    marriage.

Mahr (delayed)   Also specified in the marital contract, this is the
                    specifics of what must be paid to the bride in the
                    event of a divorce.

Makkah   The city in Saudi Arabia in which the Great Mosque
                that houses the Ka'bah is located. The city to which all
                Muslims who are able must complete the prescribed
                pilgrimage – *Hajj*.

Masjid   Mosque.

Muhammad   The last Prophet sent to humankind. The person to
                whom Allah revealed the entire *Qur'an*.

Muslim   A follower of the Islamic Faith. Literally, one who
                submits to Allah.

Prayer Clothes Special clothes that may be worn while praying.

Qadar   The timeless knowledge of Allah, His power to
                plan, and His ability to execute His plans.

Qur'an   Scripture revealed by Allah to the Prophet
                Muhammad via the Angel Gabriel.

Quwayis   Good.

Radhi   May Allah accept him.
Allaho Anho

Rakah   A unit of prayer.

Ramadan   The month of fasting for Muslims. It is the ninth
                month of the Islamic lunar calendar. During this
                month, Allah began to reveal the *Qur'an* to the
                Prophet Muhammad.

Rukn	Pillar; corner; cornerstone; essential ingredient plural is *Arkan*.
Sahabah	A companion of the Prophet Muhammad.
Sahoor	The meal eaten before *Fajr* begins by a person who is observing *Sawm*.
Salam	Peace.
Salat	The five obligatory daily prayers.
Salla Allah *'Alayhi* *Wa Salam*	The peace and blessings of Allah be upon him. A phrase said after saying the name of a prophet. Often abbreviated as "SAWS," or in English as 'pbuh.' (peace be upon him).
Sawm	Fasting; refraining from the intake of any liquids and foods, and from sexual intercourse from the first light of day through sunset.
Shai	Tea.
Shahadah	*Ushhaduan La Ilaha Illa Allah Ushhaduun Muhammad Al-Rasul Allah.* The Islamic testimony of faith that there is only one God and Muhammad is his messenger.
Sheykh	Leader or head person; chief.

Subhanna *Wa Ta'ala*	Glorified and Exalted is He! A phrase said after Allah. Abbreviated as 'SWT'.
Sunnah	The legal way or ways, orders, acts of worship and statements of the Prophets, normally applied to the Prophet Muhammad's example and model to be followed by Muslims.
Sura	A chapter in the *Qur'an*.
Tablighi *Jammah*	Translated as the group that conveys the message of Allah.
Taleem	An Islamic study circle.
Tarawih	Optional prayers offered after the '*Isha* prayers during the nights of *Ramadan*.
Tawaf	Circling (walking around) the Ka 'bah seven times.
Tawheed	The unique oneness of Allah.
The Received *Torah*	The first five books of the *Old Testament.*
Torah	The book of revelation received by the Prophet Moses.
Um	Mother, mother of.

Ummah   Community; the shared brotherhood and
               sisterhood of all Muslims.

Zabur   The book revealed to the Prophet David.

Zakat   The fourth pillar of Islam. Obligatory charity
               from all Muslims who have a surplus.